# Out of Bounds

## The Bucknell Studies in Latin American Literature and Theory
### Series Editor: Aníbal González,
### Yale University

Dealing with far-reaching questions of history and modernity, language and selfhood, and power and ethics, Latin American literature sheds light on the multi-faceted nature of Latin American life, as well as on the human condition as a whole. This series of books provides a forum for some of the best criticism on Latin American literature in a wide range of critical approaches, with an emphasis on works that productively combine scholarship with theory. Acknowledging the historical links and cultural affinities between Latin American and Iberian literatures, the series welcomes consideration of Spanish and Portuguese texts and topics, while also providing a space of convergence for scholars working in Romance studies, comparative literature, cultural studies, and literary theory.

### Titles in Series

Julia Kushigian, *Reconstructing Childhood: Stategies of Reading for Culture and Gender in the Spanish American Bildungsroman*
Silvia A. Rosman, *Being in Common: Nation, Subject, and Community in Latin American Literature and Culture*
Patrick Dove, *The Catastrophe of Modernity: Tragedy and the Nation in Latin American Literature*
James J. Pancrazio, *The Logic of Fetishism: Alejo Carpentier and the Cuban Tradition*
Frederick Luciani, *Literary Self-Fashioning in Sor Juana Inés de la Cruz*
Sergio Waisman, *Borges and Translation: The Irreverence of the Periphery*
Stuart Day, *Staging Politics in Mexico: The Road to Neoliberalism*
Amy Nauss Millay, *Voices from the* fuente viva: *The Effect of Orality in Twentieth-Century Spanish American Narrative*
J. Andrew Brown, *Test Tube Envy: Science and Power in Argentine Narrative*
Juan Carlos Ubilliz, *Sacred Eroticism: Georges Bataille and Pierre Klossowski in the Latin American Erotic Novel*
Mark A. Hernández, *Figural Conquistadors: Rewriting the New World's Discovery and Conquest in Mexican and River Plate Novels of the 1980s and 1990s*
Gabriel Riera, *Littoral of the Letter: Saer's Art of Narration*
Dianne Marie Zandstra, *Embodying Resistance: Griselda Gambaro and the Grotesque*
Amanda Holmes, *City Fictions: Language, Body, and Spanish American Urban Space*
Gail A. Bulman, *Staging Words, Performing Worlds: Intertextuality and Nation in Contemporary Latin American Theater*
Anne Lambright, *Creating the Hybrid Intellectual: Subject, Space, and the Feminine in the Narrative of José María Arguedas*
Dara E. Goldman, *Out of Bounds: Islands and the Demarcation of Identity in the Hispanic Caribbean*

http://www.departments.bucknell.edu/univ__press

# Out of Bounds

## Islands and the Demarcation of Identity in the Hispanic Caribbean

Dara E. Goldman

Lewisburg
Bucknell University Press

©2008 by Rosemont Publishing & Printing Corp.

All rights reserved. Authorization to photocopy items for internal or personal use, or the internal or personal use of specific clients, is granted by the copyright owner, provided that a base fee of $10.00, plus eight cents per page, per copy is paid directly to the Copyright Clearance Center, 222 Rosewood Drive, Danvers, Massachusetts 01923.[978-0-8387-5677-5/08 $10.00 + 8¢ pp, pc.]

Associated University Presses
2010 Eastpark Boulevard
Cranbury, NJ 08512

The paper used in this publication meets the requirements of the American National Standard for Permanence of Paper for Printed Library Materials Z39.48-1984.

Library of Congress Cataloging-in-Publication Data

Goldman, Dara E., 1971-
　Out of bounds : islands and the demarcation of identity in the Hispanic Caribbean / Dara E. Goldman.
　　p. cm.
　Includes bibliographical references and index.
　ISBN 978-0-8387-5677-5 (alk. paper)
1. National characteristics, Caribbean in literature. 2. Islands in literature. 3. Caribbean literature (Spanish)—History and criticism. 4. National characteristics, Caribbean. I. Title.

PQ7361.G65 2008
860.9'9729—dc22

2007019580

PRINTED IN THE UNITED STATES OF AMERICA

# Contents

Preface: Insular Tales    7
Acknowledgments    19

1. Between Island and Nation:
The Evolution of Hispanic Caribbean Self-Fashioning    27

2. Out Elsewhere:
The Limits of Normative Sexualities    62

3. Dancing With the Enemy:
(Post)National Borders and Contested Spaces    106

4. Out of Place:
Insular Topographies in the Diaspora    148

5. Virtual Islands:
The Negotiation of Translocal Spatiality    178

Conclusion: Beyond the Island    206

Notes    211
Bibliography    231
Index    243

# Preface: Insular Tales

FOR CENTURIES, ISLANDS HAVE OCCUPIED THE HUMAN IMAGINATION. THEY are portrayed as exotic and alluring locations filled with both potential treasures and possible dangers. Travel advertisements feature euphoric couples escaping from the drudgery of everyday life to the picturesque (and often uninhabited) landscape of a tropical island. Conversely, for contestants of the recent reality television program, *Survivor*, the island is far from an idyllic paradise. Nevertheless, the object of the game is to overcome the difficulties imposed by both the show and the setting; they must quite literally survive by managing not to get voted off the island. In both cases, the island constitutes a fundamentally alternative locale. Its value resides precisely in its disconnectedness, its separation from commonplace experiences.

Beyond these two examples, literature and popular culture have produced numerous works in which the island functions as a privileged, sacred, or unique space. Whether portrayed as enticing or as undesirable, the island repeatedly appears as a significant component in literary and cultural discourses. It would seem, therefore, that producers and consumers of these discourses are endlessly entertained—or, at the very least, intrigued—by the island as a dramatic setting, regardless of its precise characterization.

This fascination can be attributed, to some extent, to the basic nature of islands: as self-contained (and often miniature) realms, they lend themselves to symbolic interpretation. In the case of small, remote islands in particular, the borders are relatively fixed and easily apprehended. Their contents, moreover, can be more readily controlled and manipulated than in other settings. Their terrain stands in stark contrast to the fluidity of the surrounding water, and this apparent stability can be viewed as a valued attribute in the face of excessively porous borders and changing landscapes. On the other hand, the land-sea relationship can be a source of anxiety: the exposure of the island's boundaries calls attention to the inherent vulnerability of both natural and artificial lines of demarcation. In both cases, insular geography acutely dramatizes the human experience of space. Hence, they become a microcosm or exaggerated example of extra-insular phenomena.

To some extent, the value of islands as a literary topos resides precisely in their isolation, their seemingly complete separation from everyday life and social interaction. The deserted island, for example, is often depicted as a small patch of sand, just large enough to accommodate a single individual and, perhaps, a lone palm tree. This depiction may constitute an extreme exaggeration, but it nonetheless emphasizes the fundamental characterization of islands as disconnected nonplaces. Even in the case of slightly larger, remote land masses, their geographic circumstances are closely linked to primitiveness and lack. Victims of shipwrecks, from the *Swiss Family Robinson* to Tom Hanks's character (Chuck Noland) in *Cast Away*, inevitably have to negotiate the paradoxical combination of protection and perils of their new setting: their arrival on a remote island constitutes their salvation from the treacherous sea, yet they soon discover that the undomesticated nature of the island threatens their social and biological survival. They must struggle to (re)create viable social structures in the insular context. In these cases, the island is clearly depicted as a space of isolation: it is devoid of any sign, or even hope, of civilization. In most cases, however, the significance of the island lies precisely in its relationship with more quotidian spaces. Through both comparison and contrast, the insular setting functions as a heuristic device, a model that can be used to better understand how certain phenomena would play out in a larger environment.

Given their relative isolation, islands can operate as a natural site of scientific investigation. From Darwin to *Jurassic Park,* they have been viewed as an ideal setting for biological experimentation. Even though the purported containment of their ecosystems may prove less than absolute (as the characters in Michael Crichton's saga discover), the geography of these land masses allows them to more closely approximate the controlled conditions of a laboratory. As David Quammen argues in *The Song of the Dodo*, global patterns of species depletion and extinction can be more accurately assessed in an insular environment since the impact of climatic change on reproductive propagation is exacerbated. These restricted ecosystems thus offer insight into how environmental shifts will ultimately affect other populations. In this manner, the island functions as a magnified harbinger of global change and its biological consequences.

This notion of the island as a miniworld is not limited to scientific study. Similar concepts can also be traced in texts that deal with the more abstract implications of insular conditions. Countless fables, narratives and other representations, islands are portrayed as an alternative locale that, most notably, lie outside the normal parameters of everyday experience. In some cases, the island is envisioned as a perfect location for an idealized version of society: it contains a paradise that has not been corrupted by outside influences. Conversely, this notion of islands as separate spheres has also rendered them particularly well suited to act as sites of exile or banishment. Hence, both historical and fictional examples of island-prisons are often depicted as dangerous and illicit spaces, viewed as either enticing or repulsive. In other cases, the scale and circumscription of the island foster the perception of it as a magnified version of its larger and more contiguous counterparts. In a fashion similar to Quammen's study, therefore, insular society presumably offers a more readily apprehensible manifestation of the same patterns that can be found elsewhere. In all of these instances, the island is understood as a privileged space that offers special insight into the conditions found in larger scale and more commonplace settings.

The symbolic function of islands as an instructional microcosm can be largely attributed to their historical role in maritime travel: both inhabited and deserted islands have frequently constituted the first point of contact for adventuresome or wayward sailors, and they have often proven strangely unfamiliar or even inhospitable in these instances. The significance of islands, however, cannot be wholly explained based on their physical attributes or historical functions. Indeed, the fascination with insularity extends beyond the practical implications of their geography. By their very nature, islands seemingly embody fundamental aspects of the human experience. They clearly dramatize the basic dialectic of isolation and connectedness as well as the interaction between people and the world they inhabit. As a result, it is not surprising that islands are repeatedly deployed as a symbolic trope in literary and cultural production. In *Desert Islands*, Gilles Deleuze considers the persistent fascination with insular landscapes and suggests that islands represent a fundamental topos. According to the author, the nature of islands points to a basic assumption about physical space and its inherent functions. Land masses are appropriate locations for (relatively) permanent occupation and domestication. Water, conversely, is available for travel and commercial enterprise but is not well suited for human residency. The land-sea boundary therefore establishes the line of demarcation between potentially inhabitable space and the unruly natural terrain that resists civilization.

In his analysis, Deleuze makes a distinction between continental and oceanic islands. The former refers to the small land mass that even a casual observer can immediately recognize as an island. The tiny deserted island described earlier, just big enough to accommodate a single inhabitant and a lone palm tree, would constitute an extreme instantiation of an oceanic island. Even in the case of larger examples, however, these land masses are clearly circumscribed by a highly recognizable land-sea boundary, and they are often seen as incomplete or insufficient. Their separation from other inhabitable spaces may foster particular advantages but it also engenders problems or obstacles that must be overcome. In the case of continental islands, however, the circumscription of the island proves less readily apparent. Australia, for example, is undeniably an island. Given the size of the continent, its complete circumscription by water proves almost incomprehensible in the context of everyday life. Nevertheless, the insular nature of the continent can be traced in its characterization as a separate or distinct territory: it is seen as a remote and isolate location under British rule, which makes it suitable for the establishment of a prison colony, and contemporary scholars point to potential problems of sufficiency and sustainability in the face of increasing immigration and population growth. Hence, although it is manifestly distinct from the virtually uninhabitable patch of sand associated with the deserted island, Australia is still fundamentally viewed as a (de)limited insular space.

According to Deleuze, although they differ in terms of scale and legibility as islands, oceanic and continental ultimately perform similar spatial functions. In both instances, the geographic circumscription of the land mass dramatizes the underlying relationship between boundaries and territory. Social space is understood through the authoritative and recognizable delimiting of discernable terrain. Islands constitute the most overt physical incarnation of this process. Regardless of their precise political status, lines do not need to be drawn or imposed in order to identify them or to clearly divide them from neighboring lands. Instead, these boundaries are already inscribed through their natural topography. In this sense, islands circumscribe identity and produce difference; groups are defined by their location within insular boundaries and the land-sea juxtaposition simultaneously distinguishes and separates them from others.

Even though both continental and oceanic instantiations perform these spatial functions, the latter offers a more overt and immediately recognizable manifestation of the land-sea boundary. To a much greater extent than their larger counterparts, these land masses are invoked as the physical incarnation of the processes of demarcation that generate subjectivity and society. The island becomes the mythical topos of both individual and collective foundations. Given the homology between insular geography and identity parameters, it is not surprising that they become a recurring metaphor in European and American literature.[1] They embody the essential dichotomy between civilization and nature and, by extension, between a collective self and its others.

In particular, Deleuze cites Daniel Defoe's *Robinson Crusoe* as the paradigmatic example of the literary topos of the deserted island.[2] The island depicted is, first and foremost, elsewhere. The shipwreck narrated in the novel destroys the established parameters of the protagonist's social order. His new home is located outside of the quotidian social space, and, therefore, the precise relationship with his surroundings must be (re)negotiated. Through this process, the island allows the subject and civilization to be reconstituted. Furthermore, given its content and the historical context in which it was written, Defoe's novel can readily be understood as the allegorical dramatization of the imperial mission of the larger island, England. It serves as the mirror image of British imperial spatiality—an image that magnifies the objectives and obstacles of the colonial project.

*Robinson Crusoe* certainly constitutes an archetypal example of the deserted island and its metaphorical implications. As such, it is representative of a larger tradition in which islands offer particularly fertile ground for social commentary. By their very nature, remote oceanic islands present a fictional landscape that sits outside the normal terrain of human experience.[3] In some cases, they can constitute the site of a mythical origin or lost civilization; of course, the legend of Atlantis is arguably the best example of this trend. In Plato's *Dialogues*, the island is cited as a potential example of the ideal society described in *The Republic*. Subsequently, the endurance of the myth and the ongoing fascination with this lost insular paradise offer compelling evidence of the attachment to insular fables of origin. In these cases, the imagined landscapes hold out the possibility of an idealized past, perfectly preserved by the absolute isolation of the lost island. In most instances, however, the remoteness of the island is not so absolute; it may be distant and hard to reach, but most deserted islands are represented as coeval with modern civilizations. Under these conditions, the island becomes a sacred or primitive space that lies just beyond the usual territories of social interaction and structure. It is not entirely inaccessible, but it is located at a sufficient distance from other inhabited places so that regular contact and interactions are rendered, at the very least, impractical. In narratives such as *Robinson Crusoe* or *Lord of the Flies*, therefore, the forced isolation of the island drives the inhabitants to start over, to (re)construct civilization in their new environment.

Similarly, Thomas More's *Utopia* and Shakespeare's *The Tempest* depict islands that foster the development of an alternative society. In the case of More's *Utopia*, the island nation described is, quite literally, a nonspace that is wholly disconnected from contemporary society. As such, it constitutes the ideal location for a hypothetical social model. The mythical island More analyzes in his text constitutes a mirror image of quotidian society: it stands outside the parameters of everyday existence and underscores the fundamental essence of social organization.

Shakespeare's text, on the other hand, more closely parallels Defoe's.[4] The drama depicts the events that unfold when several characters are brought together on a small island. Having been removed from his home and his position as Duke of Milan by his brother and King Alonso, Prospero inhabits a small island with his daughter, Miranda. The island is also occupied by the savage, Caliban, and the ethereal spirit, Ariel. At the beginning of the play, King Alonso and Prospero's brother are returning to Italy following the wedding of the king's daughter, a route that brings them (unknowingly) into close proximity of the island where the banished duke now resides. Prospero conjures a storm, causing the occupants of the passing vessel to abandon their ship and become stranded on the island. Over the course of the play, Prospero's ability to control nature and his command of the island allow him to reverse the social order that had led to his exile. The manipulations and intrigue of Italian politics are thus conquered by Prospero's superior knowledge and power. The island therefore serves as an alternative space through which justice is achieved and social order is restored.

Of course, the characters and themes represented in *The Tempest* have engendered numerous reinterpretations and debates over the centuries.[5] To an even greater extent than *Robinson Crusoe*, I would argue, Shakespeare's play has been interpreted as a complex (and sometimes controversial) dramatization of colonialism. As Peter Hulme and William H. Sherman have demonstrated in their anthology, *The Tempest and Its Travels*, the play has inspired greatly varied responses across a wide range of literary traditions and historical moments. Among the responses featured in the volume, one of the most striking is the extraordinary resonance that the drama has had in Latin American cultural discourse. Beginning in the late nineteenth century, Latin American intellectuals have discussed the local implications of *The Tempest*. In particular, these discussions have generated two prominent essays—José Enrique Rodó's "Ariel" and Roberto Fernández Retamar's "Caliban"—each of which defines Latin American identity in terms of the character named in the title. In both these and other cases, authors have analyzed how the interactions among the characters in *The Tempest* acutely dramatize postcolonial development in Latin America.

Although the stated trajectory of King Alonso's ship presumably locates the action of the play between Africa and Italy, several scholars have suggested that Shakespeare's vision of the island may have been inspired by the chronicles of the conquest and colonization of the Americas. At the time of the play's premier in the early seventeenth century, European imaginations were largely occupied by the tales of strange and wondrous creatures and exotic lands in the New World. Whether or not these depictions of the New World directly inspired the characters and landscapes portrayed in *The Tempest*, Latin American and Caribbean readers have closely identified with the island and its inhabitants. To some extent, the connection with the play can be attributed to the role of insular arrival and shipwrecks in Spanish American colonial history. Latin American history, as such, begins with the arrival of Columbus's ships. More importantly, as Roberto González Echevarría has suggested, Columbus's *Diario* constitutes the zero-degree of Latin American writing: it is the point of departure for a discursive tradition that, by definition, inserts the Americas into a larger world view, historiography and expression. And this process begins with the textual codification of the islands of the Caribbean.

Within this discursive context, the trope of the deserted island takes on particular implications. Certainly, the symbolic function of the island as the site of mythical origins can be found in Latin American narrative traditions. Texts produced in the region often depict adventuresome travelers who discover hidden treasures, or they present the struggles of the victims of shipwrecks to civilize their adopted environment. In these cases, the narratives invariably dialogue with the documented histories of conquest and colonization. At the same time, these texts can draw from autochthonous insular traditions as well. The legend of Aztlán, for example, locates the sacred homeland of the indigenous people of southwestern North America on an intracontinental island. Although the prophecy narrated in the legend has traditionally been associated with the settlement of the early, pre-Columbian population in central Mexico, it has also been claimed within the Chicano movement as the symbol of *destierro* (unearthing or exile) and the desire to reclaim their rightful place in the southwestern United States.[6] In a contemporary context, the legend therefore becomes the tale, not only of mythical origins, but of the struggles of a repeatedly displaced population to recuperate terrain, power, and legitimacy.

In the case of the Caribbean, this palimpsestic layering of insular tales becomes even more prevalent and, at the same time, acquires increased significance. The importance of insularity in the region is undeniable. Of course, islands are the principal and most obvious geographic characteristic of the region. This condition also distinguishes the Antilles from the continental land masses that occupy the rest of the hemisphere. Although similar land masses can be found throughout the neighboring continents, no other nation or region of the Americas is comprised predominantly of islands. In fact, the Hispanic Caribbean is literally shaped by this characteristic. The Hispanic Antilles were the first to be claimed by Spain and among the last to gain their independence. Throughout its history, moreover, insularity becomes an obstacle that prevents the region from being fully incorporated into the colonial structures and shifts that take place throughout the rest of Latin America. The structures and goals of colonization implemented in the Caribbean colonies often differ from those deployed in the principal viceroyalties of the continent. These differences, moreover, are generally explained in terms of geographic disparity: the location, climate, and scale of the Antilles make them unsuitable for the imperial enterprise realized in other parts of the hemisphere. As Spanish American nations begin to gain their independence in the early nineteenth century, the geographic circumstances of the region once again engender a sharp distinction in political status. In the absence of contiguity, the proindependence armies could not readily move into the Caribbean. Although the Dominican Republic eventually managed to surmount this obstacle, the Spanish colonial forces retained power in Cuba and Puerto Rico until the end of the century. Throughout the colonial period, therefore, the Hispanic Antilles were (and were not) a product of their insularity.

In this manner, along with constituting the most prominent geographic trait, islands shape the sociopolitical and economic conditions of the Hispanic Caribbean. Consequently, the significance of insularity in literary production is greatly intensified. It is not surprising, therefore, that island landscapes function as a common setting for the narratives of the region. More importantly, perhaps, authors suggest that the nature of the characters they depict is determined by the conditions of the insular landscapes that they inhabit. In both fiction and nonfiction texts, the bound demarcation of the island becomes a defining trait of local culture and subjectivity. In their representations, authors suggest that Caribbean identity is a product of insular experience. Hence, a particular tradition evolves in the region: islands are not merely a topos that offers fertile ground for social commentary but, instead, constitute a central trope of Hispanic Caribbean identity and expression.

The relationship between island and nation thus becomes a fundamental component of productive national development. In the case of Puerto Rico and Cuba, in particular, the seemingly perfect equivalence of the boundaries of the island and the borders of the nation reinforce the attachment to insularity. In addition to purportedly shaping identity, the explicit demarcation of the island as a geographic entity suggests autonomy—even when this autonomy is not readily apparent in social or political terms. That is, although the legitimacy of Puerto Rico and Cuba as fully realized independent states may be compromised by their relationship with external powers, the existence of Puerto Rican and Cuban terrain as free-standing land masses symbolically enacts their sovereignty. In fact, even in the case of the Dominican Republic, the equation of island and nation is cited as a desirable condition that would foster progress or improvement: writers repeatedly point to the subdivision of Hispaniola as an unnatural obstacle that has disrupted the evolution of the island. In all three cases, therefore, the alignment of island and nation is persistently identified as a necessary step in national development: in order to evolve into successful independent nations, the Hispanic Antilles must achieve and maintain an appropriate insular character, in cultural as well as geographic terms.

Of course, there have been several changes in political and demographic circumstances that would presumably call the centrality of insular tropes into question. Yet insularity is persistently evoked as a defining characteristic despite these shifts. As I mentioned above, even the subdivision of Hispaniola into two separate nations does not truly displace the island-nation equation as a desired ideal. In the case of the other two Hispanic Antilles, with few exceptions, the geographic and political boundaries remain closely linked through the early twentieth century. Until recently, therefore, Cuban and Puerto Rican authors could trace an imperfect relationship between the island and the nation and circumscribe the problems of the nation in terms of a readily apparent geographic reality. During the second half of the twentieth century, however, the presumed alignment between the space of the island and the place of the nation is disrupted by the large-scale emigration of Caribbean peoples. Consequently, we might expect insularity to be displaced as a central mode of self-definition. Nevertheless, it continues to be cited as a defining characteristic of identity.

The following study focuses on these disjunctures between island and nation. In it, I analyze the significance of islands in Hispanic Caribbean writing and interrogate the persistence of insular tropes even in the absence of the geographic circumstances that had ostensibly led to their centrality. Following a concise overview of relevant theoretical and historical texts that elucidate the rhetorical role of insularity in Antillean literary and cultural production, I analyze how the underlying equation between island and nation is fundamentally challenged by queer subjectivity, territorial disputes, and migration. This discrepancy becomes ever more problematic as the analysis moves from the manifestation of an undesirable (queer) presence within the island to the occupation of a portion of the island by another nation and finally to diaspora. The instances examined increasingly reject or problematize the conventional spatiality of the island-nation, yet they continue to engage insularity as a principal mode of self-definition.

Given the centrality of this rhetorical tradition and the contradictions it engenders, the Hispanic Caribbean offers a particularly rich and complex corpus of insular tales. The topos of the island that Deleuze identifies becomes not only the foundational site of subjectivity and civilization, but also the principal trait that defines local identity and specificity. As a result, islands are persistently produced and reproduced in the literary and cultural production of the region. More importantly, perhaps, the discrepancies between the status quo of Antillean nations and the vision of what they should become is often dramatized in terms of insular misalignment. The island (or part of it) has been coopted by inappropriate entities or, alternately, the island is not providing an adequate space of national development. According to these postulates, a coterminous and harmonious relationship between the island and the nation must be achieved in order to promote the emergence of a more natural or appropriate state.

The title of the book, *Out of Bounds*, is intended as a reference to the dominant rhetoric of self-definition in the region and as a characterization of the paradoxical persistence of that rhetorical mode. Hispanic Caribbean identity has traditionally been closely linked to the physical borders of the island. According to numerous authors, artists, and intellectuals, national and regional culture are shaped by the demarcation of insular terrain. In this sense, *caribeñidad* (Caribbeanness) is born out of bounds; it quite literally emerges from the bound circumscription of space. In a contemporary context, moreover, Caribbean terrain is not perfectly aligned with the coastlines of the three islands. As a result, the production of Antillean culture cannot be neatly contained within the recognized territory of the nations. Instead, it is either influenced by an illicit, internal presence or generated from an extra-insular location. In these instances, the rhetoric of insularity is "out of bounds" since it is at odds with the "field of play" that has been traditionally designated as the foundational space of the nation.

Consequently, the geographic conditions of insularity not only shape Caribbean identity but the appropriate circumscription of insular space becomes a necessary condition of productive self-representation. In the end, this process constitutes a salient manifestation of postcolonial self-fashioning: despite changes in their political status and potential challenges to their legitimacy as self-governing nations, Cuban, Dominican, and Puerto Rican national identities are (re)inscribed through the repeated reproduction of the foundational topos of the island. Hence, the textual production of the region generates a series of insular tales that, in turn, continuously demarcate the limits of cultural discourse.

# Acknowledgments

THIS BOOK REPRESENTS THE CULMINATION OF IDEAS AND RESEARCH THAT first began in the late 1990s, when I was a graduate student at Emory. As with any project of this duration, numerous people have contributed to its development, both directly and indirectly. I am truly humbled by the quality, generosity, and consistency of support that I have received from friends and colleagues since I began my career in academia. Of course, the brief comments I will include here will never fully do justice to the ways in which my work and, in many cases, my life have been enriched by these interactions. Nonetheless, I would like to take this opportunity to acknowledge and express my gratitude for some of the contributions that have made this book possible.

First and foremost, I am greatly indebted to the extraordinary professors that I was fortunate enough to work with at Columbia and Emory. I could not have asked for a better mentor and advisor than Carlos J. Alonso. He has taught me to pursue the "ultimate critical consequences" of my work, was always patient and encouraging when I have struggled to meet that standard, and has done everything in his power to help me become a better scholar. Of course, I would not have even had the opportunity to work with Carlos if it hadn't been for the guidance and inspiration afforded by my *mamola* and *mater poetica* principal, Maria Mercedes Carrión. From our first encounter, she has been a faithful guide into the (sometimes fiery) depths of academia, teaching me to revel equally in its perils and pleasures. As professors and members of my dissertation committee, Karen Stolley and Elizabeth Fox-Genovese also offered their considerable insights and proved invaluable in helping to shape the foundation of this project. Michael Solomon, Hazel Gold, and Jean Franco also contributed immeasurably to my intellectual formation, and traces of their contributions can be found throughout this book. They offered ideas that continually excited (and continue to excite) my imagination along with admirable models of scholarly excellence. At Emory, I also met two of most cherished and faithful interlocutors, Patrick Garlinger and Lisa Tulchin. Over the years, they have imparted an array of wisdom and support that is as invaluable as it is diverse, from late-night coffee and sympathy to the most astute and discerning criticism.

I am deeply grateful for the support I have received from my extraordinary colleagues at the University of Illinois at Urbana-Champaign. Numerous members of the Department of Spanish, Italian, and Portuguese—i.e., Ann Abbott, Tony Cassell, Elena Delgado, Anna María Escobar, Eric Graf, José Ignacio Hualde, Mariselle Meléndez, Silvina Montrul, Antonino Musumeci, Diane Musumeci, Rolando Romero, Rob Rushing, Ron Sousa, Joyce Tolliver, and John Wilcox—have been a (seemingly) endless source of inspiration and comfort as well as truly exceptional mentors in both teaching and research. Antonino, Elena, Joyce, and Mariselle, moreover, offered inestimable feedback on early versions of several of these chapters, allowing me to hone the trajectory of my research. The pages of this text have also been greatly improved upon by my interactions with students at UIUC. In particular, the members of the "Mapping Identities," "Urban Desires," and "Globalization and Its Discontents" seminars helped me enormously to refine—and, often, profoundly reconsider—many of the ideas articulated here. Both within and beyond these courses, I was afforded the incalculable insights and talents of Irune del Río Gabiola, Daynalí Flores, William Hope, Michael King, Kathy León, Juliet May, Henry Morello, Sara María Rivas, Celiany Rivera, Jennifer Rudolph, and Carina Vásquez. It has been a pleasure and a privilege to be able to work with these emerging scholars, and their combination of indefatigable enthusiasm and keen attention to detail allowed me to view my work with fresh and discerning eyes.

Additionally, Gender and Women Studies, the Illinois Program for Research in the Humanities, the Center for Latin American and Caribbean Studies, Latina/Latino Studies and the Unit for Criticism, and Interpretative Theory have offered productive and welcoming spaces in which to explore the interdisciplinary implications of my work. The community of scholars in these programs and across the humanities and social sciences has afforded an embarrassment of riches too extensive to enumerate here. Nonetheless, I would like to specifically thank those individuals who have provided advice, listened to ideas, commented and/or generously shared their work as I was developing this project: Antoinette Burton, Pedro Cabán, C. L. Cole, Louis DiSipio, Augustu Espiritu, Jed Esty, Stephanie Foote, Lauren Goodlad, Andrea Goulet, Dianne Harris, Stephen Hartnett,

Debbie Hawhee, David Hays, Paul Hixson, Masumi Iriye, Nils Jacobsen, Lilya Kaganovsky, Brett Kaplan, Suvir Kaul, Lisa Lampert, Zack Lesser, Ania Loomba, Alejandro Lugo, Chris Mayo, Bill Maxwell, Jordana Mendelson, Isabel Molina, Harriet Murav, Adlai Murdoch, Lori Newcomb, David O'Brien, Michael Palencia Roth, Bob Parker, Cathy Prendergast, Naomi Reed, Bruce Rosenstock, Larry Schehr, Helaine Silverman, Siobhan Somerville, Adam Sutcliffe, David Thomson, Arlene Torres, Anghy Valdivia, Oscar Vázquez, Julia Walker, Norm Whitten, and Gillen Wood.

Without a doubt, no one contributed more to the development of this study than the members of the SIP/FLB "writing group." Ann Abbott, Andrew Herscher, Eva-Lynn Jagoe, Rob Rushing, and Yasemin Yildiz dutifully read and commented extensively (not to mention with a great deal of wit and charm) on drafts of several of these chapters, and I fear that the final product could never fully do justice to their care and critical acumen. Working with them has intensely dramatized the best UIUC has to offer, and I am—quite simply—privileged to count them among my readers. Nancy Castro and Andrew Orta also read an early version of "Dancing With the Enemy." Through their considerable expertise, they afforded a probing and challenging perspective on my argument, which contributed immeasurably to the development of that chapter and, in the end, to the overall scope of the project.

Along with these individuals, several other colleagues deserve special recognition for their extraordinary support, generosity and, at times, beneficial exigency. Michael Rothberg's depth of knowledge and commitment to utter excellence have been an unfailing source of inspiration and ideas. Matti Bunzl and Billy Vaughn, whose intellectual prowess is matched only by their inexorable *joie de vivre,* have been faithful interlocutors in an extended array of fruitful and provocative discussions about everything from inane academic gossip to the meaning of life. I cannot adequately express my deep appreciation for the seemingly endless bounty of experiences that I have enjoyed with them; suffice it to say that nothing has enriched my life in Illinois more than the time spent with them. Above all, I want to acknowledge my most cherished interlocutor and partner-in-crime, Martin Manalansan. While I may have helped him to unearth the "intellectual and social possibilities" of Chambana, he embodies the model of scholarship to which I aspire. I am continually in awe of his extraordinary generosity, exceedingly lyrical prose, and truly excellent work. He has helped and (on occasion) pushed me to more fully explore the intersections among ethnic and sexualities studies in my own research, both within and beyond this project.

I would also like to thank my colleagues in the profession who contributed extensively to this study, through their thoughtful comments in response to conference papers, articles, and drafts as well as through less formal interactions: Gerard Aching, Frances Aparicio, Jossiana Arroyo, Idelber Avelar, Efraín Barradas, Emilio Bejel, Rebecca Biron, Mary Pat Brady, Arnaldo Cruz Malavé, Viviana Díaz-Balsera, David Eng, Brad Epps, Guillermina de Ferrari, Licia Fiol-Matta, Myrna García Calderón, Judith Halberstam, Guillermo Irizarry, Robert Irwin, Larry LaFountain Stokes, Lázaro Lima, Agnes Lugo Ortíz, Yolanda Martínez-San Miguel, James Meyer, Diane Milotes, Patrick O'Conner, Suzanne Oboler, René Prieto, José Quiroga, Julio Ramos, Dierdra Reber, Juana María Rodríguez, Néstor Rodríguez, Edna Rodríguez Mangual, César Salgado, Ben Sifuentes-Jauregui, Doris Sommer, Vicky Unruh, and Keja Valens. Of course, I am greatly indebted to the anonymous readers of my work, whose rigorous, astute, and incredibly generous evaluations pointed me towards the ultimate potential of my analyses. This book is also undeniably better for having passed through the hands of Aníbal González Pérez. His assessments enabled me to better understand the implications of my work, and he has masterfully shepherded the project through its final stages.

This book would not have been possible were it not for the time, efforts and support of several key individuals and institutions. The Campus Research Board at UIUC generously provided me with the funding and release time that allowed me to complete the manuscript. I am also grateful to *Hispanic Review, Latino Studies,* and *Revista Iberoamericana* for allowing me to reproduce portions of articles published in their journals. Carol Maier and Suzanne J. Levine graciously provided the English translations of quotations from Severo Sarduy's *Pájaros de la playa* from a critical edition that they are preparing for publication (Otis Books, Seismicity Editions, 2007). Similarly, Mark Weiss generously contributed all of the English translations of Virgilio Piñera's "La isla en peso," from a forthcoming anthology of Cuban poetry since 1944, "The Whole Island," that he is preparing (University of California Press, 2008). I will be forever grateful to all three for sparing me the unenviable task of producing my own translations of the dense passages quoted in chapter 2—an effort that undoubtedly would not have produced the elegant (often inspired) renderings that they have contributed.

I am also especially grateful to Antonio Eligio Fernández (a.k.a. Tonel) and Neftali F. Lamourt for allowing me to reproduce images they created. When I first encountered it at the Museo Nacional in Havana, I was utterly entranced by Tonel's ingenious depiction of a particular, insular cosmogony. I can think of no better way to illustrate the phenomenon of how the demarcation of insular identity persists even in the face of increased transnationalism and globalization. Hence, I am greatly indebted to Tonel for allowing me to reproduce the image here. Neftali Lamourt could not have been more gracious about providing digital images and permissions. During our exchanges, she also generously and astutely engaged with my argument, offering insightful suggestions based on her own work and experiences. These exchanges offered further evidence of her deep commitment to highly intelligent and informed discourse on Puerto Rican cultures—a commitment that was already readily apparent in the website that she designed.

I also want to express my deep gratitude, admiration and love for family members who, not only lived through, but, in many ways, participated in the generation of this book. Brian Legum and Bennett Robinson both consistently exceeded the expected level of familial interest, inquiring about my progress, listening attentively to my responses, and often following up with pointed questions and astute observations. Sadly, Bennett did not live to see the realization of the ideas that he so avidly discussed with me, but the influence of his unyielding intellectual enthusiasm (and the formidable corpus of knowledge it engendered) survives in the pages of this text. Karen and Clifford Goldman have been the tireless champions of my endeavors, and they have patiently born witness to the process that culminated in this book. With their love and support, I have been able to not only survive but enjoy the journey. Finally, and perhaps most importantly of all, Elissa has helped me to laugh at the strange vicissitudes of life and, moreover, to truly revel in doing so.

# Out of Bounds

# 1
# Between Island and Nation: The Evolution of Hispanic Caribbean Self-Fashioning

> las islas son mundos aparentes.
> cortadas en el mar
> transcurren en su soledad de tierras sin raíz
> [the islands are apparent worlds,
> cut off in the sea
> moving past in the solitude of rootless lands]
> —Reina María Rodríguez, "Las islas"
> [Violent Island]

WHAT IS THE HISPANIC CARIBBEAN? WHAT DOES IT MEAN TO BE *CARIBeña/o*? Certainly, such ontological queries can be (and have been) posed in every area of the world. Nevertheless, questions of self-definition prove particularly salient in Hispanic Caribbean discourses. The literary and cultural production of the region repeatedly postulates the nature of local specificity. Not surprisingly, therefore, this corpus of material is regularly interpreted in terms of the allegories of identity codified therein. That is, Caribbean writing is often understood as a series of self-representations. According to this approach, the texts produced in the region seek to define national or regional character. Such analyses, however, rarely attend to the prominence of space and spatiality in discourses of self-definition. As writers struggle to define who and what comprises the Hispanic Caribbean, they repeatedly turn to geography as a constitutive condition, yet studies of Caribbean writing have not traditionally emphasized this tendency.

This apparent oversight is particularly surprising given the prevalence of geographic themes in Antillean writing. In fact, the question of islands and insularity constitute a principal focal point in discourses of self-definition. Historically, the island has been invoked as a foundational characteristic of national subjectivity. Processes of Caribbean self-fashioning, the literary and cultural discourses through which Caribbean identities are performed and negotiated, are thus realized by means of the relationship between the island and the nation. Within this tradition, the space of the island and the place of the nation are presumed to be perfectly equivalent. This presumption, moreover, has two critical consequences. The first of these is that the island is identified as a generative condition of national character. The second is that overt challenges to the coincidence of geographic, political, and social space become intensely problematic; if the Hispanic Antilles are understood as island-nations, any discrepancy between island and nation calls into question a principal myth of Caribbean identity.

Identity is always formed through a process of separating commonalities from differences. National or regional identity therefore implies a clear demarcation of the concomitant group, a circumscription that separates the contained community from its supposed outsiders. Notably, the geography of the Antilles conspires to reinforce this traditional process of identity formation. The carving out of island-states acts as a perfect physical embodiment of the processes of differentiation between the self and its other(s). Consequently, the islands of the Caribbean become directly linked to the authoritative delineation of a collective self. These structures therefore becomes a central device of self-definition and epistemological reflection. The interior of the island constitutes a natural space of community formation: its inhabitants are inherently unified by the shared circumscription and separation from the world beyond the island's borders. In this context, the natural evolution of the island becomes closely associated with the history of the residents. The island is literally the space of the people and their place in the world is shaped by the relationship between the land and the surrounding waters.

On April 6, 1990, the musical *Once on This Island* made its commercial debut. Based on the novel *My Love, My Love* by Trinidadian author Rosa Guy, the musical takes place on a Caribbean island during a violent thunderstorm. In order to console a young girl who is frightened by the storm, the adults tell her a story about another young girl who was caught in a similar storm. According to the fable, this peasant girl is spared by the gods and then is tested when she falls in love with the son of a wealthy landowner from the other side of the island. The story presents several principal themes of Antillean literature: the threat of a storm or hurricane and its potential for destruction, the fusion of European and African cultures, and the firm division between these cultural groups in spite of this fusion. Furthermore each of these themes is articulated in terms of insularity in the play. The storm is described as a force sent by the gods, and the paradoxical relationship between the peasants and the *grands hommes* is characterized as "two different worlds on one island."[1]

The classic fable of local history is ultimately one in which interior conflicts are resolved through the shared relationship with the surrounding waters. The internal social order that divides the romantic couple is ultimately supplanted by the more fundamental separation between the land and the sea. As in Shakespeare's *The Tempest*, the relationship among the island's inhabitants is reorganized by the disruption of the storm. At the same time, the potential for disruption also constitutes the principal narrative pretext of the drama: the story is told to a young girl in order to alleviate the anxiety inspired by an approaching storm. In this sense, mythology, ideology, and everyday experience are directly linked to the conditions of insularity. The fable emphasizes the particular characteristics of the island-nation that the characters inhabit, and the story itself must be (re)narrated because of the ongoing consequences of these characteristics.

The structure of the play, moreover, underscores the role of the island as a coadjuvant in the production of a narrative tradition. The recounting of a local myth is a direct response to the problematic relationship between the island and its surrounding waters. The style, content, and circumstances of the account conform to existing traditions of fairy tales or other didactic fables. The title, however, underscores a significant shift in narrative tradition: the conventional "once upon a time" is replaced with "once on this island." The island becomes the mythical origin of the story, the point of departure that engenders the tale. Rather than locating the story at a temporal distance, it is inscribed within the insular space of its narrator(s). This beginning is echoed in the concluding lines of the final song: "And on this island, we tell the story" (32). Through this framing device, the circumstances produced by insularity become the reason why the story is told and determine both its content and narrative form. The basic didactic tale is thereby circumscribed through the demarcation of insular space.

This relationship between insular space and the production of narrative exemplifies a trend in nineteenth- and twentieth-century Antillean literature in which the island constitutes the principal catalyst and the defining trope in the construction of cultural discourse. As in the case of *Once on This Island*, the island purportedly determines both the content of Caribbean texts and their form. Nevertheless, I do not mean to suggest that the idea of insularity remains constant throughout time. In fact, the category has been constructed in diverse and often contradictory terms. On the one hand, insularity is associated with isolation, limitation, inferiority, and vulnerability. In this case, it becomes a problem that the island's inhabitants must overcome. On the other hand, insularity is often postulated in positive terms and is associated with protection and self-sufficiency; it thus becomes a trait that facilitates self-affirmation for island communities. In "Las islas," cited in the epigraph above, Reina María Rodríguez characterizes the Antilles in terms that evoke both the positive and negative connotations of insularity: the world of the island evolves because of and in spite of the relationship between land and sea. Insularity simultaneously impedes and facilitates the successful formation of a collective self.

The consistency of this literary tradition, therefore, lies not in the specific characterization of insularity but instead in its prevalence and underlying rhetorical function. The claim of insular specificity becomes the basis for the postulation of singularity within Antillean writing. That is, whatever the particular characteristics associated with insularity may be, they become the mechanism employed to define caribeñidad. Furthermore, this discursive practice produces an ontological rhetoric of insularity that, in turn, becomes the foundation for national discourses in the region. The nature of Caribbeanness is fundamentally shaped by the conditions of insularity, and national identity is postulated in terms of either an existing or a desired relationship with islandness.

## Spatial Poetics and the Demarcation of Identity

In order to contextualize the role of insularity in Hispanic Caribbean cultural discourse, I would like to turn briefly to the question of spatial poetics. In *The Production of Space*, Henri Lefebvre rigorously challenges the idea of space as a universal physical reality. Space is not inherently endowed with fixed or readily comprehensible meaning; instead, he argues, it acquires significance through specific cultural practices. According to his assertions, not only are the social functions of sites such as parks and graveyards produced in a given context, but the very legibility of these sites is also engendered by these negotiations.

Consider the case of a large estate or a piece of property where the house is not visible from the road, for example. In these instances, a sign is often displayed at the entrance in order to mark it as private property. The presence of the sign indicates a concern (whether based on previous experience or in anticipation of potential problems) that travelers will not otherwise be able to identify the marked driveway as private. The absence of a readily apparent residential dwelling renders the driveway indistinguishable from public space. The same physical structure (i.e., a paved or gravel vehicular path) is generally interpreted as either private or public based on its visible proximity to other structures generally associated with residences.

The potential confusion implied by the presence of the sign in these cases, moreover, points to a process of special poetics. Individuals perceive the pathway as a discernable structure and understand its significance based on a specific relationship with space and spatiality. A system of encoding and decoding develops through which the physical world can be interpreted; structures are rendered recognizable and become associated with particular expectations and norms. In this sense, space functions as a language, a signifying code that perpetually negotiates the dialectics of object and meaning.

Consequently, even the fundamental dichotomy between interiority and exteriority must be understood as a construct. Cultural norms determine what constitutes interior and exterior spaces, where the precise line of demarcation between them lies, and the relative functions that each can realize or accommodate. During an undergraduate study abroad program, I witnessed how the students interpreted and reacted to a particular location based on underlying assumptions regarding this dichotomy. When I took them to visit Sagrada Familia in Barcelona, I neglected to inform them that the project had not been completed. We had already visited several other sites in and around the city, and this edifice was the final example of Antonio Gaudí's work that we would examine collectively. As we moved through the line outside and the historical exhibit leading into the towers and interior, we discussed the history of the project and its relationship with the rest of Gaudí's oeuvre. We eventually emerged into the open space of the interior, and the students were shocked to find themselves in the middle of a work in progress (complete with scaffoldings and construction materials, not to mention the absence of a roof connecting the towers and exterior walls). In fact, several of the students were clearly quite upset—even hostile—about this situation. They questioned the commonplace identification of the edifice as a church and apparently resented the required visit to an unfinished structure: they complained that the denomination of Sagrada Familia as a church or even as a building was misleading, and asked why we had come and waited so long to visit a construction site.

Of course, I am convinced that their reaction was based in large part on a misapprehension and an attempt to negotiate the discrepancy between their erroneous expectations and the structure that they encountered. Nevertheless, I would also like to suggest that their response is not merely one of disappointment or the shock of the unexpected but, instead, points to a more significant relationship with space and spatiality. Whether through religious indoctrination, relevant state ideological apparatuses, or accumulated cultural experience, the students had a clearly demarcated vision for the spatiality of Sagrada Familia that was sharply disrupted by the physical circumstance they encountered beyond the façade. Hence, the identification of this structure as a church proved offensively inappropriate. Its exterior had created a particular expectation for the interior, and the discrepancy they encountered produced an epistemological crisis. The physical circumstances were thus rendered incomprehensible since they did not contain the definitive elements of a church and, therefore, could not accommodate the fundamental functions associated with an ecclesiastic structure.

At the same time, the students also found the site incomprehensible as an architectural or historical destination. During that same trip, the students had visited ruins that contained structures in a far less complete state than Sagrada Familia and, on occasion, had participated in guided tours of buildings that were being repaired or restored (with clearly visible scaffoldings and construction material). Yet these visits had not provoked the same responses of confusion and displeasure. Their conceptualization of ancient and historic structures readily interpreted these elements as appropriate signs of decay; even if the structure was not currently complete or inhabitable, it offered evidence of an erstwhile finished and functional locale. In the case of a more contemporary edifice, however, the same elements signaled that the project was unfinished and therefore not worthy of reflective consideration. As the students climbed through and explored the interior of the towers, their hostility and discomfort diminished. Nevertheless, this contrast reaffirmed their initial objections. They continued to assert that Sagrada Familia was not what they expected. In fact, they suggested that the towers offered clear evidence of the potential significance of the edifice and insisted that the project should be completed, so that this significance could be appropriately showcased.

I offer this anecdote as a brief example of how spatiality functions in an everyday context. The students in my group had a clear sense of the relationship between physical demarcation and identification. Of course, given their inherent and often overt manipulation of space, architectural structures offer an acutely explicit manifestation of the interaction of form and function. In this case, however, the objections and discomfort of the students was not limited to the design and execution of Sagrada Familia as a building. In the end, the students could not readily understand it as a cultural site either. Their preexisting notions of space and spatiality required a clear interiority, even if this interiority was only invoked through the synecdoche of architectural remains.

The students' reaction, therefore, underscores a fundamental understanding of the social function of space. Drawing on scholarship in geography, landscape architecture, sociology, and anthropology, critics such as Lefebvre, Edward Soja, David Harvey, and Denis Cosgrove have developed innovative theoretical interpretations of space and spatiality that elucidate interpretative paradigms and epistemological crises such as the ones the students seemed to have deployed and experienced in Barcelona. As Harvey has argued, many of the fundamental categories that define modern existence are products of this codification. The relatively stable recognition of interior and exterior spaces as discernable and diametrically opposed categories does not exist a priori but, instead, is engendered through complex social, historical, and cultural processes. Moreover, through their continual demarcation and reterritorialization, interiority and exteriority become inextricably linked to the distinction between public and private and with the perpetual negotiation of the protocols associated with each category. That is, what is generally considered to be an indoor, private sphere or an outdoor, public location and, by extension, the activities and behaviors that are deemed appropriate for each are determined by the system of codification used to interpret physical circumstances. In other words, the idea of a private domestic space and the exact limits of that space (i.e., the front door, the property surrounding the structure, the vicinity surrounding that property) are negotiated through spatial codifications. Hence, social attitudes towards behavior are inevitably tied to site-specific definitions of decorum.

In this manner, the role of spatial poetics extends beyond individual perception. Certainly, as the students' rejection of Sagrada Familia as a religious and cultural site demonstrates, individuals interpret and evaluate the physical world based on an internalized sense of spatiality. At the same time, communal identity practices are also linked to the demarcation of space. Groups are identified, not only based on the common characteristics of the members, but through a shared attachment to a geographic location. Moreover, the community is formed, maintained, and regulated in accordance with its definitions and uses of space. As Foucault and Soja have demonstrated, structures of belonging, of difference, and of power are produced through the occupation and manipulation of space. Lines of demarcation are perpetually drawn and redrawn, which determines who and what constitute part of the community as well as where it is currently located. Within the community, shifting definitions of social space govern practices of inclusion and exclusion, internal hierarchies of privilege and access, codes of behavior and movement, and interactions with other groups.

Similarly, definitions of national identity are inexorably bound to particular delineations of space. Modern nations are primarily identified in terms of their attachment to a homeland (even if this homeland is a lost, ancestral one), and, as communities, their identity is continually performed through the production and regulation of territory. Not surprisingly, therefore, the internal landscape and geographic boundaries of the nation tend to function as defining characteristics. The salient geographic features are frequently invoked in literary and intellectual discourses that define national character, and the borders of the nation become a site of contestation and articulation of national identity. The nation itself is therefore represented through a particular interpretation of its physical location.

## SPACE IN THE NEW WORLD

Certainly, these tendencies can be traced in a variety of contexts. Historically, many European, African, and Asian nations have been closely identified with geographic conditions. In the context of the Americas, however, the negotiation of space acquires even greater significance. From the time of Columbus's first arrival, a tension arises between the spatial poetics of the European explorers and those of the indigenous communities. Tzvetan Todorov has asserted that the conquest and initial colonization of the Americas was comprised largely, not of a competition between military powers, but of a clash of semiotic practices. The conflict between the Old and New Worlds therefore consisted of a contest for the successful manipulation of signs, a battle waged through the codification of communication, warfare, and other cultural practices. In this context, moreover, the landscape of the Americas became the site of negotiation (and contestation) of the interpretative schema of competing cosmogonies and imperial designs.

For the European explorers and colonizers in particular, the (putatively) open spaces and natural resources of the New World were apprehended in terms of the projects of expansion that could not be realized at home. Along with specific characterizations of the native population, the landscape of the explored territory was codified in accordance with these projects. In *Ceremonies of Possession*, Patricia Seed argues that the imperial designs of the respective European powers were encoded in the rituals of acquisition that they enacted. The explorers that arrived from the various European imperial powers, quite literally, performed ceremonial acts which they believed entitled them to legitimately lay claim to the new territories.[2] The colonial projects of the different European states were thus dramatized through the particular incorporation of the space of the New World into existing spatiality.

These practices inaugurate a spatial poetics that continues throughout the colonial period. Scholars such as Annette Kolodny, Louis Montrose, and Margarita Zamora have demonstrated how the American landscapes were frequently gendered. Whether or not specific texts attended to the corporeal inhabitants of the explored terrain, the chronicles often presented the space of the New World as inherently female: it is characterized as fertile, fundamentally passive, and available for the insertion of colonial power. In her analysis, Mary Louise Pratt traces a homologous trend within later travel literature. Although not consistently gendered in the same way, throughout the two centuries following the initial arrival of European explorers, the depiction of the terrain and the structures encountered is inflected by the ideological project of the authors. The American landscape is persistently viewed in romantic (and sometimes romanticized) terms, and the space constructed in the literature produced by travelers becomes the site for projects that could not readily be realized—or even imagined—in Europe.

The rhetorical role of spatial poetics, however, is not limited to texts produced by explorers and travelers. The landscape is also a recurrent theme in the writing of Spanish American authors. In particular, during the period of nation formation and consolidation, writers frequently invoke the specific nature of local terrain. They suggest, moreover, that their communities have been shaped by the character of this terrain and that national development must adhere to (and even take advantage of) this innate connection between the environment and its inhabitants. Of course, as in the case of the European chronicles, this claim to endemic specificity can also be understood as directly tied to the authors' ideological projects. As Carlos J. Alonso aptly demonstrates in his analysis of Spanish American writing, discourses of autochthony are closely connected to the sociopolitical agenda of *criollo* writers.[3] These discourses invert the traditional colonial order that had inherently favored those individuals born in Europe. By privileging the fruits of American soil over imports, these writers inscribe their own supremacy based on their inherent connection to the space they inhabit. In this fashion, Latin American identity is persistently postulated in terms of an essential and privileged relationship with space. Nationalism, moreover, is articulated as the project of cultivating a more appropriate and productive relationship with the natural and cultural environment.

## ISLANDS AND HISPANIC CARIBBEAN SELF-FASHIONING

Given the role of space in Latin American writing, geographic circumstances take on extraordinary significance. If Latin American identity is fundamentally linked to the landscape and to the natural environment, the physical traits of a given location constitute a central element of self-definition and a key to its progress. Indeed, the most salient characteristic of the Antilles is the fact that the region is comprised of a chain of islands. It is, at once, both the most obvious unifying feature of the area and the element that most starkly differentiates it from the rest of the Americas. In the case of the Hispanic Caribbean in particular, this rhetoric relates to the larger discursive tradition of autochthony in Spanish American writing: the particular conditions of the island and the criollo specimens their geography produces become the basis for local specificity and superiority.

The scale and topography of the islands of the Caribbean are noted throughout the chronicles and early travel literature of the region, and the relationship between the land and the sea is repeatedly cited as a defining element in both daily experience and cultural practices. Once the majority of Latin America achieves independence from Spain, nations are persistently rewritten through strategic reconfigurations of a regional terrain that purportedly engenders subjectivity. In the Hispanic Antilles, "islandness" becomes the foundational characteristic for such reconfigurations. Throughout the nineteenth and twentieth centuries, Cuban, Dominican, and Puerto Rican subjectivities are constructed through the relationship with both the land and the sea as well as the interactions between them.[4]

As with the discourse of autochthony in other areas of Latin America, the role of islands in Hispanic Caribbean writing is not limited to physical descriptions of the region. Throughout the nineteenth and twentieth centuries, authors assert that national and regional character are shaped by the insular circumscription of their respective communities. The features of the island are persistently analyzed and, furthermore, are identified as the underlying cause of a wide range of traits, conditions, and circumstances. A careful review of this corpus of materials reveals a pattern of binary oppositions that purportedly either foster or hinder socioeconomic development. Isolation, for example, affords protection or creates vulnerability; it promotes self-reliance or engenders insufficiency. Similarly, the inherent openness of insular borders is linked to a fear of invasion in certain instances, yet it is also celebrated as an opportunity for expansion in others. In this manner, insularity takes on multiple connotations, all of which become closely associated with both the problems and the possibilities of the nation.

Although islands are frequently invoked as a defining characteristic in discourses of national and regional identity, the role of islands and insularity in Caribbean writing has not been widely studied or analyzed as a principal mode of self-definition. In fact, many scholars have sought unifying characteristics in order to apprehend the region as a coherent entity. These studies, however, tend to emphasize the commonalities of colonial history or—in the end—cite fragmentation and discontinuity as salient traits. To some extent, consequently, the field of Caribbean studies seems eternally plagued by a Hamlet complex: a constant questioning of its own existence that inhibits progress and through which the field threatens to destroy itself. Beyond the debates that explicitly attempt to resolve this conflict, most scholars that focus on the region struggle to establish both precisely where and what the Caribbean is. Since its incorporation into European awareness at the end of the fifteenth century, intellectuals have argued over the geographic parameters of the Caribbean as well as its relationship to other regions, and such debates continue to the present day.[5] The polemic does not subside, however, if a consensus is reached concerning geographic boundaries. In such cases, the focus merely shifts to the other principle obstacle in the attempt to postulate definitions of the region: the question of its constituent characteristics.

Definitions of the Antillean archipelago frequently disrupt the balance that must be achieved between unifying and divergent characteristics when subsumed under the aegis of a global perspective. On the one hand, arguments in favor of the pan-Caribbean approach stress the commonalties shared by the islands. On the other, attempts to recognize diversity and significant subgroupings within the Antilles challenge the cohesiveness of such a perspective.[6] Moreover, the identified commonalties themselves can further threaten the proposed cohesiveness. As Antonio Benítez Rojo points out, the very characteristics established by Caribbean scholars as unifying elements are, in fact, potentially divisive forces: "The main obstacles to any global study of the Caribbean's societies, insular or continental, are exactly those things that scholars usually adduce to define the area: its fragmentation; its instability; its reciprocal isolation; its uprootedness; its cultural heterogeneity; its lack of historiography and historical continuity; its contingency and impermanence; its syncretism, etc."[7] According to this analysis, the peculiar nature of Caribbean unity makes it incompatible with traditional approaches to regional definition.

Several scholars have attempted to resolve this contradiction by postulating alternative models of regional identity that accommodate the diversity of the Caribbean while still underscoring the cohesiveness of the area. Frank W. Knight, for example, discusses the parallel historical development of the islands in terms of a fragmented nationalism. Mark Kurlansky, in *A Continent of Islands*, stresses the common struggle of Antillean nations against imperial aggression and also argues that Caribbean reality can only be properly apprehended if the region is examined in its entirety. Both scholars postulate that the examination of a single nation or group of nations in isolation engenders only a partial or incomplete understanding since this nation forms part of a larger and purportedly indivisible collective. According to this approach, the patterns of national development studied in other areas only become apparent in the Caribbean if it is examined from a regional perspective. Therefore, although existing models of regional definition retain some validity in the case of the Caribbean, they cannot be directly applied but instead must be altered or adjusted to accommodate its peculiar specificity.

Based on this evidence, it might seem that the controversy surrounding definitions of the area persists simply because its specific elements prove difficult to synthesize. Nevertheless, when placed in the larger context of nationalism and regional politics, the Caribbean problem seems less unique. The claim for the specificity of the Caribbean case implies that it can be juxtaposed with a more typical pattern of development. Existing tools for understanding nationalism and national identity are inextricably bound to the geographic and historical circumstances through which they were developed and therefore cannot be applied to a region in which similar circumstances do not exist.

As Benedict Anderson aptly demonstrates, however, nationalism is not engendered purely by such circumstances nor even by the birth of the nation itself. Instead, it is the result of a tendency for people to conceive of themselves as part of a community and the historical changes that favor the nation as the primary structure through which to create that community. Consequently, a discussion of nationalism in the Caribbean retains validity even though the rhetorical construction of collective identities in the Caribbean does not conform entirely to the European concept of the nation that developed during the nineteenth century. Moreover, according to Anderson's paradigm, the Caribbean case does not constitute an alternative model of development but rather an additional example of patterns found in other areas since the difficulties encountered within its discourses of national identity can be explained in terms of an incompatibility between European national identifications extended and applied to the Antilles and the development of responses within the Caribbean itself to the need for collective identity.

In spite of such incompatibility, the European concept of the nation plays a significant role in the Antilles. The contemporary subdivision of the Caribbean into discrete political entities and linguistic groups is a direct result of struggles between competing imperial designs.[8] European nationalisms and national identities have been used as tools through which colonial dominance is reinforced and, therefore, become closely associated with empowerment within the islands subjugated under their influence. As Partha Chatterjee asserts, one possible response to this association is the construction of an alternative discourse through which the postcolonial subject is potentially able to resist such subjugation. In this way, the construction of anticolonial nationalism becomes a contestatory strategy through which postcolonial identities are reconstituted. The shift from a national to a regional approach in the construction of Caribbean identity could be understood as such a contestatory strategy. The division of the region in terms of individual islands or language groups reinforces the European patterns of colonization. A pan-Caribbean paradigm, however, deemphasizes the ties to the colonizers by constructing identity across European national boundaries. In this way, even though the common characteristics traced may be the result of colonialism, a discourse of pan-Caribbean identity acts as an anti-imperial strategy since it displaces the hegemony of the individual European powers.

According to Silvio Torres Saillant, however, the need for a regional approach to the study of Caribbean literature does not rely exclusively on an anti-imperialist impulse. In fact, in *Caribbean Poetics: Towards an Aesthetic of West Indian Literature*, he argues against a focus on self-legitimation or contestatory strategies in which the analysis of Caribbean literature necessarily evokes existing canonical values—even when attempting to displace them.[9] Instead, he proposes an examination of the literature on its own terms—an examination that will, by its very existence, authorize itself. "Perhaps henceforward the proper stance for Caribbeanists should be to proclaim the coherence of the region's literary production a priori. Scholars would do well to affirm the cognitive wholeness of Caribbean literature as a theoretical given. They must take Caribbean literature for granted just as one takes Western literary artifacts for granted."[10]

Rather than make a case for the unique nature of the Caribbean as a region, Torres Saillant insists that it closely parallels other areas. Unlike other scholars, he does not suggest that the fragmented nature of the Caribbean affords a singular quality to its concomitant identity but that it does create the opportunity to reexamine its nature. "Fragmentation need not be tragic. It can actually provide a principle of coherence insofar as it induces in the Caribbean artist a compulsion to sew the pieces together."[11] According to Torres Saillant, the normativity engendered by established literary criticism produces a distorted vision of Antillean writing since it evaluates it in terms of its degree of conformity with expected patterns. In fact, he argues that the discrepancies between such expected patterns and the textual evidence call into question the validity of the applied model and, by extension, its claim to universality.

Torres Saillant asserts that Caribbean literature must therefore be interpreted in terms of the predominant unifying characteristics that can be found in the writing of the region itself: "What one must keep in mind is that only Caribbean literature can explain Caribbean literature."[12] Not only does the author insist on this approach, he also follows it in his analysis of Caribbean literary production. In it, he traces common elements that can be found in the literature and interprets the poetic system circumscribed by these elements. He proposes that the similar treatment of language, religion and history as themes in the works produced throughout the West Indies define it as a cohesive corpus of literature, and he offers analyses of specific works based on these themes.

In light of his mandate, the role of insularity is notably absent from Torres Saillant's discussion. Given the author's expressed desire to examine Caribbean literature in terms of interpretative models developed within the region, this elision proves surprising. Certainly insular themes appear with notable regularity in the writing of the region. Furthermore, as I have suggested earlier, insularity is frequently cited in Antillean intellectual discourses as a defining characteristic of experience, identity, and expression. Several significant scholarly works by Caribbean authors have expressly studied insularity as a principal trope of Caribbean identity. Not only do these works offer definitions of regional identities, but they also generate a discourse through which such identities become legitimate topics of discussion. Therefore the analysis of the corpus of Caribbean writing on insularity presumably would form part of a project such as the one proposed by Torres Saillant: to arrive at an understanding of the unity of Caribbean poetics by analyzing both the literature and scholarship produced within the region itself.

According to these writings, if local geography engenders particular experiences, appropriate models must be developed in order to examine the resulting subjectivities. Antillean writers therefore emphasize the need to understand geography and its consequences. They repeatedly stress the importance of insular space as the most prominent and unifying trait of the region. The Antilles are, first and foremost, a chain of small islands. At the same time, several authors suggest that this condition and its consequences have not yet been adequately apprehended or engaged. The problems of the area are therefore assessed in terms of an inability to truly understand the implications of insular existence or to adapt to the idiosyncrasies of insular residency. These writers assert that Hispanic Caribbean peoples do not fully understand the role of insularity or, even if they have a conceptual grasp of its significance, have not yet successfully developed a productive relationship with this condition.

The insistence on insularity as a defining trait therefore constitutes a recurring theme in Hispanic Caribbean intellectual discourse. Islands ostensibly shape local culture and expression. Despite this consistency in the avowed significance of islands, a vast array of characteristics are attributed to this formative space of local culture and expression. In fact, to some extent, the supposed importance of insularity transcends any specific consequences; instead, the attachment to insularity, in and of itself, becomes the central trope of Antillean cultural discourse.

One of the most salient cases of such argumentation, to my mind, occurs within the dialogue between Juan Ramón Jiménez and José Lezama Lima that is represented in the latter's text, *Coloquio con Juan Ramón Jiménez*. This text is one of the earliest works published by Lezama and purportedly represents a conversation that took place during Jiménez's visit to Havana.[13] The published version of the dialogue includes an introductory comment in which the Spanish poet indicates that his recollection of the conversation does not concur entirely with Lezama's, although he is willing to accept his interlocutor's liberal recreation of the dialogue: "But that which I don't recognize as my own has a quality that nonetheless obliges me to not abandon it as alien. Furthermore, the dialogue is at times fused, not belonging to one or to the other but instead to the time and space in between . . . I preferred to collect everything that my friend attributes to me and make it my own to the greatest extent possible, to protest it with a non-signature, as is necessary at times with the supposed writing of others and facile dialogians."[14] In fact, whether or not *Coloquio* constitutes an accurate transcription of the conversation that actually occurred between the two writers may prove irrelevant. The printed text is the conversation as Lezama chooses to represent it and, as such, it becomes part of his literary project.

In Lezama's text, an extensive portion of the dialogue focuses on insularity. Lezama suggests that Cuban poetry is marked by "insularism" and inquires whether the Spanish poet has noticed this quality. Lezama defines insularism as a concept that transcends geographic circumstance and defines Cuban sensibility. Jiménez is persistently skeptical as to the specificity of Cuban "insularism" and claims that similar geographic and poetic sensibilities can be found in other traditions:

> Porque si Cuba es una isla, Inglaterra es una isla, Australia es una isla y el planeta en que habitamos es una isla. Y los que viven en islas deben vivir hacia adentro. Además, si se habla de una sensibilidad insular, habría que definirla o, mejor, que adivinarla por contraste. En este caso, ¿frente a qué, oponiéndose a qué otra sensibilidad, se levanta este tema de la sensibilidad diferente de las islas?
>
> [Because if Cuba is an island, England is also an island, Australia is an island and the planet we inhabit is an island. And those that live on islands should live inwards. Furthermore, if we are to speak of an insular sensibility, it must be defined or, better yet, divined by contrast. In this case, against what, opposed to what other sensibility is this theme of the different sensibility of the islands raised?][15]

Although the topic of insularity is introduced within the context of eliciting Jiménez's perceptions of the poetry he has encountered, it soon becomes clear that the question forms part of a rhetorical agenda in which insularism plays an already established role. In spite of repeated inquiries as to the nature of this insular sensibility and requests for specific examples from Cuban poetry, Lezama seems reluctant to give a more specific definition of the phenomenon. Instead, he continues to insist on its existence and discusses its implications. In this way, insularism acts as a rhetorical device that must be accepted as a specifically local experience—despite any evidence to the contrary—in order to legitimize a unique poetic tradition. Arnaldo Cruz-Malavé discusses this function of insularity in his analysis of the evolution of Lezama's poetic system:

> Against the univocal weight of tradition and the history that subordinates, marginalizes or limits the possibilities of the creation of the modern and the American, Lezama proposes this "myth of insularism"; a total poetic system whose objective is to convert the marginalization of the contemporary and the American into a transcendental center, an origin of infinite possibilities. Centering the island of Cuba and centering its uprooted historical evolution . . . returning to the paradisiacal image of the island, this is the goal of the *Colloquium*'s "myth of insularism."[16]

Even though later texts do not address this myth of insularity as directly as *Coloquio*, the theme and its rhetorical function continue to appear in Lezama's writings.[17] In a subsequent essay entitled, "X y XX," Lezama clarifies the relationship between insularity and a particular poetic sensibility that he alludes to in his conversation with Jiménez. This piece is also written in the form of a dialogue and could be interpreted as a rewriting of *Coloquio*. Although the dialogic form itself does not necessarily invoke the earlier exchange (since the intellectual dialogue is an established literary device within Western writing), the relationship between the two texts is enhanced by similarity in their content as well as references to *Coloquio* in the later essay.

Unlike in the earlier dialogue, Lezama does not claim explicitly that insularity constitutes the defining element of a Cuban poetic sensibility in "X y XX." Nevertheless, the discussion itself between the two interlocutors—the 'X' and 'XX' of the title—focuses on the nature of both insular and poetic experiences. In the advice he offers, XX suggests that there is a link between geography and poetic sensibility by claiming that the *siesta*—a custom associated primarily with tropical climates—can allow for transformational meditation.[18] And this improved awareness is linked to poetic function. Immediately following the instructions on how to alter understanding through the siesta, XX adds that "[e]n la poesía, en su sustancia, es como la voluntad logra manifestarse con más dignidad, se hace totalmente invisible" [in poetry, in its substance, is how volition manages to manifest itself with more dignity, it becomes totally invisible].[19] Moreover, not only does geographic circumstance impact upon one's potential for comprehension, but insular circumstances in particular afford unique opportunities that are impeded by other settings:

> Mientras en los continentes la síntesis tiene que ser superada por el concepto de sentirse deudor; en las islas, la suspensión que hay que vencer para llegar hasta ellas, no hacen la síntesis continental de lo blanco y de lo negro, sino de raíces oscuras, cambiantes y ligerísimas.
>
> [While on continents the sythesis must be overcome by the concept of feeling indebted, on islands, the suspension that must be beaten in order to reach them, does not make the continental sythesis of black and white, but, instead, of dark, changing, and very light roots.][20]

This association between insular and poetic experiences becomes increasing significant when considered within the larger context of the essay itself. As Rubén Ríos Ávila states, "X y XX"—as with many of Lezama's essays—can be read as an explanation of the author's own understanding of poetry and poetic systems. In other words, beyond the individual comments made by the two speakers, their conversation acts as a vehicle through which Lezama addresses fundamental relationships among islands, language, and poetry. Within this system, insularity is a characteristic of language itself and poetry the medium in which language overcomes this characteristic.

The establishment of insularity as an organizing axis within language and poetry potentially could detract from Lezama's claim for a particular Cuban sensibility. If in fact insularity is an inherent characteristic of language itself that poetic language manages to transcend, then it necessarily exists in all language and is not produced by location or geographic circumstance. However, the correlation Lezama establishes between such circumstances and insight creates precisely the opposite effect. He argues that the coincident geographic condition enhances the insular poet's understanding of this fundamental characteristic and, thus, affords a privileged perspective.

For Antonio Salvador Pedreira as well, insular conditions can have a profound effect on the island's inhabitants. In his now famous essay, *Insularismo*, he postulates insularity as the foundation of local sensibility.[21] Pedreira, however, takes this hypothesis to its furthest consequences and presents a definition of Puerto Rican identity based on this geographic circumstance. But *Insularismo* is not just an exercise in national definition; the rhetoric of the text creates instead the nationalistic cause of salvation. That is, Puerto Ricans have not realized their full potential and the essay is designed both to explain the consequent discrepancy and to indicate a possible resolution. To this end, Pedreira presents a diagnosis of the problem—or infirmity, to use his terminology—affecting Puerto Rican national identity and encourages his reader to attempt to resolve this problem.

Pedreira's definition of Puerto Rican identity relies on a deterministic model in which he establishes an essential character inherent in all Puerto Ricans and traces the effects of history on this essence.[22] According to the author, the repeated interruptions in the process of historical development have thwarted the evolution of national character. Since this disrupted trajectory has left the underlying essence of Puerto Rican identity in an immature, underdeveloped state, the process must somehow be recuperated or reinitiated. In order to accomplish this goal, Puerto Ricans must be able to recover this underlying essence as well as to overcome the past. For this reason, Pedreira ends his essay with a chapter entitled, "Juventud, divino tesoro" (Our Most Precious Treasure: The Young) in which he advocates a new beginning, a rebirth of national evolution founded upon contemporary youth as its starting point.²³

According to the author, geography also impacts national character. The physical characteristics of Puerto Rico—especially when these have been linked psychologically with certain consequences—have engendered tendencies that further inhibit the progress needed. As the title of the essay indicates, insularity is a key component in the development of Puerto Rican identity. Nevertheless, insularity itself does not present a problem. Instead, it is the relationship with this condition created by specific historical circumstances that has impeded the evolutionary process. Therefore, the concept of insularity as an integral component of the Puerto Rican psyche must be reconstituted. Pedreira cites the absence of an impulse to explore and seek knowledge from outside the island as well as the consequent propensity towards exaggerating or universalizing the significance of local production. As a possible cause of this phenomenon, he offers historical evidence of external threats; Puerto Rico has consistently been attacked and invaded by outside forces.²⁴

> Abierto por los cuatro costados a la codicia aventurera y conquistadora, nuestra isla fue fácil presa de piratas y expediciones internacionales, y tuvimos que defendernos isla adentro.²⁵

> [Open on all four sides to adventurous avarice and conquest, the island was easy pickings for pirates and international expeditions, and because Spain's naval power did not dominate these waters we had to defend ourselves by moving inland.]²⁶

He presents this problem in terms of a symbolic fear of the Dutch pirate that is waiting to assault anyone who dares to venture beyond the island's borders and insists that Puerto Ricans must be willing to venture forth despite this perceived threat.

The role of insularity in the project proposed by Pedreira becomes increasingly significant when viewed in light of the metaphors used in his text. One metaphor Pedreira repeatedly evokes in the presentation of his argument is that of ocean travel.²⁷ In this way, Pedreira presents both the problem of Puerto Rican evolution and its solution in terms of the relationship between the island and the surrounding waters as well as movement through those waters. The metaphor is linked to the historical trajectory presented in *Insularismo*. In her introduction to the essay, Angélica Barceló de Barasorda describes Pedreira's vision of history as "allegorically represented as an ocean voyage."[28] In this way, the metaphor reinforces the connection between geographic circumstance and historical development. Furthermore, the symbolic journey not only mirrors the dynamic between the problem and its causes proposed by the author but also addresses the rhetorical operations of the essay itself. The phrases Pedreira uses to describe the various periods of Puerto Rican history—i.e., "levando el ancla," "buscando el puerto," "intermezzo: una nave al garete" ("Weighing Anchor," "Looking for Safe Harbor," "Intermezzo: A Ship Adrift")—also serve as titles for the individual chapters of the text. Moreover, toward the end of *Insularismo*, Pedreira announces that, "[h]a llegado el momento de abandonar al lector, para que siga solo en esta peregrinación hacia la patria"[29] [The time has come to take our leave to the reader so that he may proceed alone on his pilgrimage toward the homeland].[30] In this way, the apprehension of the rhetorical problem itself is linked to both the geographically and historically insular circumstances that have engendered it. The reader must progress towards a certain intellectual relationship with insularity in order to reach the salvation that the author proposes.

What is most significant about *Insularismo*, however, is not necessarily the specific definition of Puerto Rican subjectivity advanced by the author. In fact, most of Pedreira's claims have been called into question by subsequent scholars. Nevertheless, even those writers who challenge and reject the arguments made in *Insularismo* assert the importance of the text itself. This importance transcends the author's conclusions precisely because Pedreira initiates a legitimate discourse of Puerto Rican self-definition. Juan Flores underscores this function of *Insularismo* in his analysis of the work: "From this point onward it could no longer be said of Puerto Rico that it lacked the kind of self-interpretative essay enjoyed by other Latin American countries. *Insularismo* put Puerto Rico on the intellectual map, and lent its claim to nationhood, however belated and mimetic, a measure of authority and, one might add, respectability."[31] In this way, Pedreira's essay performs a particular rhetorical function within the discourse of national identity that had been previously lacking in the case of Puerto Rico. Therefore, as in Lezama's writing, insularity becomes a trope that legitimizes the articulation of a specific local identity, and this legitimating function supersedes the elements of the argument itself.

For Benítez Rojo as well, in *La isla que se repite [The Repeating Island]*, insular circumstances constitute a defining factor within Caribbean sensibility. He presents an argument similar to Torres-Saillant's and suggests that the characterization of Caribbean reality in negative terms may be, in part, a consequence of the models used to understand it. When viewed according to paradigms that do not correspond to Antillean circumstances, therefore, the region is defined in terms of discrepancy and lack. The author argues, however, that the incompleteness, instability and other characteristics circumscribed by this approach can be recast in more positive terms if Caribbean reality is apprehended more appropriately. Drawing on chaos theory, Benítez Rojo proposes that internal rhythms and patterns of organization can be found in the Antilles.

> Pero la cultura del Caribe, al menos el aspecto de ella que más la diferencia, no es terrrestre sino acuática; una cultura sinuosa donde el tiempo se despliega irregularmente y se resiste a ser capturado por el ciclo del reloj o el del calendario. El Caribe es el reino natural e impredecible de las corrientes marinas, de las ondas, de los pliegues y repliegues, de la fluidez y de las sinuosidades. Es, a fin de cuentas, una cultura de meta-archipiélago: un caos que retorna, un *detour* sin propósito, un continuo fluir de paradojas; es una máquina de *feed-back* de procesos asimétricos.[32]

> [But the culture of the Caribbean, at least in its most distinctive aspect, is not terrestrial but aquatic, a sinuous culture where time unfolds irregularly and resists being captured by the cycles of clock and calendar. The Caribbean is the natural and indispensable realm of marine currents, of waves, of folds and double-folds, of fluidity and sinuosity. It is, in the final analysis, a culture of the meta-archipelago: a chaos that returns, a detour without a purpose, a continual flow of paradoxes; it is a feed-back machine with asymmetrical workings.][33]

Consequently, the very attributes that are condemned by traditional approaches may provide the key to deciphering the unique structures of the area.

One of the principal elements that Benítez Rojo focuses on in his reexamination of the region is the island. According to his analysis, the individual islands and the relationship among them constitute a central organizing axis of this chaotic Antillean order. That is, Caribbean reality is comprised through the conjoining of repeated reproductions of finite structures, and the island nations of the Antillean archipelago constitute concrete manifestations of this process. Once again, the nature of islands afford a singular quality to the region and, in turn, the need to develop interpretative paradigms appropriate to this unique reality.

Benítez Rojo's posture at times parallels Lezama's reticence in the *Coloquio* when it comes to defining the exact characteristics that set Caribbean writers apart from their counterparts in other regions. Although he does identify and specifically address many such characteristics, he also reserves an essential quality within the realm of indefinable perception. Benítez Rojo specifically uses the phrase "a certain way" to describe such characteristics, insisting that it cannot be described more precisely but rather that it must be apprehended.[34] Once again, the geographic reality of the Caribbean is inscribed within a rhetorical project that reserves a unique sensibility for the region—and its literary production in particular—that authorizes a process of self-definition.

Through the focus on insularity in multiple definitions of Caribbean identity, the trope transcends individual articulations: insularity moves beyond each author's definition to an omnipresent rhetorical condition within the discourse of Caribbean self-definition. Moreover, the role of insularity is not limited to the texts discussed here—or even those that explicitly address issues of identity—but forms part of a larger tradition of texts in which Antillean geography provides the setting for the inscription of regional identity.

Not only does the pervasiveness of the trope suggest that it is linked to a rhetorical need, but the repeated postulations of it also indicate that it does not satisfy this need. The continual resurgence of insularity implies that it responds to a rhetorical necessity that it is simultaneously unable to sufficiently address. In spite of inherent rhetorical flaws, authors in both Latin American and the Caribbean invoke a positivistic model in which local geography circumscribes subjectivity. As a result, that geography both legitimates local discourse and becomes inextricably bound to the identity it legitimates. In the case of the Caribbean, the sea and the relationship between the islands and their surrounding waters constitute the primary indigenous geographic circumstance through which authors attempt to construct such identities. This tendency produces a tradition of self-inscription that draws upon and, later, reformulates this autochthonous discourse. Caribbean writers postulate land-sea oppositions and explorations of the sea itself as a strategy through which they define and redefine identity. More specifically, in the works examined here, insularity ultimately functions as an essentialist concept on which a Caribbean or island-specific ontology is based. Nonetheless, the Caribbean specificity that is demarcated through this rhetorical tradition is not entirely stable or consistent. Instead, authors repeatedly reconfigure the boundary between land and sea in the construction of a discourse of identity.

Admittedly, the discursive construction and contestation of borders has also been examined outside of the Caribbean. In fact, boundaries often circumscribe these constructs in diverse contexts and registers. Even though they construct distinct arguments, Homi Bhabha and Gloria Anzaldúa, have each examined how the border can either reinforce or subvert existing articulations of national identity.[35] Of course, this function of boundaries is not restricted to the inscription of geographic divisions either. As Foucault asserts in *Madness and Civilization*, for example, this practice is the very foundation of normative discourse: national identity and power are constructed through the separation of the purportedly disruptive and productive elements in a given social order. And in his reflections, Derrida has rigorously interrogated the limits of writing and signification. In this case, the construction of boundaries constitutes the concrete manifestation of the underlying system. Since Derrida insists that the nature of writing renders the location of absolute meaning impossible, signification has to be understood as a process. In "Signature, Event, Context," he argues that the sign always inscribes a separation or displacement and that this differentiation renders it interpretable: "The force of rupture is due to the spacing which constitutes the written sign: the spacing which separates it from other elements of the internal contextual chain . . . , but also from all the forms of a present referent . . . that is objective or subjective. This spacing is not the simple negativity of a lack, but the emergence of the mark."[36] Hence, the legibility of the written sign is produced through its circumscription. According to these theories, boundaries and circumscription constitute fundamental mechanisms in the construction of subjectivity.

Although this interpretation of the rhetorical function of boundaries can be applied to Caribbean writing as well, the role of circumscription also becomes more significant in the Antillean context because of the specific role of boundaries in the articulation of singularity. Throughout Caribbean writing, the island frequently occupies a central role and, furthermore, becomes the foundation of the textual project. In the case of the Hispanic Caribbean in particular, the postulation of the island as the defining trope of national identity privileges insular boundaries. As in other discursive contexts, therefore, boundaries constitute the site of negotiation and reconfiguration of subjectivity. More importantly, the rhetoric of insularity becomes a foundational fiction of Hispanic Caribbean writing that engenders both discourses of national identity and the project of Antillean writing. The narratives perpetually reconfigure insular boundaries and contribute to an overarching literary enterprise that repeatedly reiterates and reinscribes these boundaries.

## Tales of Insularity in
## Hispanic Caribbean Literature

Of course, the prominence of insularity is not limited to texts that explicitly address the nature of Hispanic Caribbean identity or self-expression. In the literary production of the last two centuries, these themes are persistently invoked. Again, the problems and possibilities of the nation are often articulated in terms of a particular relationship with the island. Its boundaries are drawn and redrawn in a manner that offers a critical vision of Caribbean development. As with the examples of intellectual discourse discussed above, the evolution of the islands depicted in these fictional universes has been hindered by an inappropriate relationship with Antillean geography. The writing of the late nineteenth century, in particular, postulates projects of self-determination and advancement. More importantly, several texts produced during this period strongly emphasize geographic demarcation in the articulation of these projects. In particular, *La peregrinación de Bayoán* (1863) and *La vuelta al hogar* (1877) overtly dramatize how insular geography shapes Hispanic Caribbean literary discourse. At the same time, however, these texts showcase a trend of spatialized conflict that can be traced in other works of the period as well.

Eugenio María de Hostos, the nineteenth-century Puerto Rican author, political activist, and educational reformer, engages in this rhetorical dynamic in his novel, *La peregrinación de Bayoán*, and rewrites the arrival narrative of Caribbean literature. Through this rewriting, the author also examines the impact of insular boundaries on national and regional development. In *La peregrinación*, Hostos constructs a dichotomy between the Caribbean region and the sea beyond it, but the specific articulation of the rhetoric of insularity in Hostos's text also engenders problems that ultimately must be resolved through the production of even more writing.

The novel takes the form of a personal diary and is narrated almost exclusively through the dated journal entries of the protagonist, Bayoán. In many of these entries, he comments on the political situation of the Hispanic Antilles and argues for the need to negotiate a healthier and more productive relationship among Caribbean nations and with the exterior. At the beginning of the novel, Bayoán reflects on his travels and his ambitions as he embarks on a journey to Spain where he plans to argue for a refined relationship between his homeland, Puerto Rico, and the colonial powers that govern it, a new compact that will lead to a more autonomous existence for the island. Before leaving for Spain, he meets Marién, and the two fall in love. Although Bayoán is torn between his love for her and his sense of patriotic duty, he opts for the latter and decides to leave. This conflict is resolved, nevertheless, when Marién's parents, along with their distraught daughter, decide to accompany Bayoán on his trip to Spain. However, the solution is short-lived, since Marién's health proves directly dependent upon proximity to the Antilles, and Bayoán is once again caught between contradictory obligations: he is unwilling to abandon his mission but is also acutely aware that its pursuit is jeopardizing Marién's health. In the end, Marién succumbs to her illness and Bayoán renounces his political ambitions and resigns himself to total defeat. The plot of the novel, therefore, does not allow for a synthesizing closure since Bayoán's simultaneous desire to realize incompatible projects leads to their mutual destruction.

Bayoán's pilgrimage is narrated through a series of journal entries that chronicle his travels as well as the difficulties he encounters and the dilemmas he experiences as a result of these difficulties. Toward the end of *La peregrinación*, Bayóan is unable to continue to document his experiences. The missing information is provided, instead, through journal entries written by the supposed editor of the text. Although most of the story is narrated through the protagonist's first-person chronicle, the insertion of the editor's comments and interventions in the diary underscore the status of the account as a written (and repeatedly revised) text. In this sense, Hostos presents the diary as a mediated and, to a large extent, rewritten account of Bayoán's experiences. At the same time, this narrative device also intensifies the intertextuality between the protagonist's diary and earlier chronicles. Not only does Bayoán retrace Columbus's foundational voyage through the Antilles; this parallel is also presented through Bayoán's self-conscious narration of his travels in his journal in a clear allusion to and repetition of Columbus's seminal *Diario*. In this way, *La peregrinación* presents itself as a complicated—perhaps even unstable—palimpsest, since it constitutes the rewriting of an already problematic reproduction.

This self-sustaining rhetorical structure becomes increasingly significant when examined in terms of the foundational aspirations of the novel. Not only is *La peregrinación* cited as one of the seminal texts of modern Puerto Rican literature by contemporary critics, but Hostos himself underscores the role of his text as the origin of a literary tradition.[37] At the time of the novel's publication, national literatures were emerging in both the Caribbean and Latin America. In the case of Puerto Rico, the first and second *Aguinaldo puertorriqueño* were published in 1843 and 1846 respectively along with *Album puertorriqueño* (1843) and the first version of Manuel Alonso's *El Gíbaro* (1849).[38] Although Hostos does not make explicit reference to this incipient literary tradition, he emphasizes the seminal character of his narrative through specific textual elements. The most obvious of these is the intertextual dialogue between Bayoán's travel journal and Columbus's *Diario* mentioned earlier, since the latter's text constitutes not only the supposed record of the voyages of discovery but the putative origin of American letters. Therefore, by establishing *La peregrinación* as a rewriting of this text, Hostos suggests that his novel will perform a similar function and constitute the point of departure of a new narrative tradition.

In this end, *La peregrinación* is a novel about beginnings that resists the idea of origins. The narrative project of Hostos's novel generates a discourse machine, which, in turn, constitutes the source of a self-sustaining literary tradition. Furthermore, the discourse machine that Hostos produces is a fundamentally insular one. His text repeatedly rewrites the relationship between insular territory and the terrain beyond its border. It articulates the project of Puerto Rican writing, moreover, in terms of a perpetual (if not self-perpetuating) circumscription of the arrival narrative of Latin American letters.

In a similar fashion, Salvador Brau dramatizes the foundational significance of insular boundaries in his play, *La vuelta al hogar*. *La vuelta* constitutes a paradigmatic example of how issues of national identity, romanticism, and theater interact and produce a critical vision of the developing project of nationalism. The work was first performed in Mayagüez in 1877 and focuses primarily on a love triangle among the three principal characters: Gabriel, Consuelo, and Tristán. Consuelo is a noble young woman who was raised by Gabriel's parents after she was orphaned. Tristán is a suitor who attempts unsuccessfully to win Consuelo's love. Gabriel, the young man who has left Puerto Rico in order to seek better economic opportunities, returns home at the end of the second act. At first Gabriel's return is widely celebrated: not only are his parents overjoyed by his unexpected and safe return, but he also develops a romantic interest in Consuelo, whom, he discovers, is already in love with him. It quickly becomes apparent, however, that Gabriel's "fortune" is based on his exploits as a violent pirate. Therefore, Consuelo rejects the possibility of any future happiness for the pair, and Tristán seizes the opportunity to eliminate his rival by denouncing him to the local authorities. Of course, Gabriel promises to repent in order to become worthy of Consuelo's love, but he is not able to escape from Tristán or the authorities, and he is presumably killed in the final scene by his persecutors.

On the one hand, *La vuelta* presents a version of the classic romantic triangle in which the union of the principal characters is impeded by the relative social status and power of the third member of the triad. On the other, however, Brau's play also dramatizes the central conflict of insular development. Through the relative displacement and confinement of the respective characters, the play highlights the problems and possibilities afforded by the relationship between the island and the surrounding waters. Access to the sea provides Gabriel with opportunities that had not been readily available to him within the confines of insular society. Nevertheless, the sea does not consitute an appropriate space of social formation, and his status as a successful pirate becomes an impediment when he attempts to return home. As with *Once on This Island* and more paradigmatic examples such as *The Tempest* cited earlier, the threat of an approaching storm also highlights the precarious nature of the land-sea boundary—an instability that fuels the principal conflict of the play.

More importantly, perhaps, significant components of the drama take place outside the visible space of the performance. In this sense, the staging of the play mirrors the dynamics between the interior and exterior of the island that are portrayed in *La vuelta*. Hence, the action depicted both relies upon and is thwarted by what can only occur beyond the representational space of the performance. The interior territory of colonial Puerto Rican society and the island are in constant and necessary tension with the space beyond its boundaries. In this fashion, Brau suggests that the contradictory relationship between the island and its surroundings is simultaneously (and paradoxically) a response to the limitations of colonial society and a possible obstacle in the development of productive nationhood. The plot and structure of the play thus repeatedly showcase the importance of the confines of both insular and dramatic space.

In Brau's play, therefore—as in Hostos's novel—the impossible romance is framed and foiled by the geopolitical circumstances of Puerto Rico. Not surprisingly, perhaps, these works dramatize the failed family romance of Puerto Rican literature. As Doris Sommer has cogently argued and critics such as Juan Gelpí and Arnaldo Cruz Malavé have discussed in the Puerto Rican context specifically, the literature of the region repeatedly retells the story of impossible unions. Of course, *La vuelta* constitutes an early example of this master narrative: as with Jorge Isaac's *María*, for example, the female lead is an orphan who is adopted by the male lead's family. Given the status of the two children, the genealogical potential of the family is, at best, already problematic. Yet the pairing of the adopted orphan and the lost son offers the possibility of restoring or healing the familial (and, by extension, social) structure.

In this case, however, the principal foil is the inability of the potential new progenitors to successfully develop within the established parameters.

Hence, the inevitable displacement of Gabriel ultimately leads to the impossible (re)unification of the seminal pair. In the end, the unproductive insufficiency of available components on the island thwarts the generation of a new national identity. In Lacanian terms, Gabriel is, almost literally, the missing element that is desired but cannot be fully attained. More importantly, however, Gabriel's unattainability is engendered by the fundamentally irreconcilable need to both transgress and respect existing boundaries in order to fulfill his role as a desirable and productive male protagonist. Hence, ironically, the very characteristics that allow Gabriel to become Consuelo's object of desire also render him unacceptable as a partner. In this way, beyond its status as yet another example of failed foundational drama, the plot structure, themes, and representational mechanics of *La vuelta* highlight the binary opposition between interior and exterior spaces in Puerto Rican national discourse.

Certainly, other texts that feature pirates or maritime themes also emphasize the paradoxical relationship between the interior and exterior of the island that Hostos and Brau present in their texts. In these cases, the surrounding sea offers a conduit of access to the outside world (access that proves essential in the pursuit of a modified relationship with external powers) on the one hand and a principal threat to insular existence on the other. These texts acutely dramatize a particular relationship between spatial limitations and national development that can also be traced in other works that do not share their thematic content. Although they do not necessarily engage insular geography explicitly, nineteenth century sentimental novels produced in the Hispanic Caribbean also dialogue closely with the emergent tradition of insular self-expression.

In particular, Gertrudis Gómez de Avelleneda's *Sab* (1841) and Manuel de Jesús Galván's *Enriquillo* (1881) narrate the struggles of their respective protagonists to carve out an appropriate space for themselves in Cuban and Dominican society respectively. In both cases, the title character is an ethnically marked or racialized other who gains a privileged position in the colonial social order through education and the apparent internalization of European ideals. In the end, however, their privilege does not ultimately allow them to realize the desired union with a beloved member of colonial society.

As in the case of *La peregrinación* and *La vuelta*, these texts focus on a romantic coupling that is thwarted by the presence of a superfluous suitor and the restrictions of social norms. At the same time, however, the central conflict of the novels is also intensely spatialized in both texts. The absence of an adequate location for the protagonist within colonial society and the more general problem of insufficient room for appropriate development are persistently highlighted as the plots of these novels unfold. The protagonist is an outsider that struggles to be incorporated into the mainstream community, and the success of this struggle depends on his ability to navigate a Foucauldian path from the marginal spaces of alterity to the more centralized enclosures of normative domesticity.[39]

In the end, Enriquillo is able to maneuver through the limits and limitations of Dominican society and overcome his initial marginality. Despite his economic success, however, Sab is not able to liberate himself from his original confinement and reposition himself within plantation society. Through these trajectories, moreover, the project of national development is dramatized in terms of displacement and confinement. The idealized vision of the nation that the characters strive to realize is posited in terms of their need to develop a more suitable relationship with the excessively circumscribed social space of the island. They attempt to foster a productive relationship with confinement and demarcate appropriate and, to some extent, protective boundaries that will allow for the successful evolution of the social and economic structure of the island-nation.

As Doris Sommer has compellingly demonstrated, these novels focus on themes that can also be found in national romances of continental Spanish America. Nevertheless, in these cases, the desired development of the nation is ultimately impeded by predominantly spatialized tensions. Not only are the Antillean protagonists unable to form the appropriate unions and thus engender the (narrative) future of the nation, but this impossibility is closely tied to territorial conflicts. The characters cannot appropriately inhabit the demarcated spaces of colonial Caribbean societies nor relocate to a suitable alternative location of productivity without compromising the proposed union. Hence, lack of space becomes the locus of enunciation for Antillean self-fashioning. In this sense, the foundational fictions of the Hispanic Antilles are fundamentally insular: they inaugurate a tradition of writing in which the problems and possibilities of the nation are expressed through the demarcation of space.

Indeed, the tradition initiated by these works continues to thrive in subsequent writing. Throughout the literary production of the twentieth and early twenty-first centuries, authors repeatedly postulate the perils and potential of Caribbean expression in terms of a relationship with insular topography. Recently, in fact, Reina María Rodríguez has hypothesized that the idea of the island has become a trap that confines Caribbean writing.[40] By persistently returning to the island as the defining trope of subjectivity, Antillean writers reinforce the master-narrative of insularity. According to

Rodríguez, the pervasiveness of this master-narrative, in turn, limits textual production.

Although the excessive attachment to spatialized self-fashioning may impede the evolution of Caribbean expression, the rhetoric of insularity has proven surprisingly malleable; Caribbean writing has remained fundamentally insular, but this attribute is not limited to a single manifestation or set of implications. In the end, Caribbean authors construct insularity in vastly different terms and in a variety of contexts. Hence, insularity in fact acts as a catalyst in the generation of distinct and even contradictory projects. As I have argued earlier, the rhetoric of insularity can underscore the need to preserve existing boundaries and protect the island from invasion, on the one hand, and the need to overcome the separation between the internal and the external on the other. Furthermore, the reconfiguration of boundaries can incorporate previously marginalized or excluded components of Caribbean culture.

The development of a literary corpus that encompasses all of these possibilities implies that the island acts as a mechanism of production rather than one of confinement. Insularity is not bound to a particular definition but can acquire multiple and even incompatible meanings. Similarly, the rhetoric of insularity can construct boundaries as a problem to be solved or as a potential to be activated. Nevertheless, because of the possibilities available for the rhetoric of insularity, the latter engenders fundamental contradictions that cannot be resolved internally. Insular tropes demarcate the fundamental discrepancy between the current status of bound territory and the vision of the place that the nation should ideally come to occupy. Whether they construct insularity as possibility or conflict, Caribbean authors engage in a contestatory poetics since they continually postulate discourses of identity in terms of the very circumstance that they desire to overcome. Hence, Caribbean literature has become the record of the repeated attempt to resolve this conflict, and to write itself out of the confines—not of insularity itself—but of the rhetoric of insularity that it has generated.

## The Shifting Topographies of Caribbean Island-Nations

As is characteristic of discourses of nationalism, this mode of Caribbean self-fashioning continuously articulates a vision of the nation that will never be fully achieved. Nevertheless, until recently, the underlying equation between the physical borders of the nation and the boundaries of the island had remained relatively stable and unquestioned. Authors have traditionally associated insularity with a vast array of positive and negative attributes, yet, in both cases, they could readily cite the fixed demarcation of insular terrain as the symbol of a standard to be emulated. The island and nation were generally seen as coextenstive, even if the current consequences of that relationship were less than ideal.

Since the middle of the twentieth century, however, the desired equation of island and nation has been further challenged by two significant trends: the island is occupied by increasingly visible individuals or groups who cannot readily constitute part of the nation and, at the same time, a significant portion of the Hispanic Antillean population has begun to reside beyond the island's borders. Consequently, as these contradictions have developed, we might expect a concomitant shift in the discourses of self-definition. Yet insularity persists as a primary rhetoric of Hispanic Caribbean self-fashioning. In these cases, the boundaries of the island and the nation cannot be readily identified as equivalent, but authors nonetheless have continued to claim that insular geography defines national character.

As a result, the discrepancy between insular boundaries and national borders becomes increasingly problematic in Hispanic Caribbean literary and cultural production. Given the avowed role of insular geography in the formation of Antillean identity, the island functions as the principal space of social formation. How, then, can Caribbean identity be produced or maintained when the island becomes unavailable or fails to adequately perform this function? Similarly, since the desired equation between the space of the island and that of the nation constitutes a fundamental component of national development, political and demographic movement away from this equation poses a direct challenge to traditional notions of national identity. The following chapters examine particular instances in which the island-nation equation is called into question and analyze how this rhetorical crisis is negotiated in contemporary literary and cultural production.

Chapter 2, "Out Elsewhere," explores how queer subjectivity is articulated in insular terms. As the nineteenth-century texts demonstrate, the island-nation equation presupposes an absolute binary between the appropriate subjects who reside on the island and the aberrant others who are located beyond its borders. The manifestation of queer subjects within the boundaries of the island disrupts the presumed dichotomy. As in other contexts, gay, lesbian, bisexual, and transgendered individuals have often been viewed as aberrant, subversive dissidents who cannot readily constitute part of the (re)productive state in the Caribbean. Because of the spatialized vision of national development, this conflict is expressed in terms of a problematic dialectic between the interior and the exterior. In other words, the island must be occupied solely by legitimate, appropriate, and (re)productive citizens. If we were to pursue this logic to its furthest consequences, queer subjects would have to be physically removed from the community and could only be introduced as ostensibly productive citizens if they are successfully reeducated or reconstituted by this experience. And if there is no place on the island for queer subjects, their citizenship can only be formed, if at all, in the space of an alternative island.

"Out Elsewhere" examines how Caribbean writers have problematized this vision of the island-nation. I analyze how the works of Virgilio Piñera, Severo Sarduy, and Mayra Santos Febres challenge conventional representations of national space and their concomitant normative limits. The alternative spaces constructed by these authors fundamentally destabilize the characterization of the delimited island as a natural phenomenon rather than a cultivated social construct. Each of these works presents subjects that are "out elsewhere" and therefore underscores the limitations from and within which the nation has constituted itself. The negotiation of queer insularity thus highlights the fundamental processes of Hispanic Caribbean self-fashioning: the desired identity is circumscribed through the demarcation of insular terrain and subjectivity.

As I suggested earlier, the geographic circumstances of the Antilles conspire to create and reinforce a vision of national autonomy (even when this autonomy has not been achieved in political terms). Consequently, the presence of another sovereign power within the borders of the island severely challenges the appearance of self-governance naturally afforded by the physical circumstances of the islands. Chapter 3, "Dancing with the Enemy," explores several key instances in which the islands become subdivided or a portion of the island is claimed by a separate sovereign nation. Specifically, I analyze three instances in which the island is subdivided between the nation and the other against which the nation defines itself: the relationship between Haiti and the Dominican Republic on Hispaniola and the impact of the U.S. naval bases in both Guantánamo Bay, Cuba and Vieques, Puerto Rico.

In these situations of insular subdivision, the battle for political power and for the control of space become conflated. Hence, territorial claims become intensified, and the presence of the opponent within the island necessarily becomes a threat that must be symbolically, if not literally, eliminated. The three instances examined here, therefore, expose the false dichotomy through which the nation is always already defined by a symbolic separation from outside forces. The nation is demarcated in opposition to an other that is putatively located beyond its boundaries. In these cases, however, the manifestation of the enemy's presence within the delimited space of the island highlights the underlying paradoxical relationship with this other and therefore constitutes a crisis of identity that must be overcome.

In both of these cases, the rhetorical crisis is provoked by an alternative presence within the confines of the island. The presumed dichotomy between the island and the world beyond its borders is disrupted by an internal heterogeneity or diversity that cannot be readily subsumed within existing visions of the nation. To an even greater extent, however, the movement of the traditionally internal population beyond the space of the island constitutes an even greater threat to insular self-fashioning. Hence, the increasing prevalence of the diaspora emerges as the largest and most obvious challenge to conventional notions of the island-nation as the formative space of cultural identity. If Caribbean people are located outside the Antilles, how can their identity be fundamentally shaped by insularity? The final two chapters examine how Caribbean literary and cultural production has attempted to sustain insular self-fashioning despite the demographic shifts that would presumably displace its centrality.

Over the course of the twentieth century, there has been a sustained emigration of Hispanic Caribbean people; Cubans, Dominicans, and Puerto Ricans increasingly reside outside of the Antilles. Consequently, the island no longer constitutes the exclusive or even primary site of their communities. At the same time, developments in communication, travel, and international commerce have fostered greater interconnectedness between the islands and the United States. Given these changes, we might expect a corresponding shift in the Hispanic Caribbean rhetoric: as the primacy of the island diminishes, the rhetoric of insularity would presumably be rendered insufficient and anachronistic. Instead, however, insularity continues to function as a principal trope of self-definition. Even in the diaspora, the historical attachment to insular borders continues to shape cultural production. In fact, marketing trends in the U.S. favor geographically bound paradigms of identity. Hence, Antillean spatiality is often reproduced in the diasporic context, which can engender a fundamental contradiction in the codification of diasporic subjectivity.

Chapter 4, "Out of Place," examines how Caribbean spatiality is (re)inscribed in contemporary caribeña popular culture and fiction. In particular, it focuses on how insular topographies are reinforced through the commodification of artists such as Ricky Martin and Marc Anthony and in Cristina García's *Dreaming in Cuban*. In both cases, the formation of identity relies on a particular spatiality, one that emphasizes the alterity and displacement of the subject. In these cases, not only does insularity continue to function as a primary trope of caribeñidad, but it is articulated in terms that privilege the geographically bound space of the island. Hence, the particular codification of U.S. Caribbean cultures found in these texts render the space of the diaspora inherently lacking or inferior.

Finally, chapter 5, "Virtual Islands," also analyzes diaporic literary and cultural production. In this case, however, the materials demonstrate how conventional notions of insular self-fashioning can be adapted to the changing landscape and spatiality of Caribbean cultures. Historically, the role of insularity has persisted despite political, cultural, and demographic shifts that might otherwise have called it into question. Nevertheless, this persistence has not always been counter-productive. In fact, given its inherent attachment to fixed demarcations, the rhetoric of insularity has proven remarkably malleable. As with discourses of identity in other contexts, it has been reconfigured in innovative terms—terms that, at times, have critically interrogated the rhetorical tradition itself. Not surprisingly, therefore, recent articulations of insular topographies have called into question the direct attachment to geographic location. They underscore the limitations of bound demarcation and, in particular, the contradictions that this mode of self-fashioning engenders for increasingly translocal populations. "Virtual Islands" traces the reterritorialization of insularity in contemporary Hispanic Caribbean cultural production.

In particular, the chapter focuses on the function of cyber-spatiality on Puerto Rican Web sites. The representations of insular space on these sites engages the circular migratory patterns and the more formalized political relationship with a transinsular national space in the Puerto Rican context. The insular tropes deployed on these sites resituate conventional tropes of landscape and autochthony in more fluid terms. They construct real-and-imagined spaces of Puerto Rican experience that, in the end, underscore the very translocal spatiality of the Hispanic Caribbean diaspora. In this context, insular boundaries do not circumscribe the sacred space of the Antilles; instead, they create new spaces in which diasporic subjectivity can be inscribed. These sites therefore problematize (rather than reinforce) the primacy of the Antilles as the principal locus of cultural production and self-formation. Consequently, the representation of insular iconography on Puerto Rican Web sites negotiates the paradoxical convergence of a geographically bound trope and an alternative (not to mention inherently mobile) locus of cultural enunciation. The cases analyzed in this chapter critically engage the complexity of translocal insularity. Through these reconfigurations, moreover, the reified space of the homeland is transformed into an allegorical spatiality that can be productively reterritorialized.

In all of these instances, the texts examined address the disjunctures between national geography and territory and, in doing so, offer a portrait of the rhetoric of insularity at its limits. They highlight contexts or circumstances in which insular self-fashioning is seemingly "out of bounds"; the traditional attachment to geographic demarcation presumably becomes an inappropriate or even counter-productive mode of self-definition that potentially undermines the legitimacy of the identity these works seek to codify. Given the apparent inappropriateness of geographically determined models, it is precisely the perseverance of this mode of self-definition that makes these works the most intriguing and significant manifestations of the tradition. The fundamentally paradoxical or contradictory status of insular tropes in these cases brings their underlying operation into stark relief. They reveal complex negotiations of spatiality and demonstrate how insularity transcends geography and comes to function instead as a legitimating structure of identity. In the end, Hispanic Caribbean discourse persistently inscribes itself in the interstices between island and nation and, in doing so, creates its own authoritative space.

# 2
# Out Elsewhere:
# The Limits of Normative Sexualities

A FEW YEARS AGO, A FRIEND RELATED AN INCIDENT THAT SHE HAD EXperienced in the reading room of a local café along with several colleagues. After perusing the wide array of periodicals on display, the three women inquired if the café carried the *Advocate*. The employee responded curtly that they did not carry it because the café was a "family establishment." My friend pointed out that magazines such as *Cosmopolitan* and *Maxim*—featuring scantily clad and sexually provocative images of women on the cover—were prominently displayed, but the employee simply informed them that the periodicals available had been specifically selected by the owner.

This anecdote offers evidence of a well-established trend: despite political correctness and the increasing visibility of gay culture in the media, homosexuality is often equated with decadence and aberrant self-indulgence and is considered to be fundamentally antithetical to mainstream family values.[1] Although this equation is most commonly attributed to religious fundamentalism (especially in the United States), it is also the product of the Foucauldian link between heteronormativity and spatiality in postindustrial societies.[2] That is, societal codes regarding conduct, domesticity, and labor fundamentally favor the nuclear family as the central structure of production and reproduction, and queer sexuality inherently threatens the stability of these codes since it challenges their underlying organizing principles. Consequently, non-normative sexuality must remain socially "closeted": it can be tolerated in carefully circumscribed and marginalized locations, but it cannot be overtly visible in mainstream spaces of interaction and consumption.

For the most part, Hispanic Caribbean cultures do not constitute an exception to this rule. In fact, Cuban, Dominican, and Puerto Rican histories offer numerous examples of heteronormative, homophobic, and—in some cases—anti-gay policies that are directly tied to discourses of national development. More importantly, given the intense identification with insular boundaries in this context, the displacement of non-normative sexuality becomes a heightened anxiety within projects of national self-definition: the coterminous equation of island and nation presupposes a similarly absolute dichotomy between national territory and normative subjectivity. Hence, the manifestation of queer subjectivity within the boundaries of the island-nation fundamentally destabilizes the spatialized vision of appropriate development.

Arguably, the most salient example of this trend can be found in the first decade of Fidel Castro's leadership following the Cuban Revolution. During the 1960s, laws against homosexuality were regularly enforced and gay men were routinely arrested and interned in military reeducation centers, commonly referred to as UMAP (Military Units to Aid Production) camps. In other words, suspicions of same-sex activities or desires could not be readily incorporated into the vision of the "New Man" that Castro and Ernesto "Che" Guevara had advocated. Homosexuals—gay men in particular—were deemed inherently guilty of counterrevolutionary sedition and were therefore removed from Cuban society so that they could be "reeducated" and reformed as appropriately (re)productive comrades.

Of course, this historical episode and other state-sanctioned regulations of sexuality in the Caribbean certainly have their counterparts in other geographic contexts.[3] Nevertheless, what is particularly striking in Hispanic Antillean discourses is the exceptionally overt link between sexuality and spatiality. The case of the UMAP camps illustrates this trend: not only is queer sexuality viewed as a threat to (re)productive society, but the ensuing conflict is dramatized in highly spatialized terms. These individuals must be removed from the quotidian social space and contained in a particular locus of confinement and potential reconfiguration. In this fashion, the fundamental dichotomy between the interior and exterior of the island carries heteronormative connotations: in order to develop appropriately, the territory of the island-nation must be inhabited exclusively by (re)productive citizens. And queer subjects must be removed from the dominant social space of the nation, be effectively reeducated and/or be circumscribed in a manner that allows them to perform an appropriate (and nondisruptive) social function.

Of course, this dominant vision of self-fashioning and social regulation has not been universally accepted. In fact, it has frequently been criticized or called into question within Antillean cultural production. Paradoxically, however, this counter-hegemonic discourse often reproduces the underlying equation of insularity and nationhood even as it critiques how this equation has been conventionally deployed. This chapter will examine how queer Hispanic Caribbean authors have challenged dominant demarcations of subjectivity in their work and presented an alternative configuration of insularity. More specifically, Virgilio Piñera, Severo Sarduy, and Mayra Santos Febres all portray the limits of insularity in a manner that fundamentally problematizes the dominant spatialized configuration of normative sexuality. As I will argue here, desire cannot be productively or adequately contained within the confines of the islands they depict, and this impossibility exposes the arbitrary and artificial nature of the heteronormative insular binary. In this manner, the alter-insularity they construct significantly interrogates the normative function of spatiality in Hispanic Caribbean self-fashioning. At the same time, however, their vision of spatiality reproduces the very relationship between sexuality and space that they seek to contest. As a result, their alternative demarcations do not fundamentally destabilize insularity as the dominant paradigm of self-definition.

## Insularity at its Limits:
## Normative Sexuality and the
## Urgency of Space in Puerto Rico

As I have asserted earlier, one of the purported consequences of insularity is insufficiency. That is, given the limited confines of the island-nation and its relative isolation, Caribbean discourse often insists on the maximization of internal resources. This sense of urgency applies not only to material commodities, but to citizenship, sexuality, and space: the (inter)actions of the inhabitants who coexist within the confines of the island must be as efficient and productive as possible in order to avoid a potential crisis of scarcity.

This exigency is articulated with particular intensity in the case of the smallest of the Greater Antilles, Puerto Rico. Puerto Rican discourses of self-definition persistently evoke the diminutive size of the island as a characteristic of identity and culture. Writers as diverse as Euguenio María de Hostos, Antonio S. Pedreira, René Marqués, José Luis González, and Rosario Ferré—to name a few salient examples—have all explored the pressures that are engendered by the relative smallness of the island. The dynamics of scarcity and insufficiency that can be traced throughout the Hispanic Caribbean are therefore rendered in especially salient terms in the Puerto Rican context.

The limitations and impediments associated with this spatial insufficiency, moreover, are frequently linked to questions of sexuality. The refrain of a song popularized by El Gran Combo de Puerto Rico, for example, announces the problem of a required commodity for which necessity exceeds availability: "No hay cama pa' tanta gente" (There ain't enough beds for so many people). The song describes a Christmas party that several famous Caribbean musicians and other individuals involved in the music industry attend. The duration of the festivities, however, is restricted a priori by the lack of sufficient space for the guests to sleep in the house. That is, as individual guests begin to show signs of fatigue, another attendee warns that appropriate sleeping accommodations cannot be provided. Therefore, some of the individuals present literally must be thrown into the street because there simply is not enough room to accommodate everyone.

On the one hand, the song constructs a playful allusion to professional competition, given that El Gran Combo itself is named among the guests of the party. Hence, the insufficiency of the house ultimately engenders the inability for the performers of the song and their professional colleagues to inhabit the same space for an extended period of time. The insistence on limited accommodations could therefore be understood as a allusion to the competitive difficulties of the relatively saturated market of popular Caribbean music. One the other hand, this competition for limited resources is articulated in implicitly sexual terms. The excessive number of individuals who have convened at the party, and their shared desire to produce music, could potentially lead to inappropriate, excessive and, thus, counterproductive unions. The chorus and refrain of the song continually insist that the attendees cannot simply go to bed together, and some of the guests must be ejected from the house in order to avoid this possibility.

Not surprisingly, the exigencies of limited resources put even greater pressure on the normative function of the state. That is, the state must regulate the behavior and productivity of the island's inhabitants in order to maximize the potential of available assets, which leads to the intense scrutiny of sexual unions. As Eileen Findlay has cogently asserted in *Imposing Decency*, the legal regulation of marriage can be directly linked to changes in political and economic status in Puerto Rico: this regulation is used to incite the more efficient and appropriate incorporation of the colony into global systems of exchange. Hence, because of their inherent inability to conform with traditional conceptions of family and genealogy, queer subjects cannot constitute productive members of the proposed society and, consequently, have no legitimate place on the island.

Similarly, in Puerto Rican literature, national subjectivity is perpetually articulated, contested, and reterritorialized in terms of normative and non-normative sexualities. Once again, these processes of subject formation and regulation are inexorably tied to insularity. Over the past two decades, several prominent scholars have astutely underscored how sexuality is both demarcated and deployed in Puerto Rican texts. In her article, "Community at Its Limits," Agnes Lugo Ortiz examines the literal and figurative (r)ejection of queerness. She analyzes "¡Jum!" a short story by Luis Rafael Sánchez that was originally published in *En cuerpo de camisa*, the author's first book. In "¡Jum!" a young man is forcibly ejected from his town because of his disconcerting effeminate demeanor. That is, he does not conform to the established paradigm of normative masculinity to which the rest of the community subscribes, and therefore he must be expelled. According to Lugo Ortiz, the process dramatized in Sánchez's story represents the dynamics of national identity. She argues that the protagonist's alterity threatens the underlying episteme of communal identity and, therefore, that his elimination constitutes a necessary reaffirmation of the *polis*: "It is as if Trinidad's son is perceived to disrupt not only the logic of established categories (masculine/feminine, black/white) but also to retreat from the same instrument for the construction of this logic: verbal language—the instrument on which the community has established its foundations (and the nation, Puerto Rico, its identity)."[4] In the end, not only must the protagonist be verbally assaulted by the community; he must also be physically removed in order to ensure its preservation.

In this fashion, Sánchez's story fundamentally dramatizes the function of normativity. In her analysis, moreover, Lugo Ortiz underscores how this normativity is both physically and discursively circumscribed in the construction, affirmation, and—by extension—empowerment of community. Non-normative sexuality cannot legitimately be embodied or articulated in the dominant social space. According to this logic, queer subjects must be both literally and rhetorically eliminated in order to ensure the productive development of the community (and, of course, the nation).

This dynamic becomes increasingly significant given the role of *En cuerpo de camisa* within Puerto Rican literary history. As Juan Gelpí argues in *Literatura y paternalismo*, Sánchez's text can be read as a response to the crisis of national identity that had been played out within its immediate antecedents. Gelpí argues that Marqués's play, *Los soles truncos* (1958)—*The Fanlights*—represents the culmination of this crisis.[5] Often compared to Checkov's *Three Sisters*, Marqués's play presents the struggle of the principal triad to preserve an increasingly anachronistic existence and the eventual failure of this project. In the dénouement of the play, the protagonists burn down the house that they had inherited from their father and within which they had attempted to insulate themselves from the changes occurring beyond its walls. According to Gelpí, this gesture constitutes a necessary liberation from the literary constructs of national identity that engender confinement and claustrophobia:

> *The Fanlights* unfolds in an extreme way all the previous rhetoric, framing it in and, to some extent, subordinating it to the totalizing metaphor of the house. The work ... reunites [the canonical metaphors] to consume them ... It is about a decisive moment in the canon which arrives at the work of René Marqués in a "pure" state; after this play, hybrid writings will be produced such as those of Luis Rafael Sanchez, Magali García Ramis, or Edgardo Rodriguez Juliá breaks with the paternalist canon will occur, in Manuel Ramos Otero, Rosario Ferré, and Ana Lydia Vega.[6]

That is, *Los soles truncos* clears the ground for a new beginning and invites the construction of an alternative metaphor of national identity.

Marqués's play, moreover, establishes this new beginning in spatialized terms. It takes the metaphor of insularity to its furthest consequences. The three sisters are unable to successfully participate in the ever-changing system of (re)production in Puerto Rico. They attempt to conserve or recuperate the past by shutting themselves in the only terrain they can still control, their house on Cristo Street in Old San Juan. The strategy proves unsustainable, however, since the protagonists do not have sufficient resources to fully isolate themselves. In the end, they destroy the space of their self-imposed confinement and the last vestige of the former colonial and agriculture system rather than allow themselves to be fully subsumed into the increasingly industrialized and U.S.-identified systems of exchange. *Los soles truncos* therefore "plays out"—in the sense that it both dramatizes and exhausts—the paradigm of bourgeois domesticity and thus facilitates the development of alternative spaces of subject formation in Puerto Rican literature.

As Gelpí suggests, Sánchez's *En cuerpo de camisa* becomes the foundation for the next generation of Puerto Rican authors. These writers—often referred to as the *nuevos narradores* (New Narrators)—introduce innovative representations of both national identity and individual subjectivities. In his introduction to the anthology *Apalabramiento*, Efraín Barradas argues that the *nuevos narradores* differ from their predecessors in their treatment of alterity:

> These narrations stand out based on the fusion of the narrative voice and the voice of the characters, on their fascination with the historical understood in aesthetic terms, on the new identification that they establish with the Puerto Rican proletariat, with the Antillean world and with the rest of Latin America, on the employment of the language of the economically lower classes as the basis for the creation of their own literary language, on the indirect presentation of the decadence of the middle class that has its roots in the nineteenth century, on their contribution of a feminine and feminist point of view, on their conciousness of the literariness of the texts themselves.[7]

In this way, elements that had been marginalized in earlier works become the main focus of these texts. [8] Furthermore, Sánchez's publication initiates a literary movement in which the authors are complicitous with the alternative universe they represent: "the Puerto Rican short story writers that began to publish their works after the appearance of *En cuerpo de camisa* . . . are imbricated, directly or indirectly, with the reality they potray, whether collective or individual."[9] According to these scholars, therefore, the publication of Sánchez's work signals the beginning of a new era in Puerto Rican literary production, one marked by changing attitudes toward not only gender and class but the hegemonic values and phallologocentric norms that had characterized earlier canonical texts.

More importantly, perhaps, Sánchez's work also marks a shift in the space of Puerto Rican literature. In *En cuerpo*, the principal setting for the construction of national identity has literally moved outside the claustrophobic confines of the house—as in *Los soles truncos*—and into the streets of San Juan. Nevertheless, as Lugo Ortiz clearly demonstrates, the liberation from the restrictions of an enclosed edifice does not guarantee emancipation since it does not eradicate the problems of such restrictions. In the end, the space of the town in "¡Jum!" also proves insufficient and incapable of accommodating diverse subjectivities. That is, the putative openness of the outdoors is deceptive. The boundaries and their concomitant limitations have not been erased in *En cuerpo*; instead, they have simply shifted to circumscribe a geographic area rather than an individual structure. And this problematic becomes a defining aspect of the project of the *nuevos narradores*: they focus on previously marginalized or excluded elements, but this attempted inclusiveness inevitably engenders additional displacements or exclusions.

In this manner, the emergence of an erstwhile marginalized or subordinated perspective exposes the fundamental interdependence of heteronormativity and the bound demarcation of national space. Given the relationship with space in Hispanic Caribbean self-fashioning, these inexorable links become even more significant: the salient equation between the borders of the island and those of the nation highlights and intensifies the negotiation of sexuality in the Hispanic Antilles. The combined perception of limited resources and the commitment to defending the autochthonous—and consequently more legitimate—interior from the threat of either insufficiency or external invasion requires that insular territory be vigilantly guarded against contamination by inappropriate elements. Under these circumstances, homosexuality is equated with vulnerability. The homosexual is therefore an aberrant subject that cannot be reconciled with the imagined reproductive community that the state is attempting to create. And this irreconcilability requires not only the negation of the homosexual subject but the physical removal of non-normative individuals from the sacred space of national formation: the island.

In their work, Piñera, Sarduy, and Santos Febres develop a poetics of limits that destabilizes these assumptions. The narratives that I will analyze here center on characters that strive to carve out a space for non-normative desires and, in doing so, interrogate the master narratives of insular self-fashioning. They construct an alternative vision of the island-nation that, although it does not displace insularity as a rhetorical mode, fundamentally challenges the presumed equation of heterosexuality and insular subjectivity.

### Virgilio Piñera's Assaulted Bodies

Few Hispanic Caribbean authors have developed a more persistent and complex poetics of limits than Virgilio Piñera. Throughout his writings, the author repeatedly considers the implications of bound demarcation, normative circumscription, and insularity. Not only does Piñera comment on the importance of insular geography in his expository writing, but he also offers evidence of its effects in his literary work. In fact, in several of the author's texts, the division between the internal and external itself defines Piñera's subjects and, at the same time, threatens to destroy them.

During the latter half of the twentieth century, Piñera became an increasingly recognized (and recognizable) figure in Cuban literary studies. Furthermore, his work has received even greater attention over the last decade. In his analysis of gay literature in Cuba, for example, Emilio Bejel underscores the growing prevalence on the author's work and the critical discourse that has been produced about it. The majority of recent Piñerian studies have focused on the writer's relationship with the revolution, his participation in literary journals or his sexuality; at the same time, these analyses examine the diverse array of complexities in Piñera's work (and, in many cases, his life) and ultimately construct an overarching vision of the author's poetic system. Nevertheless, Piñera's work has proven provocatively elusive. As Ana García Chichester asserts, the writing that Piñera produced throughout his life both supports and refutes—paradoxically enough—any monolithic analysis of his oeuvre. In fact, as I will argue here, Piñera's poetics is fundamentally one of resistance. To some extent, since it continually questions and resists the validity of totalizing, hegemonic systems, his work can only be interpreted in terms of a hermeneutics of polyvalence and contradiction. At the same time, however, a detailed analysis of Piñera's texts reveals several central themes, including a constant exploration of corporality and insularity as defining characteristics of subjectivity.

The critical reception of Piñera's work by a variety of scholars over the last fifty years follows a common yet also highly significant pattern of extreme changes. Both the author and his work have been recognized and greatly respected since he began publishing in Cuban literary journals. Until recently, however, this visibility had been limited to a relatively specialized reading public. More importantly, the increasing attention that the author's work has received in recent years cannot be easily attributed to a unified political or ideological position. Hence, the inevitable questions of "Why Piñera?" and "Why now?" cannot be readily answered by the identification of a particular value system or agenda that is codified within his texts. The extent of his appeal must be explained instead in terms of the very multiplicity that makes his work so elusive.

Whatever the specific focus or methodology of the studies may be, most analyses of Piñera's work evoke aspects of his life. Yet this tendency is not surprising given the importance of Piñera as a literary and historical figure. Piñera had a complex and controversial relationship with the Cuban Revolution, and he published several pieces—both under his own name and under the pseudonym, "El Escriba" (The Scribe)—in which he advocated significant changes in Cuban politics and society. He was, of course, also involved in the development of the journal *Orígenes*, and his relationship—textual and often personal—with other writers associated with the journal is also well known. In particular, the polemic between Piñera and Lezama has been so widely discussed that it, on occasion, has become the principal subject matter of critical work on the two authors. In fact, the author's politics and interactions with literary colleagues often constitute the primary focus of Piñerian criticism. More recently, Piñera's sexuality has also become a major focus of studies. Néstor Almendros and Orlando Jiménez Leal's film, *Mauvaise conduite*, and other works on the subject have documented how Piñera—like many of his colleagues—was persecuted and ostracized during his lifetime on account of his sexuality. In, "The Death of Virgilio," Guillermo Cabrera Infante recounts a (by now) widely cited anecdote in which Piñera's work is also subjected to such treatment: when he encounters a copy of the author's *Teatro completo* on the shelves of the Cuban Embassy in Algiers, Ernesto "Che" Guevara hurls it against the wall and berates the ambassador for including work by that "foul faggot" in the embassy's collection.[10]

This tendency to conflate the man and his writing, however, is not limited to his persecutors. The extraordinary prevalence of a biographical focus within contemporary Piñerian criticism suggests that the author's work is fated to be continually read in terms of his life. On the one hand, this approach is not surprising given the importance of Piñera as a literary and historical persona. This tendency, moreover, is common among controversial figures, especially when this controversial status can be attributed to political activism or sexual orientation. As with scholarship that deals with the work of Federico García Lorca or Oscar Wilde, for example, Piñerian criticism often insists on a biographical hermeneutic that risks reducing the author's literary production to a series of manifestos or coded personal declarations.

This biographical approach also often engenders significant interpretative problems. One major difficulty that critics face when they examine Piñera's writing in these terms is the complexity of the author's life. Piñera's life itself presents substantial contradictions and does not readily offer a stable matrix through which one may begin to understand his literary production. In her overview of studies on the writer's work, García Chichester argues that several of the critics tend to overlook important aspects of his writing because each one focuses excessively on specific themes or concerns within his work. Adriana Kanzepolsky, on the other hand, does not make the mistake of overly limiting her analysis, but instead confronts the impossibility of interpreting Piñera's work in terms of all these themes and concerns. She reads the author's literary project according to the attitudes that he expresses in his essays and journalistic pieces: "Virgilio, the homosexual, the polemical, the fearful, is here—among other things—electing how he wants to be evaluated when he dies."[11] Her references reveal, furthermore, the same complexities that can be found in Piñera's fictional prose. His changing position on the definition and role of Cuban literature, for example, not only reflects the shift in sociopolitical context marked by the events of 1959, but also underscores the construction of an authorial subjectivity in each of the pieces. Therefore, although these works are certainly worthy of critical analysis, they can not be read as transparent statements nor provide a "reader's guide" for the interpretation of Piñera's prose.

Even some critics who argue that the interpretation of Piñera's work should move beyond the predominant attention paid to his life ultimately focus on the latter in their analyses. In her article on *Cuentos fríos*, Teresa Cristófani Barreto observes that reactions to the author's life have impeded the necessary attention that should have been paid to his writing. Through an interpretation of specific elements, she examines Piñera's minimalist literary style in his short stories. She establishes a connection between the images of consumption in "La carne" ("The Meat/Flesh"), for example, with a narrative self-consumption in which texts are reduced to individual elements such as description, action, or characters. Nevertheless, Cristófani Barreto finally explains this narrative system in terms of the rivalry between Piñera and Lezama. She argues that the former's minimalism is, in fact, a reaction against Lezama's neo-Baroque style: "Virgilio Piñera, inventor of a "laundry literature," directed himself, on the contrary, towards the ex-centric. He rejects the aestheticism imposed by Lezama, denying any manifestation of a poetics of eroticism."[12]

In his opening plenary address at a conference dedicated to Piñera, Enrico Mario Santí also initially advocates a textually-based approach but then reverts to a biographical one. He suggests that the conference participants are the best qualified to generate criticism that does not conflate biographical and literary analysis: "No one better than this group of specialists to comprehend and explicate the marginal character of Piñera's work. And no one better to distinguish between that marginal character and the marginalization, the ostracism, the civil death to which this writer was subjected after 1970."[13] The discussion that follows, however, focuses almost exclusively on Piñera himself. Moreover, Santí concludes by asserting that the two are ultimately inseparable: "With all of these antecedents, how can we not read the work of Virgilio Piñera, after 1965 . . . as a vast parable of these observations [on the situation of his country] (63).[14]

Yet it is precisely this difficulty or complexity that can constitute the foundation of a queer interpretation of Piñera's writing. That is, the elusiveness of Piñera's discourse underscores a sexual poetics without insisting on a predetermined or fixed identification.[15] In his analysis, José Quiroga examines this complexity and argues that Piñera's transcendence as a homosexual author lies in the perpetually indefinable system of codification that can be found in his writing. He does not explicitly advocate or disavow the biographical approach to Piñera's work in his article, "Fleshing Out." Quiroga argues instead that the author constantly skirts the identification of autobiographical elements in his writing by eliding sexuality or, at the very least, codifying it in elusive terms. "Piñera says (but he does not say—his silence says it for him) that this is the only power that faggots may have, what allows them to subvert and at the same time reaffirm the blindness of masculinity. It is, moreover, a silence that is an assertion of the passivity of power, the presentation of the pharmakon that actively refuses to come out in script."[16] In fact, in his chapter on the Cuban writer in *Tropics of Desire*, Quiroga further underscores the complex difficulty of interpreting his work according to an overtly homosexual poetics: "But Piñera's work not only speaks in code: it likes and seduces code, and it encodes its own interventions. To rupture the complexity I have deployed in this essay for the sake of a politcs of outing does not do justice to the particularities of the work itself: it neutralizes Piñera and confines him to a space that Piñera himself could not have forseen."[17] According to the critic, the interpretation of Piñera's writing must engage the discursive intricacies that actively resist a stable identification of the author's sexuality or—to some extent—even his subjectivity.

Quiroga avoids forced and limiting readings of Piñera's writing and examines instead the code that the author constructs. Nevertheless, as the critic himself astutely points out, the interpretation of this code tends to engender biographical readings which enclose the text in a politically (over-)determined interpretation. Hence, paradoxically, the author's silences prove as significant and as elusive as that which he articulates, and they point to the reductive insufficiency of the homosexual approach to his work. Taken to its furthest consequences, the poetic system that Piñera constructs resists the totality of hegemonic norms not only of politics but also of textuality. In the end, his poetics fundamentally call into question the ideological limits of any system of signification and thus constructs a radically counter-hegemonic positionality. In this sense, Piñera's work dermarcates a queer space as its principal locus of enunciation.

Although many critics have addressed Piñera's representation of islands and insular geography in his writing, this aspect has not been the primary focus of their work. Nevertheless, several recent studies have begun to address how insularity functions within the author's poetics. Alan West presents a careful analysis of the real and imagined geographies Piñera constructs. In "Virgilio Piñera: On the Weight of the Insular Flesh," Quiroga argues that the author's treatment of insularity reflects his relationship with Lezama and underscores a poetics of homosexuality. Alberto Moreiras does not specifically focus on insular tropes in his analysis of Piñera's work, but he does examine how the author postulates a cleansing and an escape to an alternative space in his texts. Moreiras argues that, through this poetics of displacement, Piñera inaugurates a distinct narrative project: "If the Latin American cave has always been an anti-Platonic one, conceived of as a place of redemption or of preparatory resistance, Piñerian concealment is neither resistant nor redemptive. In any case, his resistance is not a transitive one (resistance against or resistance of) but instead preservative resistance, where what is preserved is preservation itself, its pure possibility."[18] According to this interpretation, it is the construction of space and the circumscription of interiority that defines Pinera's writing. Insularity, therefore, could constitute a foundational component of this spatial poetics.

In the end, however, the multiple manifestations of insular tropes throughout the author's oeuvre and their implications have not been thoroughly examined. Moreover, when viewed from the perspective of theoretical discussions of space and spatiality in the formation of traditional subjectivity, Piñera's use of insularity becomes increasingly significant. The complex and contradictory representation of insular tropes in Piñera's work reflects a fundamental problematic in his poetics. And this problem points to a vision of alternative subjectivity that destabilizes conventional discourses of identity. Piñera's work repeatedly highlights questions of space, displacement, and claustrophobia. More importantly, these motifs do not merely reflect a central or recurring theme in the author's oeuvre; instead, they constitute the incarnation of a resistant subject—in every sense of the phrase.

An early poem, "La isla en peso" (1943), constitutes one of the most obvious manifestations of insularity within Piñera's writing. The poem presents a crisis to which the primary response is a lament. Several aspects of the crisis are expressed, and the underlying source that purportedly engenders them is irreconcilable opposition. Each aspect is comprised of a binary opposition, a dichotomy in which the divided categories threaten one another rather than complement or facilitate a mutually beneficial synthesis.

The first of these dichotomies is the separation of land and water. The poem begins with a description of insular circumstances and their effect:

> La maldita circunstancia del agua por todas partes
> me obliga a sentarme en la mesa del café.
> Si no pensara que el agua me rodea como un cáncer
> hubiera podido dormir a pierna suelta.[19]

[The curse of being surrounded by water on every side
forces me to sit at this café table.
If I didn't think that water encircled me like a cancer
I'd be able to sleep like a lamb.][20]

Not only is the boundary between land and sea a salient theme in the poem; Piñera consistently presents this boundary as disruptive and problematic. Throughout the poem, both water and the sea are characterized as a limitation, a threat and a force capable of destroying the island and its inhabitants.

El horroroso paseo circular
el tenebroso juego de pies sobre la arena circular
el envenenado movimiento del talón que rehúye el abanico del erizo
los siniestros manglares, como un cinturón canceroso
dan la vuleta a la isla
los manglares y la fétida arena
aprietan los riñones de los moradores de la isla.[21]

[The horrific circular stroll
the shadowy play of feet on the circle of sand
the poisonous movement of a heel avoiding the urchin's spine
the sinister mangroves, like a cancerous belt
force the island back
the mangroves and the fetid sand
squeeze the kidneys of the island's inhabitants.][22]

Given this constant threat, the island must protect itself against the invasion of such destructive elements or against the suffocating confinement they can engender. Nevertheless, Piñera presents contradictory responses to the situation. The poem repeatedly establishes the desire to achieve a more complete division between land and water through increased separation. At times, however, the imagery suggests that the separation itself is the problem and that the two elements must be fused or combined in order to overcome the problem of the present dichotomy.

This conflict, moreover, is not limited to the opposition of land and sea; the poem includes similar contradictory responses to the other dichotomies it establishes. At several points, the poem constructs a clear distinction between the island and the world beyond it. On the one hand, this distinction characterizes the island as relatively underdeveloped and lacking and suggests that it, therefore, must overcome its limitations through the expansion of its confines. The poem implies, for example, that the islander lacks the ability to comprehend processes of change on a larger scale: "todas esas historias, leídas por un isleño que no sabe lo que es un cosmos resuelto"[23] [All these stories, read by an islander who doesn't know what a defined cosmos is]. [24] Furthermore, the putative ignorance of the readers is especially problematic given the presence of an alternative historiography in the poem. In one section, a reconstructed history of the island is presented as a potential force of resolution. Therefore, even if the conflict of insular nature could be counteracted through the writing of such a history, the impact of this solution would presumably be reduced by the limited interpretative capabilities of its readers—a limitation that is engendered by their isolation. On the other hand, the poem presents the relative isolation of the island as potentially advantageous: "afortunadamente desconocemos la voluptuosidad y la caricia francesa"[25] [Luckily we're familiar with neither voluptuousness nor the French caress].[26]

Beyond the specific geographic circumstances of insularity, the dynamics of binary opposition in "La isla en peso" extend to additional internal and external elements. The dichotomous dynamic determined by the island's physical attributes both circumscribes and defines insular existence: autochthonous and foreign plants and animals are contrasted, along with black and white, light and dark, and past and present. In each case, the poem underscores both the need to resolve the conflict these oppositions engender and the need to maintain the separation, since the juxtaposed elements are capable of destroying one another. The arrival of light, for example, is represented as a violent invasion:

> Pero la claridad avanzada, invade
> perversamente, oblicuamente, perpendicularmente,
> la claridad es una enorme ventosa que chupa la sombra,
> y las manos van lentamente hacia los ojos.[27]

> [But the light advances, invades
> perversely. Obliquely, perpendicularly,
> the light is an enormous mouth that sucks the shadow,
> and you raise your hands slowly to shield your eyes.][28]

The problem, however, is neither light nor darkness in and of themselves. The destructive force emanates from the transitional process in which one state of illumination is continuously disrupted by the other: "los cuatro momentos en que se abre el cáncer: madrugada, mediodía, crepúsculo y noche" [the four moments when the cancer opens: dawn, noon, dusk, and night].

In this way, Piñera presents a series of volatile dichotomies that parallel his treatment of the physical conditions of insularity, a parallel that Piñera reinforces through his use of metaphor. At several points, natural elements are characterized as bodies or body parts. Within this symbolic system, human and natural elements interact directly: "El trópico salta y su chorro invade mi cabeza / pegada duramente contra la costra de la noche"[29] [The tropic leaps and its flow invades my head / pinned fast to the crust of night].[30] Not only does he use corporeal metaphors throughout the poem, but—as with the juxtaposition of other physical elements—the boundary becomes the focal point within this bodily imagery. For example, it is the crust or scab of the night against which the head beats. Similarly, the skin and body orifices become the site of negotiation between the external and the internal: "Confusamente un pueblo escapa de su propia piel . . . /La piel, en esta hora, se extiende como un arrecife / y muerde su propia limitación"[31] [In confusion a people escape their skin . . . / Their skin, at this hour, stretches like a reef / and bites its own boundary].[32] Hence, the island and its contents are represented as an individual body. Furthermore, the poem again emphasizes the role of the surface: it is the skin that defines this collective body and its possible transformation.

The cumulative effect of these elements creates a system based on the contrast between opposing internal and external elements. In the poem insular existence is determined by this conflict. Furthermore, the dynamics established within the text indicate that this existence requires the continual maintenance of a delicate balance between the opposed elements. This representation of binary opposition acquires even greater significance given the geographic and rhetorical equation between the borders of the island and those of the nation. As Eithne Luibhéid cogently argues in her analysis of U.S. immigration policies, the control of political borders is not limited to the mere application of regulations that exist a priori. Instead, the very practices developed for patrolling the border have often produced definitions that differentiate between normal and aberrant subjects; officials charged with policing characteristics such as decency and sexuality must therefore develop a system that renders these traits visible and recognizable, which in turn engenders a particular code of sexuality. In a similar fashion, insular dichotomies in the poem do not simply reflect a dialectics; instead, the boundary between the interior and the exterior constitutes a line of demarcation through which norms are defined. Hence, through the manipulation of the surface or the membrane that marks this division, these norms are controlled, reinforced or, at times, reconfigured.

In "La isla," Piñera constructs a system in which both national identity and his poetic system are determined by the dynamics of insularity. In other works by the author the subject of insular geography is not explicitly addressed. Nevertheless, these works focus on the same problems of the dichotomous juxtaposition of internal and external elements just examined in the poem. In this manner, the tropes that are identified with insular existence in Piñera's poetry become the predominant themes in his prose writing as well.

In the collection, *Cuentos fríos*, Piñera develops the dichotomous paradox in which elements must be both conjoined and protected from one another. Several of the stories present the disruptive encounter between opposing entities. Although this encounter proves destructive, it is not unequivocally negative, since the conflict is not necessarily an obstacle to be overcome or eliminated. Rather than transcend the destruction, the narrative culminates in an irreducible binary. In this way, the juxtaposition of external and internal elements determines both the initial conflict and the dénouement in these works.

Piñera explores the consequences of total isolation in "La carne." In this story, the inhabitants of a particular town are limited to a restricted diet because of a shortage of meat. One resident of the town, however, discovers that his own flesh can serve as a substitute. The other townspeople then begin to feast on their own bodies until they eventually consume themselves. Ironically, the people of the town are quite willing to destroy themselves since the eradication of their own bodies is not nearly as distasteful as the prospect of being deprived of meat. This irony, moreover, is underscored in Spanish by the double meaning of *carne*: the inhabitants of the town literally destroy their own flesh in order to avoid being deprived of (animal) flesh.

As in "La isla," the opposition of the external and the internal is exaggerated through a synecdochic representation of corporeal entities. Not only must the town negotiate the disruption in contact with the world beyond it, but the sudden absence of an external element to be ingested forces the body to digest parts of itself as a substitute. Through its use of hyperbole, this story underscores the dependence of the internal on the external. Piñera elucidates the need to protect the internal from destructive invasion in other instances, but in "La carne" he suggests that it cannot be fully separated from the external either. For when the inside is completely deprived of outside resources, its only means of becoming absolutely self-sufficient is through self-consumption, by recreating the lost division between the interior and exterior within itself.

In this way, the story also highlights the intersection of difference or alterity and the physical or corporeal realization of desire. In her discussion of how gender categories have functioned within queer studies, Biddy Martin addresses the problematic role of masculinity and femininity in the analysis of homosexual relationships. According to Martin, the apparent absence of heteronormative difference in homosexuality can lead to a compensatory recasting of the expected otherness. "[W]e still wonder why femme-butch couples are so frequently made visibly different by way of skin color and what it means that the femme's indifference or lack of difference from heterosexual women is often represented in terms of whiteness . . . . Disidentification from assigned gender is accomplished through darkness, as if whiteness and femmeness counld not be differentiated and as if blackness were pure difference."[33] Martin thus questions the complicated implications of a system that fundamentally insists on difference as a constitutive characteristic of desire.

In a sense, "La carne" presents a corporeal situation that mimics or metaphorizes the problem that Martin analyzes. The story depicts a system in which the traditional and clearly external object of desire has disappeared. This absence does not eradicate desire, however, but instead the conventional drive is redirected inward and thus becomes hyperbolically narcissistic. In this manner, the reconfiguration of desire in response to the absence of the meat/flesh the characters seek engenders a highly autoerotic and self-destructive impulse. Hence, the story explores the very question that Martin discusses in her essay and satirically problematizes the absolute insistence on a libidinal economy based on difference.

"La carne" may be the most explicit and extreme dramatization of this intersection of desire, scarcity, and self-consumption. Nevertheless, the theme is also reproduced in other texts and thus engenders a poetic system based on physical limits that repeatedly emphasizes the potential (and dangerous) consequences of the traditional parameters of desire. The characters in "La cara" ("The Face"), for example, confront a problem that also explores the perils of conventional definitions of desire: over the course of the narrative, they pursue (and, in the end, require) a relationship that depends simultaneously on intimacy and distance. The narrator receives a mysterious phone call from a man who is desperate for prolonged contact with another person. He explains that his face is so repulsive that he has been unable to sustain a relationship with anyone who has seen it. Therefore, he has resorted to dialing random telephone numbers in search of interlocutors. However, the limitations of several conversations with a stranger have rendered this solution unsatisfying. The two characters attempt to develop sustained contact without meeting face to face, but the narrator soon discovers that he has an overwhelming desire to see his new friend's extraordinary countenance. The narrator resolves the situation by cutting out his own eyes. This strategy, however, cannot be understood solely as a repetition of the literary precedents of self-inflicted punishment, such as—most notably—Oedipus's self-mutilation at the end of Sophocles's *Oedipus Rex*. Instead, the gesture is presented as a felicitous resolution of the characters' dilemma:

> Una vez estuve sentado en mi sillón le hice saber que había saltado los ojos para que su cara no separase nuestras almas, y añadí que como ya las tinieblas eran supérfluas, bien podrían encenderse las luces.[34]
>
> [As soon as I was seating in my armchair, I told him I had poked my eyes out so his face wouldn't separate our souls, and added that since the darkness was now superfluous, the lights could very well be turned on.][35]

In this story, Piñera again constructs a situation in which two characters must negotiate their need for contact and the concomitant danger that the desired contact will ultimately separate them. Through various strategies, they struggle to resolve the situation by maintaining a controlled, partial connection. In the end, however, the narrator must destroy a part of himself—more specifically, a part through which he apprehends the world—in order to maintain the relationship.

The narrator of "El muñeco" ("The Doll") devises a strategy to protect a body against external threats through the creation of another body. In order to protect the president, he proposes the construction of a dummy that could fulfill the public functions of the president. The reproduction is so effective, however, that the characters—including the president himself—prove unable to distinguish between them, and the dummy eventually supplants the leader that he was intended to protect. In this case, the reproduction of a body presents the opportunity to resolve the conflict between the desire to guard the corporeal self against external threats, on the one hand, and the need for the body to overcome the limitations of its own containment on the other. The body cannot be completely isolated nor fully exposed, and the possibility of a "fake" reproduction allows an individual to transcend corporeal limitations without directly disrupting the boundary between the internal and the external. Nevertheless, the results of the process suggest that the coexistence of putatively external and internal bodies also destroys the individual while it protects him since it limits him to a lifeless, purely corporeal existence. Hence, as in "La carne," the separation of oneself from the outside world leads to an erosion of the self.

Not only does Piñera explore irreconcilable dichotomies in *Cuentos*, as Cristófani Barreto argues, the stories are often reduced to a fundamental opposition of two elements. The first story in the collection, "La caída" ("The Fall"), can be read as a *mise en abyme* in which this narrative strategy is taken to its extreme. As in the other examples just discussed, the two characters in "La caída" struggle to protect themselves from the threat of destruction. At the beginning of the story, they are climbing a mountain. One character slips and, because they are joined by a rope, they both fall. The narrator explains that he and his partner are each obsessed with a specific body part: he with his eyes and his partner with his beard. Their bodies become increasingly obliterated by the fall, and the narrator is eventually forced to choose between protecting his partner's cherished beard and devoting his one remaining hand to the preservation of his beloved eyes. He opts for self-preservation but points out in the last line of the story that tragedy has been averted: "Pero no pude hacer lamentaciones pues ya mis ojos llegaban sanos y salvos al césped de la llanura y podían ver, un poco más allá, la hermosa barba gris de mi compañero que resplandecía en toda su gloria"[36] [But I couldn't complain; my eyes landed safe and sound on the grassy plain and could see, a little ways off, the beautiful gray beard of my companion, shining in all its glory].[37]

This reduction of individuals to their essential characteristics could be understood as a poetics of the short story. That is, "La caída" would represent a narrative system in which all excess is eliminated and writing is reduced to its fundamental aspects. According to this interpretation, the repeated opposition of irreconcilable elements in the stories would constitute part of this system. However, this explanation proves insufficient since the problems explored in *Cuentos* also appear in Piñera's novel, *La carne de René*. *La carne*, perhaps the author's most frequently read and studied work, is an extensive exploration of the conflicts engendered by physical boundaries. The novel presents the continual dilemma of a corporeal subject that must both overcome his physical confinement and protect himself from the threat of penetration. Furthermore, through the repeated thematic representation of this conflict, Piñera ultimately constructs a battle between competing forces of expansion and penetration that is waged over René's flesh.

Along with his flesh, René's skin frequently becomes the primary focal point and site of negotiation. In fact, several episodes in the novel underscore its purportedly singular quality. René is determined to protect his skin from puncture and penetration. Other characters, however, are equally determined to achieve such penetration. In the first scene of the novel, René's skin attracts the attention of a neighbor, Dalia Pérez. She contemplates his appearance and describes the intense attraction that this potentially permeable surface inspires:

> Si no posee los músculos del atleta, en cambio en la calidad de su piel reside su belleza. Pero más que esto, lo que lo hace irresistible es la seducción de su cara. En ella la nota dominante que está pidiendo protección contra las furias del mundo. Y cosa extraña: ese aire que pedía protección se manifestaba en su carne de víctima propiciatoria. La señora Pérez la imaginaba herida por un cuchillo o perforada por una bala o pensaba en su uso placentero o doloroso.[38]

> [While he doesn't possess the muscles of an athlete, his beauty resides in the quality of his skin. But more that this, what makes him irresistible is the seductiveness of his face. Its dominant quality is the appearance that it is appealing for protection against the furies of the world. And something curious: that appearance manifests itself in his sacrificial victim's flesh. Mrs. Pérez imagined his flesh wounded by a knife or punctured by a bullet, or she thought about it being used for pleasure or pain.][39]

In this description it is the inherent instability of René´s corporeal boundary that incites desire. Although René is presumably unaware of his neighbor's reaction, he is soon confronted with a similar threat. Later in the chapter, he observes his mother treating the flesh wounds that his father has received as a butcher. René is obviously repulsed by these lesions, and is even more distressed when his father warns him that he should prepare himself for a similar fate: "No seré yo quien te hunda el cuchillo en el pecho, hijo mío, pero piensa que el mundo hay millones de manos y millones de cuchillos"[40] [I won't be the one to stick the knife in your chest, son. But consider that there are millions of hands and millions of knives in this world].[41]

Penetration again becomes a device that foreshadows René's destiny when his father introduces him to "The Cause" and the role he expects his son to play in its defense. Early in the novel, René discovers that his father belongs to a secret society or cult that has devoted itself to the search for chocolate. Ramón informs his son, moreover, that he is expected to sacrifice himself to the Cause as its principal martyr. This rite of passage, during which René is first made aware of his intended fate, is introduced through a symbolic reference. Just before explaining the history of the "chocolatófilos" and the need for René to sacrifice his flesh on their behalf, he presents René with a portrait of the martyrdom of St. Sebastian in which René's face has been superimposed on the punctured figure.[42] Once again, René is disturbed by the image of his penetrated skin. The protagonist clearly finds the initiation deeply disconcerting, but his reaction centers on the representation of perforated martyrdom; what is repulsive or disturbing is not the potential endangering of his life but the threat that his father's plan poses to his skin.

Soon thereafter, René is sent to an academy to be indoctrinated into a cult of pain and thereby prepare himself for his role. The school is devoted to familiarizing its students with pain and inculcating an appropriate response to experiencing it. Skin also constitutes a primary focus in this training. In his quarters, each pupil finds a portrait similar to the one René's father had commissioned of the martyrdom of St. Sebastian, and the students are instructed to emulate this depiction. As the course progresses, the directors of the school repeatedly express concern that René is not developing an appropriate relationship with carnal suffering. Furthermore, René's skin is identified as the clearest manifestation of his resistance. A colleague notes the petrified quality of René's skin and insists that it must be softened in order to be successfully subjugated:

> Roger lamió profundamente la frente de René. Movió la cabeza con aire de duda. Pasó la lengua por los labios del rebelde. Volvió a mover la cabeza.
> —¿Qué pasa, Roger?—preguntó Cochón.
> —Pétrea—se limitó a decir Roger.[43]

> [Roger licked René's forehead profoundly. He shook his head in doubt. He passed his tongue over the rebel's lips. He shook his head again. "What's wrong, Roger?" Swyne asked. "Hard as a rock," was all he said.][44]

Several of the instructors and students therefore follow Roger's example and begin to incessantly lick René's entire body in an attempt to dominate the resistant surface.

As in "La isla en peso," the desire for protective isolation in *La carne* is juxtaposed with the need for fusion between the external and the internal. The conflict between these irreconcilable forces is concentrated on the surface that separates the body from the world that surrounds it; René fights to protect his skin from the threat of invasion while others strive to permeate this boundary. Through the episodes that present this struggle, René's skin becomes the divide that must be traversed or—conversely—protected in the battle over his flesh.

René is reproduced through plastic depictions but he is also replicated through the presence of doubles. Like the characters in "El muñeco," the "chocolatófilos" employ doubles to protect their leader. Although this replication does not lead to confusion of the original and its copy in *La carne*, René is severely constricted by the presence of his doubles in the novel. The doubles successfully protect René as a potential public figure, but they simultaneously threaten and limit him as an individual. In the end, René repeatedly finds himself restrained by these reproductions of his physical self.

At several points in the novel, a double appears just as René is on the verge of escaping from the "chocolatófilos" and he is literally detained by the encounter. René first discovers his doubles in an elevator. In an intensely claustrophobic scene, the protagonist finds himself enclosed with several of his decoys:

> Al abrir la puerta del ascensor empezó el doblaje. Un grupo de cuatro personas—probables vecinos del edificio—entraron conversando animadamente. Eran cuatro seres humanos, pero René los vio como cuatro maniquíes—dobles de su propia persona.[45]

> [The doubling began as the elevator door opened. A group of four people—probably neighbors from the building—entered engaged in animated conversation. They were four human beings, but René saw them as four mannequins—doubles of himself.][46]

At a later point, when René is determined to flee from his fated martyrdom, he unexpectedly meets another double. To his dismay, this double is intent on remaining with René and unknowingly circumvents the planned escape. Hence, both René's physical movement and his personal development are delimited by the presence of his multiple reproductions.

Beside the plastic and living reproductions, René also encounters an inanimate imitation of his body. After spending the night at Dalia's house, he discovers a mannequin that resembles himself floating in the bathtub. The neighbor explains that she had acquired the mannequin to satisfy her desire for René's flesh, but that she had been dissatisfied with the imitation. Like the "chocolatófilos" and Ramón, she has used a reproduction to manipulate René and realize her carnal desire for him. René is repulsed by the mannequin, but he responds more directly to the appearance of the replica's skin than to its presence or Dalia's use of it. He comments on the strange, soft quality of submerged skin: "Su carne parecía blanda y hasta fofa, por efecto de la hinchazón, seguramente"[47] [His flesh seemed soft and even spongy, surely due to the swelling].[48] Ironically, it seems that Dalia has achieved with the mannequin what René's companions at the school were unable to accomplish with his skin: through the creation of this double, Dalia has been able to come close to the desired subjugation of René's flesh.

The doubles determine René's future, and they also restrict his movement. Through their interventions René is systematically prevented from moving beyond a limited geographic area. His freedom from his father and from his planned martyrdom requires that he distance himself physically from these elements. However, he is repeatedly drawn back toward the epicenters of the forces that contain him. The consistent reinforcement of René's containment makes his destiny seem increasingly inevitable. At one point, René finds himself across the street from the very building from which he has been trying to escape, the headquarters of La Causa (The Cause). Rene's desire for escape is repeatedly thwarted by his enclosure in spaces that are controlled by The Cause.

Because of this enclosure, René often feels confined or trapped by the external desires to control his flesh. This problem is acutely represented in a scene in which he unexpectedly encounters Dalia and another neighbor, Powlavski. When she finds René, Señora Pérez places him on a bench between the two neighbors: "Por así decir lo arrastró hasta el banco y lo sentó entre ella y Powlavski"[49] [One might say she dragged him over to the bench and sat him down between her and Powlavski].[50] In this situation, René is literally surrounded by characters that he fears, but this circumstance leads him to accept his fate rather than flee from it. The dramatization of this entrapment leads him to conclude that he will not be able to completely protect his flesh from outside forces, but, instead, that he may choose to which of these forces he will subject himself.

Along with physical manipulation and confinement, language is also used to control René. During the first lesson, each pupil at the school receives a muzzle. According to René, the restriction is designed to improve their experience of pain and, thus, facilitate their education: "De pronto, recordó la expresión del señor Mármolo: <<Sufrir en silencio . . . >> Era evidente que el bozal impediría el sufrimiento clamoroso, pregonado, a gritos"[51] [He suddenly remembered Mr. Marblo's expression: "Suffer in silence . . ." It was obvious that the muzzle would prevent clamorous suffering, public, shouted out loud . . . ].[52] Through this restriction, the instructors force the students to experience pain exclusively in terms of the flesh. This technique suggests that the inability to articulate their experience of physical pain increases the intensity and the purity of that experience.

In addition to the restrictions on verbal expression, the pedagogical techniques at the school foster a specific relationship with written language as well. After the placement of the muzzle, the students proceed to a room filled with electric chairs. In this room, the students are tortured with a series of increasingly stronger electric shocks. Apparently, however, the simple receipt of the shocks themselves is not sufficient. Instead, the instructor periodically administers the electric current during the reading of a text. The professor of René's class, however, is extremely disconcerted when the system malfunctions and the electric current is not delivered to the students:

> No pudo continuar [el profesor]. La voz se le había rajado en la garganta y allí se quedó como un cadáver. El dedo se revolvía histéricamente sobre el botón, amenazando desarraigarlo . . . . Una risa amordazada, pero no menos burlona, se clavaba en la dignidad del profesor, haciéndole perder toda compostura.[53]

> [He was unable to continue [the professor]. His voice had cracked in his throat, and there it lay like a corpse. His finger was hysterically pressing down on the button, threatening to rip it apart altogether . . . . Muzzle laughter—no less mocking for being muzzled—pricked the professor's dignity, causing him to lose his composure altogether.][54]

The episode demonstrates that the manipulation of the students' response to a text is an important aspect of their education, and that the failure to effectively control this response constitutes a serious threat to the power of the instructors.

In the end, subjectivity is determined in Piñera's novel by the perpetual negotiation of boundaries. Characters are defined through the struggles to preserve or alter the limits that circumscribe them. René's plight, moreover, can be understood as the inability to transcend or escape traditional gender roles. René is repeatedly reconstructed as the object of desire throughout the novel and he struggles to elide the desiring gaze of other characters. The potential effacement of René's subjectivity, however, is not produced only by the proliferation of desire for him but also by his inability to constitute himself as a desiring subject. At the end of the novel, he resolves this conflict by accepting his fated role and resigning himself to the impossibility of an alternative subject-position. The conflict lies, therefore, in the Manichaean division between masculine and feminine roles that delimit subjectivity. René is unable to effectively articulate an authoritative subjectivity throughout most of the novel because he can neither accept his role as the desired other nor construct a desirable other for himself. Hence, René is ultimately constrained by a totalizing paradigm of gender in which he is constructed as the feminine.

In Piñera's writing, therefore, the role of the body as the traditional locus of heteronormativity is fundamentally challenged. The assaulted bodies in his texts constitute, instead, an elusive sign that resists monolithic processes of signification. The resistant—and, thus, counter-hegemonic—sexuality he constructs both perpetually displaces and excessively circumscribes conventional definitions (and demarcations) of the corporeal. And the complexities that are underscored by this process are inexorably linked to the space of the island and its rhetorical conflation with normative nation-building.

As David Eng and David Kazanjian astutely assert in their analysis of Asian and Asian American cultures, queer sexuality tends to be formed in exile, in a space that is removed from the restrictions of family ties and national infrastructures. Given this underlying connection between displacement and non-normative sexuality, queer subjectivity is fundamentally associated with the experience of loss and mourning. Piñera's work does not trace comparable circumstances of exile, transnational migration, or globalization. Nevertheless, queer subjectivity is characterized in similar terms of displacement and alienation. The spatial configuration of the island-nation and boundaries in his texts establishes an absolute dichotomy between the normative interior and externalized aberrant subjects.

Given the diverse representations of assaulted and contested "bodies" —whether individual, collective, or insular—in Piñera's writing, the struggle between its inside and outside not only becomes a defining factor of insularity but also engenders subjectivity. The juxtaposition of opposing forces that offer, respectively, either protection or expansion is articulated in terms of the limits of an individual body. In this manner, both national identity and subjectivity are constructed through a sustained conflict between the internal and the external. In the end, Piñera constructs a poetics of corporeal resistance that fundamentally calls into question the limits and limitations of conventional systems of knowledge and power.

In this sense, Piñera takes the question of bound demarcation to its furthest discursive consequences. He constructs a poetics that continually circumscribes and problematizes the limits of normative self-fashioning. In fact, as I asserted earlier, few authors have dealt with the issue of Caribbean spatiality and its implications in such a fully developed manner. Nevertheless, Sarduy and Santos Febres also engage the intersections of insularity and sexuality. More specifically, Sarduy's final novel, *Pájaros de la playa*, depicts an island of infirmity and decay that offers a hyberbolic critique of the logic (and policies) of non-normative displacement, and Santos Febres's *Sirena Selena vestida de pena* critically juxtaposes the relative regulation of non-normative sexuality in Puerto Rico and the Dominican Republic. In these works, both authors construct alternative visions of insularity that simultaneously underscore and challenge the hegemonic spaces (and spatiality) of Hispanic Caribbean nation building.

## Severo Sarduy's Other Island of Alterity

By the time he published *Pájaros de la playa* (1993)—Beach Birds—Sarduy was already well known as an accomplished neo-Baroque writer. Through his novels and essays published during the 1960s and 1970s, Sarduy developed a particular literary code of elusive language and desire. In *La ruta de Severo Sarduy* (1987), Roberto González Echevarría examines the corpus of work that the author had produced at that point. He traces the evolution of a transformational poetics, and analyzes how the author's work takes up the concerns of Latin American master narratives of modernity and the boom and transforms them into a postmodern artifice of language and symbols.

For the most part, Sarduy's work has not suffered the same fate as Piñera's. Earlier novels such as *De donde son los cantantes* and *Colibrí* are not read in exclusively or even predominantly biographical terms. Of course, the author's sexuality is often cited or invoked in critical analyses of his work. Even a cursory glance at the corpus of criticism published on Sarduy's writing reveals a wide array of thematic focuses and methodological approaches. Scholars frequently cite the author's essayistic production about writing (i.e., *Ensayos generales sobre el barroco* and *Escrito sobre un cuerpo*) and his involvement with the Tel Quel group and structuralist/poststructuralist thinkers in Paris. A strictly biographical hermeneutic, however, is not as prevalent as in the case of Piñera.

*Pájaros*, nevertheless, tends to be the one exception to this rule. The novel is Sarduy's final work and was published posthumously. The author was suffering from AIDS when he wrote the novel. Given his experiences during this period, along with his training as a medical student, it is not surprising that Sarduy began to focus on illness, isolation, and deterioration in his writing. Hence, the biographical contextualization and analysis of the novel proves logical almost to the point of inevitability. In his analysis of Sarduy's oeuvre, René Prieto notes the significance of this correlation between the author's life and his work: "The degraded walking carcass in *Pájaros de la playa* ... is the narrator's own, painstakingly described until it becomes confused with that of Sarduy, who was dying of AIDS when he wrote these pages."[55] At the same time, however, Prieto's analysis is not limited to such biographical interpretation. In fact, he asserts that the degraded body cannot be tied to a single meaning but instead develops into a corporeal semiotics in Sarduy's work. Along these lines, biographical circumstances can function as a critical point of departure without necessarily becoming a reductive interpretative lens. In fact, a careful analysis of the text reveals that *Pájaros* indeed deals with the issues that Sarduy himself was facing as he wrote the novel yet also constructs a poetics of limits and normativity.

As with Shakespeare's *The Tempest*, Sarduy's novel takes place on a small island filled with strange—and, one might argue, wondrous—creatures.[56] The precise location of the island is not specified, but several of the names and references establish clear links with the Cuban (historical) landscape.[57] *Pájaros de la playa* is set on a small island that has been converted into a medical sanitarium for the chronically ill. The novel traces the experiences of Siempreviva, a patient who arrives at the island refuge to recover from her own debilitating illness. In the end, however, Siempreviva does not fit neatly into established parameters. The hyperbolic exaggeration of her supposed femininity, for example, not only underscores the way that her beauty has been ravaged by the passage of time and her illness, but ultimately destabilizes itself, casting her either as a failed diva or a drag queen. And her attempts to recuperate something she has lost—or, to an even greater extent, gain access to something that she never had—are persistently undermined by the inevitable presence of deterioration, decay, and compensatory excess.

Siempreviva struggles to reconstruct herself from within the peculiar insular context. The setting, however, does not prove conducive to her recuperative enterprise since it is characterized by erosion and decay. Not only is the island itself subjected to the forces of geological time, but the presence of such forces is magnified by the island's inhabitants. Many of the patients described suffer from conditions such as severe anemia and leprosy in which their bodies are, quite literally, progressively consumed by their illness. Nevertheless, even those patients who do not suffer such apparent outward decay, such as the protagonist, find themselves constantly battling the destructive effects of their condition as well. "Siempreviva sufría, como todos los otros recluidos y a pesar de su buen talante, los exámenes regulares que denunciaban o excluían la presencia del mal"[58] [Immortelle, like all the other inmates, and despite her good demeanor, was subjected to the regular examinations that denounced or ruled out the presence of the malady].[59] On the surface, she appears to be relatively healthy. Medical analyses, however, go beyond this superficial appearance and confirm or eliminate the persistent threat of an illness that could be lurking beneath her (deceptively) healthy outward appearance. In this fashion, the clinic also performs the Foucauldian function of rendering the aberrant visible and effectively removing it from the social body until (or unless) it can be reconstituted.

Along with repeated comments that she feels physically and emotionally drained in a metaphoric sense, Siempreviva also points out the more literal draining of her bodily fluids that her treatment requires. She refers to the medical personnel who draw her blood, for example, as vampires. In a cycle reminiscent of the pathology of humors, the eradication of illness requires the systematic extraction of corporeal entities as potential sources of contamination. In this case, however, Siempreviva's treatment is based on a concept of disease in which malady is posited in terms of an external invasion rather than as an internal impurity.[60]

In addition to combating the physical symptoms of her illness, the protagonist is determined to recover and recuperate her past. In fact, the desire to revert to a former self becomes her primary objective:

> Siempreviva no tuvo más que una idea. Fija, por definición. Una obsesión, más bien: quería rejuvenecer. Ir tiempo atrás, volver a ser la que había sido, la que fue hace cuarenta años, cuando dio una fiesta azul y plateada para recibir a Bola de Nieve, de regreso de París.[61]

> Immortelle had only one idea—fixed, by definition. Or rather obsession: she wanted to be rejuvenated. Go backwards in time, return to being who she had been, herself forty years ago, when she threw a blue and silver gala party to receive Bola de Nieve who had just returned from Paris.[62]

Along with traditional medical treatments and Afro-Cuban remedies, Siempreviva invokes her memories in order to return to her lost youth. This use of memory, however, undermines the recuperative enterprise. As a rhetorical reconfiguration of the past from the perspective of the present, memory cannot recover the past; instead, it reinvents it.[63]

This inherent contradiction ultimately impedes the realization of Siempreviva's desires: the reconfiguration of history does not allow her to revert to a former (imagined) self. On one level, the structure of the novel advances this project. The narrative itself becomes a persistent oscillation between the past and the present. The linear account of Siempreviva's experiences on the island is repeatedly interrupted by earlier episodes in her life. One such episode, for example, recounts the party at which Siempreviva receives Bola de Nieve.[64] The party had been mentioned earlier in the novel, when Siempreviva alluded to it in the passage just cited, but it had not been described or narrated in detail. In this fashion, the temporal intercalation of the novel realizes Siempreviva's stated objectives. Nevertheless, the juxtaposition of competing or contradictory historical narratives persistently marks the temporal displacement that the protagonist strives to eradicate or overcome. In this sense, the character's persona is indeed constructed through the juxtaposition of present and past selves. The resulting subjectivity, however, does not successfully insert Siempreviva into existing parameters of identity. She is notably different from the fellow inhabitants of the island, yet she is also too distant from healthy, (re)productive citizens to function in mainstream society.

This recuperative project does not fail solely based on issues of nonconformity; it is consistently subverted by multiplicity and excess. The physical space of the narrative is characterized by repeated reterritorialization. In an ironic juxtaposition with its current status, the island itself is portrayed as having once been occupied by nudists described as youthful and athletic. In fact, the novel begins with a description of these supposed former occupants and their activities:

> Los nudistas . . . alzaban los brazos hasta que las manos se tocaran sobre la cabeza, inspirando aire puro, el aire vivo de la costa; luego iban bajándolos poco a poco, expulsando el mismo aire ahora contaminado por el interior del cuerpo opaco y pulmonar. Eran pájaros de la playa antes de emprender el primer vuelo, ensayando las frágiles alas, prestos a afrontar el viento en remolinos del mar.[65]

> [The nudists stood on the highest rocks, raising their tensed arms until their hands touched above their heads, inhaling the pure air, the live air of the shore; then they began to lower them little by little, expelling the same air now contaminated by the insides of their opaque pulmonary bodies. They were beach birds just before embarking on their first flight, rehearsing their fragile wings, ready to tackle the oceanic whirlwinds.][66]

The persistent use of the phrase—"pájaros de la playa"—to refer to the subsequent inhabitants of the island underscores both the discrepancy between the two groups and the desire of the patients to achieve the putative status of these predecessors. Nevertheless, Sarduy's description immediately undermines this goal. Although the nudist may exemplify a level of physical health that the patients strive for, they are also characterized as suffering from imperfection and dissatisfaction: the nudists are juxtaposed to a harmonious natural purity that they approximate but are unable to fully incorporate. In fact, as the description quoted above indicates, these former occupants of the island must confront the discrepancy between the outward appearance of purity and an internal (if not internalized) corporeal impurity. In the end, they reach the boundary between their corporeal selves and their surroundings, yet, they cannot overcome it.

The competition between linear and recuperative movement is also reflected in the onomastic structure of the novel. Multiple meanings and historical references often converge in the names and other terms used to characterize the island's inhabitants. The use of the phrase "pájaros de la playa" not only conflates distinct inhabitants of the island but it also invites multiple interpretations of their status. On the one hand, the phrase underscores a paradoxical contradiction between the confinement of marginalized patients and the potential freedom of birds that could leave the island at will. On the other, however, it is also a coded allusion to queer subjectivity since "pájaros" is a term that is often used to refer to homosexuals. In this sense, the characters' marginal status is linked to non-normative sexuality. Furthermore, the inhabitants are characterized in terms of polyvalence and uncontainability: they cannot simply be identified as either effectively normal or abnormal subjects that could be neatly circumscribed within the boundaries of the island.

Similarly, most of the island's inhabitants in *Pájaros*—both patients and medical attendants—are identified by their given names at some point in the novel. They are more commonly referred to in the narrative, nonetheless, with a sobriquet that they have acquired while on the island. Since each name is directly linked to a specific spatiotemporal phase of their lives—i.e., prior and subsequent to their arrival—the intercalation of the two parallels the oscillation between past and present in the text. The opposed names represent the consubstatial current and former selves that fight for primacy in each character. This denominative duplicity does not simply mirror the tensions between past and present identities; it also reveals an underlying discrepancy between an expected or desired identification and an existing one.

The sobriquets tend to reduce each character to an exaggeration of a defining attribute. The doctor who tends to Siempreviva, for example, is referred to as Caballo (horse) because of his equine physical appearance and mannerisms: "Grande y fornido. Con mucho pelo y cara de caballo. Cuando entra en un lugar parece oler el aire, como asustado. Avanza a zancadas. Muestra las encías cuando se ríe,"[67] [Big and strong. With thick hair and a horse face. When he comes into a place he seems to sniff the air, as if afraid. He walks with big strides. He shows his gums when he smiles].[68]

Nevertheless, individuals frequently also possess traits that contradict their anthropomorphic characterizations. Although both Caballo and Caimán earn their nicknames through manifest similarities with the suggested creatures, their behavior does not completely adhere to the nature of their biological namesakes. In the narration of a conflict between the two, Sarduy first outlines the attributes of each animal and then examines how the actions of the characters diverge from the resulting expectations:

> Pasemos en la balanza de la saña zoológica, las aptitudes de los contrincantes . . . un caballo puede reventar a un caimán a patadas, o bien, cabreándose sobre él, asfixiarlo, comprimirlo hasta que vomite su baba verde . . . un caimán puede, en una voltreta, atrapar una pata del caballo con la mordaza de sus quijadas, como un cepo, y así inmovilizarlo hasta la muerte. Como siempre sucede con las previsiones—literarias o no—, el desarrollo de la acción fue totalmente distinto.[69]
>
> [Let's weigh the abilities of the two opponents on the scale of zoological rage:
>   \* a horse can kick a Cayman to pieces, or better yet, rear up on him, asphyxiating and compressing him until he vomits his own green saliva;
>   \* a Cayman can, with one somersault, trap a horse's hoof, clamping it in his snare-like jaws, thus immobilizing the horse until it dies.
>   As always happens with predictions, literary or not, the action unfolded in an entirely different manner.][70]

Throughout this description, the narrator asserts that each character is capable of destroying the other through the employment of specific innate abilities; however, he also avers that their behavior does not reflect this zoological analysis. In fact, the two characters resort to indiscriminately and violently attacking one another. In doing so, they reveal equivalent fundamental instincts that negate their particular characterizations as a given animal. By the end of the fight, they become indistinguishable and inextricably bound entities: "Eran emblemas de constelaciones, enrevesados y borrosos, anegados en el polvo estelar de sus sangres mezcladas,"[71] [They were emblems of constellations, twisted and blurred, drowned in the starry dust of their commingled bloods].[72]

In a similar fashion, even when the contradiction between the sobriquet and the fundamental nature of the characters is not explicitly addressed, the assumed name points to a desired, unfulfilled potential. The denomination of the protagonist, Sonia, as "Siempreviva," for instance, ironically underscores the very status that she fails to achieve in the novel. On the one hand, this appellation effectively codifies the ostensible distinction between her outward appearance and that of the other patients at the sanitarium. More poignantly, perhaps, the name is a constant reminder of lack or loss that characterizes all of the inhabitants. In stark contrast to the eternal youth suggested by her moniker, the protagonist is closely identified with death and decay.

Along with its inhabitants, the island is also subject to deterioration over time. At several moments in the novel, the narrative focuses on the geological cycles that cause shifts in the boundary between land and water. This parallel is reinforced, moreover, in Sarduy's equation of the geographic limits of the island with the inherent limitations that the characters strive to overcome. For both the nudists and the patients, the edge of the island represents the concrete manifestation of their insuperable confinement. At the end of the novel, Siempreviva attempts to escape from her situation by fleeing from the hospital and the island. Nevertheless, in the end, Siempreviva's reconstruction fails because she is unable to eradicate the existing occupants of her surroundings. The island in *Pájaros* becomes an allegory for the characters' mission to redraw boundaries and construct an alternative history and, thereby, an alternate self. The inherent limitations underscore the inability to sustain contradictory identities within a finite structure.

Through the representation of bodies and desire in *Pájaros*, Sarduy creates a palimpsest in which the characters are repeatedly rewritten in an attempt to more closely approximate an idealized subjectivity. In this sense, the "other island of alterity" becomes the locus of a history of inclusion that will purportedly incorporate the desired objects that the characters lack. In the end, however, the alternative space proves rhetorically equivalent to the one it supplants. Therefore, rather than eradicate or escape from the decay engendered by corporeal and insular confinement, the alternative historiography ultimately reaffirms the inevitablility of limitation.

In this way, Sarduy confronts the fundamental incompatibility of an emancipatory impulse and a discourse of identity based on geographic confinement. The characters eventually become "pájaros de la playa" in the sense that they exist at the liminal boundary between the normative spatiality of the island and the elusive expanse beyond its borders. To a certain extent, the narrative universe Sarduy constructs adheres to the normative logic of insularity: non-normative subjects are removed from the dominant social space and confined in the alternative insular locale of the sanitarium. In a gesture highly reminiscent of the UMAP camps and the mandatory reclusorios in which AIDS patients were interned, the patients are imprisoned in this remote site.

At the same time, however, Sarduy's island functions, not as a counterpoint that effectively reaffirms the hegemony of the dominant social space, but instead as a hyperbolic and excessively baroque mirror image of insularity at its limits. Through exaggeration, inversion, and contamination, *Pájaros* calls the underlying binary logic of insularity into question. The characters repeatedly attempt to rectify their corporeal selves and thereby reconfigure themselves as legitimate desiring subjects. Yet, at the same time, they cannot be readily contained in the prescribed corporeal or spatiotemporal boundaries. Neither their aberrant subjectivity nor the desired reconfiguration can be appropriately circumscribed on the island. The linear, discursive production of monolithic, normative subjects proves unattainable because of the inevitable polyvalence of signs and the simultaneity of competing historical narratives. The space of the novel is palimpsestically overpopulated and thus incapable of fully functioning as the locus for hegemonic subject (re)formation. The putative function of the alternative island Sarduy depicts is the reconstruction of the patients' bodies and their lives. The space of the island should therefore reconfigure them as healthy, productive citizens. In the end, however, the narrative persistently underscores the impossibility of this proposed project. *Pájaros de la playa* focuses on the very boundaries that demarcate subjectivity and spatiality and, in doing so, calls into question the conventional limits of insularity.

## Marya Santo Febres's "Global Divas"[73]

Unlike Piñera and Sarduy, Santos Febres was not a widely recognized author when she published *Sirena Selena vestida de pena* (2000).[74] In fact, although she had an established reputation as a Puerto Rican writer and scholar, her work was not widely read—or even known—outside of "national" literary criticism. Consequently, for many readers of *Sirena Selena*, the novel constitutes their first encounter with the author. At the time of its publication, little was commonly known about her as a person, and the information that was readily available did not immediately suggest a strong, autobiographical connection between the author's personal life and the narrative content of her work. The back cover of the novel's first English edition, for example, emphasizes the author's academic and professional training and experience but does not make reference to any details about her personal life other than her place of birth:

Mayra Santos Febres was born in Puerto Rico. In 1991 she received her doctorate in literature from Cornell University, where she has since taught as a visiting professor. She has also been a guest lecturer at Harvard, as well as numerous other American and European universities, and is currently Associate Professor of Literature at the University of Puerto Rico. She has published two books of poetry to wide acclaim, and her short stories have won many prizes, including the 1994 Letras de Oro Prize from the University of Miami, and the 1997 Juan Rulfo Prize, awarded by Radio Sarandi in Paris. In 1997 her two collections of short fiction were translated into English under the title *Urban Oracles*.[75]

In this way, the biographical data offered situates Santos Febres as an author, but it presents only minimal information about her as a person. More specifically, it does not draw any possible connections between the writer and the narrative content of the novel itself.

Under these circumstances, it is not surprising that Santos Febres's work is not subjected to the same biographical hermeneutic as the previous works that I have discussed here. As with other queer fiction, the content of *Sirena Selena* has often led readers to assume that the author is homosexual. Nevertheless, this assumption does not direct them to read the work as a narration of the author's personal experiences, per se. In fact, this interpretation could be understood as the converse of the critical trend discussed earlier: the literary content leads to assumptions about the author's personal life rather than information about the author's personal life engendering a particular analysis of the work. Hence, even in these cases, the novel is not viewed as a dramatization of the writer's personal experiences. Instead, critics have focused on the characters' complex (and sometimes problematic) negotiation of their sexuality.

Indeed, this approach highlights the striking unwillingness of the novel to present a clear narrative of the protagonist as a coherent—and, of course, legible—subject. On both an *intra-* and an *extradiegetic* level, the elusiveness of the eponymous central figure provocatively frustrates the attempts to fully circumscribe her/him. Similarly, the characters in *Sirena Selena* perpetually search for an appropriate space in which to express and realize their desires. The spaces they encounter, however, prove dystopic: although each new space affords opportunities that had been lacking in the previous one, they also impose new—and equally problematic—restrictions on their occupants. In the end, desire and sexuality prove fundamentally uncontainable and, thus, call into question the limits of normative spatiality.

Although the narrative intercalates the experiences of other characters, most of the novel centers on the evolution of its title character. Santos Feberes's work focuses predominantly on the experiences of the protagonist, whose exceptional talents and attributes are recognized and pursued by several characters in the novel. In short, Sirena Selena is extraordinary. In addition to her mesmerizing voice, she is capable of hypnotizing her audience through a seductive glance, a coquettish gesture, and the utterly convincing femininity of her drag performance. At the same time, Santos Febres's protagonist is also captivating and seductive as a young boy, a quality that is attributed to his suspiciously feminine physical appearance and movements on the one hand and to the disproportionately large size of his penis on the other. In other words, Sirena Selena is the ultimate drag queen and, as such, is utterly irresistible.

In this sense, the protagonist of Santos Febres's novel seems to have the best of both worlds. At the same time, however, several of the principal conflicts of the novel arise from the intersection of competing desires for and about Sirena—while, of course, the protagonist's own desires remain tantalizingly elusive. At first, Sirenito is condemned to a marginal existence, living on the streets of San Juan in an area populated by transvestites and prostitutes. Hence, even in a world of non-normative figures, the protagonist has not been able to access the established systems of exchange. Once Miss Martha Divine—a veteran drag queen—discovers Sirenito (the nickname used to refer to the younger and more masculine persona of the protagonist) and his talents, she takes him on as her protégé and helps him to realize his potential as Sirena Selena. As they soon discover, however, desires cannot be so easily manipulated. The existing constraints on systems of exchange and the coexistence of competing desires constantly destablize the proposed trajectories of Sirena, Martha Divine, and the other characters that they encounter over the course of the novel.

Miss Martha sees Sirena's combination of attributes as a ticket to international success. She believes that her young protégé's transformative abilities will allow her to transcend conventional social and national boundaries along with traditional demarcations of gender. As the novel demonstrates, however, this mobility is not so easily achieved. Sirena's performative abilities become the catalyst for movement and indeed allow the two characters to gain access to certain spaces and power in the novel. This movement, however, is not wholly synonymous with freedom nor does it lead directly to the type of success Miss Martha Divine had envisioned.

When Miss Martha Divine first encounters the young Sirentito, his singing can only be heard in the alleys of San Juan. Martha immediately recognizes Sirenito's potential and seizes upon the opportunity to achieve the level of international success that had alluded her as a performer. Paradoxically, however, Sirena Selena's singular talents cannot be appropriately showcased and cultivated in Puerto Rico since restrictions on child labor laws are stringently enforced on the island. Nevertheless, Martha will not allow her plan to be thwarted by this legal obstacle. Hence, she takes Sirena to Santo Domingo where legal restrictions will not prevent her young protégé from performing in night clubs.

Once they arrive, the alternative location indeed provides opportunities for the pair that were not readily available in Puerto Rico. At the same time, however, the restrictions of the new context also introduce additional obstacles that thwart the realization of Martha Divine's vision of success. In fact, the contradictory combination of problems and possibilities afforded by the Dominican Republic first becomes apparent when the pair arrives from San Juan. In order to gain access to the subculture of drag performances in Santo Domingo, Martha Divine and her protégé must pass through the scrutiny and control of national borders. As they move from the airplane into the customs area, Martha is reminded of how precarious a situation this can be for them:

> Empezó a sentir miradas sobre su cuerpo y el de su ahijada. <<Ay, Jehovah Dios de los ejércitos, dame valor. Esto es lo que más odio de los aterrizajes.>> Por más que trató de tranquilizarse, de nuevo a Martha el ansia se le volvió un tumor vivo en el estómago. Comezaron de nuevo las dudas. ¿Y si le notaban algo raro por las esquinas del maquillaje, y si a ella le pasaba lo que a la Maxine, que la leyeron tan pronto se bajó del 747 y le hicieron pasar vergüenza tras vergüenza en las oficinas de aduana? Casi veinte horas la tuvieron detenida, los guardias burlándose de ella, revolcándole las maletas, rompiendo los frascos de maquillaje contra el piso.[76]

> [She began to feel eyes on her and her adopted son. "Please, Jehovah, God of the armies, give me strength. This is what I hate most about landing." Despite her attempts to calm herself, Martha again felt the anxiety turning into a living tumor in her stomach. The doubts came back. What if they noticed something strange around the edges of her makeup, and if what happened to Maxine happened to her? They figured her out as soon as she got off that 747 and they put her through shame after shame in the customs offices? Almost 20 hours they detained her, the guards making fun of her, dumping out the contents of her suitcases, breaking jars of makeup on the floor.][77]

Martha's situation parallels the experiences of the transvestite Maxine who had been humiliated by the customs officials: as with any transgendered individual, she inevitably runs the risk that the officials might notice something "unusual" in her appearance. But her situation is also further complicated by the presence of Sirenito. Consequently, the usual processes and screenings to which all passengers are subjected become a test of the pair's ability to successfully maintain the illusion of a "normal" mother and son:

> Pagaron impuesto de entrada, dieron certificado de nacimiento, cambiaron unos cuantos dólares en dinero local. Nada que declarar. Por suerte no le abrieron las maletas. Si no, ¿cómo explicar las tres combinaciones de camisetas y mahones para el nene y el maratón de trajes y pelucas de mujer que ni siquiera eran del tamaño de la señora. (21–22)[78]

> [They paid the arrival tax, showed their birth certificates, changed a few dollars into local currency. Nothing to declare. Luckily they didn't have to open their suitcases. If they had, how would they have explained the three sets of sport shirts and [jeans] and the array of dresses and wigs that were not the señora's size.][79]

In a gesture similar to Julia Álvarez's deployment of the converse—*Something to Declare*—the phrase, "nada que declarar," underscores their desire to remain undetected: they do not want to claim or announce their transgendered status to the border officials, and having "nothing to declare" may allow them to avoid the intense scrutiny (of both their bodies and their possessions) that might undermine the desired concealment. In the end, Martha and Sirenito are able to "pass," and the combination of contradictory gender markers remains undetected by the customs officials.

Yet, although they are able to overcome the initial hurdle of the border crossing, this accomplishment only marks the beginning of their struggle. Of course, the border has traditionally been a space of negotiation and contestation. Nevertheless, as Luibhéid cogently argues in her analysis of U.S. immigration policies, the control of political borders is not limited to the mere application of regulations that exist a priori. As cited earlier, when U.S. immigration officers were charged with denying entry to "indecent women," for example, they were not provided with specific instructions on how to evaluate decency. In these situations, immigration officers become the de facto mechanism of the state that translates the national vision of normativity into juridical practice.

Luibhéid's study is based on a careful historical analysis of the U.S. context. Nonetheless, her conclusions point to a significant intersection between borders and normative boundaries that extends beyond the specificity of her case study. That is, borders often constitute the site for enacting a vision of the nation that is desired but not necessarily achieved. When border patrols exist, their function, by definition, is not only to monitor but to control the individuals and goods that are permitted to enter the territory of the country. In this sense, an idealized version of a national "us" is fundamentally opposed to an externalized and less desirable "them." The border thus becomes the contested space that guards the nation against the perceived threat of penetration and contamination.

In this sense, the unease that Martha Divine experiences upon arriving in Santo Domingo is doubly significant. Not only does it represent a moment of intense scrutiny by local officials but it also constitutes the first encounter with the values and restrictions that they will have to confront in the new context. Not surprisingly, therefore, Martha continues to experience anxieties about the precariousness of their situation even after they successfully pass through customs. She must take extra caution in her negotiations with the hotel manager since they are—to some extent—at the mercy of his sponsorship. Therefore, when Sirenito disappears from the hotel, Martha is unwilling to inform the hotel manager or seek assistance from local officials—in spite of her maternal concern.

As it happens, several of Martha's worst fears were justified. Sirenito has left the hotel in the company of Hugo Graubel, an international businessman who lives on the island. He has convinced Sirena to give a private performance at his home for his family and friends. From the first moment he sees the young performer, Graubel is attracted to her. In the end, the two become lovers, and Graubel is able to experience a *jouissance* that had eluded him previously. The protagonist's emotional state and underlying desires remain—as always—intangible. Nevertheless, s/he clearly chooses a life with Graubel over the career that Martha had envisioned and seems satisfied with this decision. The apparent happiness that Sirenito and Graubel find together, however, is achieved at the expense of Martha's desires. When she discovers that her protégé will not be returning to the hotel, she must abandon her dreams of international stardom and begin to seek more modest economic opportunities.

To some extent, what makes Sirena Selena such a valuable commodity is her elusiveness. Given the combination of feminine and masculine attributes along with the ambiguity of youth, she is the perfect commodity to be marketed in a transnational and "borderless" context. Santo Domingo does not ultimately provide them with a gateway to this global citizenship; instead, they find themselves outside the parameters of official control in a manner that affords both opportunity and vulnerability. Santo Domingo proves to be a space of transnational capital, private consumption, and domestic desires and thus fails to function as a vehicle for mobility and international stardom.

In *Sirena Selena*, the desired freedom of this parallel existence is nonetheless truncated by the homologous limitations that are reproduced rather than diminished in the alternate space. Santo Domingo indeed affords opportunities that were not available in Puerto Rico. Geographic displacement holds out the possibility of transcending the limitations of normative sexuality: by moving beyond the boundaries of the nation and, by extension, of the island the characters hope to gain access to spaces and opportunities that prove inaccessible within their island of origin. To some extent, this strategy proves successful. In the end, however, the two islands are excessively similar since, in the Dominican context, one set of possibilities and limitations is simply substituted for another. Hence, the emancipatory potential of the new location is ultimately subverted by the underlying equivalence of the insular spaces that the characters inhabit.

Sirena Selena sets out to achieve the borderless and utopic mobility of a global diva, yet her exceptionalism inevitably exposes the pervasive and ubiquitous limits of normative subjectivity and citizenship that are reproduced rather than dislodged by the shift to a transnational context. The characters, and the protagonist in particular, cannot be neatly inserted into established paradigms of mainstream or marginal social rules. As with *La carne* and *Pájaros*, the novel thus constructs subjects that are "out elsewhere": they are "out" sexually and they strive to move outside or beyond the normal boundaries of circumscribed social spaces. By introducing both the possibilities and the problems of trasnational mobility, moreover, *Sirena Selena* fundamentally destabilizes the supposed dichotomy that always already locates non-normative subjectivity on the other side of the insular borders.

Consequently, the novel underscores the limitations from and within which the nation has constituted itself. The principal characters' aberrant desires lead them to seek opportunities beyond the boundaries of the island-nation and, in doing so, attempt to gain access to a more adequate space of subject formation. The putative difference of the alternative locale thus points to the possibility of transcending the national. The problems that they strive to escape from, however, are not limited to the specific constraints of either nation but are tied instead to the underlying equation of island, nation, and normativity itself. At the same time, their queer subjectivity positions them in a perpetual state of "elsewhereness"; they will always be critically displaced from the hegemonic normativity on which conventional definitions of nationhood and citizenship are based. The insularity posited through translocation fundamentally calls into question the hegemonic and totalizing configuration of the island-nation, but this alternative spatiality proves incapable of fully overcoming the regulatory function of national borders that it purportedly subverts.

## SEXUALITY AND BORDER PATROL

In Tomas Gutiérrez Alea's film, *Fresa y chocolate*, the communist militant Miguel insists on the need to guard the island against inappropriate invasions: when one of the principal characters, David, suggests that they should be more tolerant of their homosexual comrades, Miguel exclaims that "la revolución no entra por el culo." [revolution doesn't enter through the ass].[80] In this rather memorable line, Miguel concisely articulates the fear of penetration and contamination that equates sexuality and national development. Excessively feminized men (i.e., men who allow themselves to be penetrated) cannot function as the source of productive evolution; on the contrary, they constitute a threat that could potentially compromise the nationalist mission of the Cuban Revolution. The presence of homosexual subjects within the borders of the island therefore disrupts the desired absolute dichotomy between the normative and appropriate citizens on the island and the non-normative or aberrant subjects beyond its borders.

This equation of sexuality and nationalism is certainly not limited to the Caribbean. As I have mentioned earlier, Luibhéid's analysis of border patrol cogently traces how the desire to insulate the nation against inappropriate penetration leads to a particular codification of (sexualized) immigrant bodies. According the author, legislation that has adjudicated the requirements for admission to the United States, such as the Page Law and the McCreary Amendment, has often enumerated restrictions without offering concrete guidelines for implementing or enforcing those restrictions. Hence, immigration officials were required to deny admission to anyone who appeared to be indecent or to be seeking entrance to United States for "immoral purposes," yet they frequently received little or no instruction on how to recognize or assess these characteristics. The border thus became a site of incarnation as well as implementation; that is, immigration officers constructed policies, tests, and measures that were designed to identify—and, consequently, interpellate—individual bodies as appropriate or undesirable.

Under these conditions, moreover, immigration policies and practices wield the discursive power of the state and, through their interpretation of legal mandates and proscriptions, render sexuality visible and thus available for evaluation. As the author explains in the introduction, her study proposes to address the question of how the law negotiates the epistemological elusiveness of sexuality. In fact, the introduction begins with a quotation from a student who once asked Luibhéid, "How would the Immigration and Naturalization Service (INS) know if someone was gay, anyway?"[81] Of course, the question can easily be altered slightly to encompass the "mysteries" of promiscuity, seductiveness, and fecundity that immigration policies sought to control. The officers charged with carrying out these policies and realizing the necessary assessments must differentiate between women's bodies that are capable of (re)producing appropriate citizens and those that could "infect" the nation with unwanted sexuality and/or genealogy. They attempt to guard the nation against inappropriate penetration and, in doing so, create a specific code of normative and non-normative behavior.

Although the border offers a particularly rich site of negotiation and contestation for studies of sexuality, the territorial conflict can often be traced in intranational spaces as well. In his study of gay Philippino immigrants, *Global Divas*, Manalansan analyzes the complex relationship between queer transnational sexuality and modernity. More specifically, in his chapter entitled, "Out There," he examines how queers of color are geographically and rhetorically distanced from the mainstream through both physical displacement and the reterritorialization of "alternative" spaces. Similarly, in their work, David Eng and Alberto Sandoval Sánchez have discussed how the diaspora functions more readily than the homeland as the space of homosexual self-fashioning. For these scholars, therefore, queer sexuality is fundamentally tied to the extra- or transnational. The space of queer subjectivity not only relies on the "uncoupling" of family and capitalist production—as John D'Emilio has averred—but is always already situated in a perpetual "elsewhere" that lies outside the dominant space of national subject formation.

In the case of the Hispanic Caribbean, as I have suggested earlier, the vexed relationship between queer sexuality and national space is further intensified by the close identification with the geographic demarcation of the island. Hence, in a performative expulsion reminiscent of an episode of Mark Burnett's reality television show, *Survivor*, certain individuals are either literally or figuratively "kicked off the island." The "tribal council" convenes and determines that they are not worthy of membership since they are not contributing as effectively to the advancement of the group. Removing these individuals therefore enhances the remaining members' chances of survival and, of course, success. And, as Lugo Ortiz has demonstrated in her analysis of "¡Jum!" the community performs its identity through the ritualistic and violent expulsion of the aberrant element that ostensibly impedes this progress.

According to this logic, there is literally no space for the queer subject within the dominant social space of the island. The three authors I have examined here take this logic to its furthest and most perverse consequences: they present an extreme poetics of limits in which spaces and characters are inevitably defined in terms of normative insularity yet, at the same time, prove fundamentally uncontainable. More importantly, the three novels initially accept the dichotomous logic of insularity, and their protagonists must therefore seek alternative possibilities outside the dominate social space of the island. Nevertheless, in all three cases, the authors also underscore precisely those desires that cannot be neatly inserted into or contained within the prescribed boundaries of the island-nation. Through hyperbole, elusiveness, and displacement, their work calls into question the epistemic conflation of insular and (re)productive space.

On the one hand, the alternative space that the authors postulate or construct stands against the island as a counter-hegemonic space of queer subjectivity. On the other, however, the alter-island ultimately proves excessively equivalent to the hegemonic one it opposes. Hence, Piñera, Sarduy, and Santos Febres fundamentally destabilize the supposed sexual/spatial binary of Hispanic Caribbean insularity: they interrogate the specific conditions that purportedly necessitate or engender that binary and offer a critique of spatialized normativity. In this manner, *La carne de Reñe*, *Pájaros de la playa,* and *Sirena Selena*—in particular—underscore the impossibility of a totalizing system in which subjects are so hyperinterpellated that they cannot function. They expose the foundational myth of Hispanic Antillean subjectivity as both arbitrary and manipulative. In the end, their work suggests that the survival of the nation does not necessarily depend on the removal of aberrant subject but, instead, that power and privilege are derived from an insistence on (and an apparent "naturalization" of) this underlying binary logic.

In his work, Homi Bhabha has asserted that the other is never outside or beyond us. That is, although the nation defines itself in direct opposition to a purportedly external other, difference is never truly eradicated by this rhetorical operation. In fact, discourses of nationalism are sustained by the need to perpetually efface or neutralize the other that can never be fully externalized. The alter-insularity of queer subjectivity discussed in this chapter challenges the false dichotomy through which the nation asserts itself. The alternative space constructed by these authors fundamentally destabilizes the configurations that present the delimited island as a natural phenomenon rather than a cultivated social construct. Each of these works presents subjects that are "out elsewhere": they are both located outside the island and are out sexually. Through the uneasy negotiation of insular spatiality that these subject enact, moreover, the works critically interrogate the limitations from and within which the nation has constituted itself.

# 3
# Dancing With the Enemy: (Post)National Borders and Contested Spaces

> A charter flight from Miami to Havana takes
> forty minutes or so.
> They pass out the plastic cups of cola, you
> drink, and as they collect the cups,
> the plane is descending already.
> —Ned Sublette, *Cuba Classics 2:
> Dancing with the Enemy*

IN 1991, A COMPILATION OF CUBAN MUSIC ENTITLED *DANCING WITH THE Enemy* was released. The title of the compilation underscores the paradoxical status of this music, framing it in terms of both its political and artistic value. And the language on the back cover explores this duality: "Are politics our enemy? Are governments our enemy? Can music be our enemy? Can communists have a good time? Can we have a good time? Is a music communist? Can it be capitalist? Do you enjoy it more either way? You need this record. Have a cigar."[1]

The repetitive—and, one might argue, trivializing—language and elaboration of the rhetorical questions posed here highlight the inappropriate conflation of politics and music. That is, political boundaries should not dictate aesthetic appreciation. Yet, if this is understood to be the principal message of the questions, the final imperative seems to be a nonsequitur. In the end, however, the questions invite the consumer to enjoy commodities that political conflicts have rendered, both inappropriately and provocatively, inaccessible: Cuban music and cigars.

To some extent, Ned Sublette's more extensive contextualization of the project that is included in the liner notes echoes this contradictory portrayal of the value of Cuban music. As he suggests in his discussion of the relative invisibility of current Cuban music in the United States, the title of the album refers to the very legislation that impedes access to Cuban cultural production. "Dancing with the enemy" inevitably alludes to the "Trading with the Enemy Act" which prohibits U.S. citizens from purchasing any goods and services from Cuba. The appeal of the album is thus derived from its ability to provide access to illicit material.

More importantly, perhaps, this framing of the music underscores a fundamental instability in the purported relationship between the two opposing nations of Cuba and the United States. In the description quoted in the epigraph above, Sublette points to the startling proximity of the two national territories. The subjective and quotidian experience of the distance between the southern tip of the Florida peninsula and the island of Cuba (an experience measured in terms of the commonplace practices of consumption generally associated with air travel) dislodges the conventional conception of an enormous gulf between the two: however inconceivable it may seem, the distance can be traversed in approximately the time required for in-flight beverage service. That is, although residents in the United States have been made acutely aware of the physical proximity of Cuba through specific historic events (i.e., the Cuban Missile Crisis, the arrival of numerous *balseros* (raft people) by means of transportation as minimal as an inner-tube), the ease with which the trip to Havana can be realized proves nonetheless shocking. Irrespective of how close the two nations may be in physical terms, the distance between them is nonetheless portrayed as seemingly insuperable.

In this sense, the description of traveling to Havana metonymically represents the project of the album. According to its packaging, *Dancing with the Enemy* provides access to contemporary Cuban culture in a manner that presumably dislodges the conventional wisdom or dominant discourses that codify the relationship between the opposing political spaces of the United States and Cuba. The juxtaposition between these two nations, following the Cuban Revolution in 1959, is generally presented as an absolute dichotomy, but the album introduces an alternative: it suggests that cultural expression—when it is allowed to cross political borders—can transcend and even transgress this type of division.[2] And, moreover, the album sells itself as an opportunity to subvert foreign policy through transcultural consumption and enjoyment.

At the same time, however, the phrase "dancing with the enemy" also points to a more subtle and complex codependency with the juxtaposed adversary. The more the two nations insist on an absolute separation from one another, the more inseparable they become. In this sense, the title also offers a metaphorical representation of this relationship: the two nations become locked in a perpetual embrace and thereby enact a dance generated by both the insistence on absolute division and inevitable permeability of clearly demarcated boundaries. "Dancing with the enemy" can therefore be understood as a reference to the art that is created through the "pa'lante-pa'trás" (back-and-forth), the movement of a sustained engagement between the nation and its declared enemy.[3] The relationship between the two is thus characterized as a delicate balance: they must maintain a mutual distance that preserves their separation and, at the same time, reinforces the ever-present threat of invasion and the concomitant need for constant vigilance. Understood in these terms, the interaction of Cuba and the United States is not primarily one of hostility or military conflict; instead, the two nations sustain a highly convenient tension.

Nevertheless, this characterization of the U.S.-Cuban relationship proves surprising in the current context of geopolitical shifts and transnational consolidation. According to the epigraph quoted above, the proximity and resulting accessibility of the island constitute an uncanny disruption within conventional notions of the distance that separates the island from the United States. In contemporary cultural discourse, however, it is more common to express astonishment at the relative inaccessibility of places or information. Over the past several decades, divisions engendered by both physical distance and political borders have been supplanted by geopolitical shifts that foster greater interconnectedness. Accordingly, the characterization offered by *Dancing with the Enemy* might seem anachronistic, a remnant of Cold War politics that is fundamentally out of place in contemporary society. Yet the obstacles that thwart direct interaction between Cuba and the United States are persistently redrawn by politicians in both countries. More importantly, the paradoxical relationship with space that Sublette presents is not limited to Cuba. In general, Hispanic Caribbean discourses of identity perpetually reinforce insular boundaries in spite of geopolitical shifts that would presumably minimize their significance. Consequently, a curious duality can be traced in contemporary cultural production between the reification of traditional political borders and quotidian experiences that seemingly contravene the historical importance of these borders.

In a sense, the geographic circumstances of the Antilles conspire to reinforce the historical notion of national borders even when demographic changes would otherwise call these notions into question. Hence, in the face of a changing geopolitical context, a contradiction emerges between the spatiality of the national imaginary, on the one hand, and the literal place of the nation, on the other. Not surprisingly, perhaps, the most salient example of this tension can be found when an external force invades the island since this presence destabilizes both political sovereignty and insular self-fashioning. The subdivision of Hispaniola, to cite the most overt case, fundamentally disrupts the equation of island and nation. Although the neighboring islands of Cuba and Puerto Rico are not subdivided between two sovereign nations, complex and often controversial relationships with the United States have evolved over the course of the twentieth century. More specifically, the discourse and cultural production engendered by the U.S. military installations in Cuba and Puerto Rico perpetually negotiate the incommensurability of an external force within the confines of the island. As I will argue here, this occupation of insular terrain leads to strategies of denouncement, repression, and carnavalesque parody that ultimately reinforce the absolute dichotomy of insularity. The conventional spatiality of the nation is continually reproduced in spite of—and, in some cases, in response to—fundamental challenges to the logic of self-definition.

In this fashion, the title of the anthology of Cuban music serves as an appropriate metaphor for the dynamic that develops between the national imaginary and the geopolitical circumstances of the Antilles. "Dancing with the enemy" is a recasting of the more common phrase, "sleeping with the enemy." To some extent, both phrases suggest an excessive—and therefore perilous—intimacy with a purported adversary. The substitution of dancing for sleeping, however, relocates that relationship: the two entities represented are still connected and interdependent, but the more complete (and more completely sexualized) metaphor is mitigated through the metaphoric displacement of the enemy to the slightly safer distance of an alternative embrace. The enemy is not eliminated or neutralized but, instead, is kept at arm's length. Rather than the excessive intimacy of being in bed together, the relationship is reconfigured as one of mutual engagement between highly proximate partners that are, at the same time, adversaries.

In this chapter, I will examine specific cases in Cuba, the Dominican Republic, and Puerto Rico through which the absolute dichotomy of insularity is challenged by the inappropriate manifestation of the extranational enemy within the boundaries of the island. I will focus on a moment of historical transition or a particular incident that highlights the disconnect between the idea of the island-nation and its geographic, sociohistorical conditions. The precise circumstances of and responses to the crisis provoked vary greatly across the three cases. Nonetheless, they all dramatize the underlying conflict between the insistence on a perfect binary and the inevitable permeability of the national borders. In all three cases, moreover, this inevitable permeability is recast in terms of proximity: the nation must effectively lay claim to its insular terrain and then "shore up" its borders to protect itself from the excessively imminent threat of invasion and occupation. According to this logic, the enemy within the island must be relocated or circumscribed in a manner that displaces its more immediate challenge to national self-definition.

In the end, these cases underscore a fundamental condition of Hispanic Caribbean self-fashioning: the problem of insufficient space and the inappropriate presence of the extranational "other" are themselves locked in a dance that must be endlessly rehearsed and reenacted. This duality engenders twin anxieties around the excessive presence of the enemy on the one hand and the absence of a fully formed island-nation on the other. As a result, the relationship between insular and national space is persistently reiterated in a manner that insists on proximity and interconnectedness with the nation's other while it also negates full imbrication. The enemy within the borders of the island cannot be explicitly acknowledged; yet, at the same time, it is externalized and thus recast as a (potential) threat lurking just beyond the borders. Consequently, it must be actively kept at the precise distance of arm's length.

## Divided Islands: The Archetypal Contested Space of Hispaniola

The island of Hispaniola has been shared by Haiti and the Dominican Republic for over three centuries, and it is one of the few Caribbean islands in which imperial powers and their postcolonial counterparts have cohabited for such an extended period of time. In this way, Hispaniola presents a microcosm of the competing political and economic interest that can be traced throughout the region. At the same time, however, many of the internal tensions found within specific areas of the Antilles —i.e., class systems, competing affiliations with distinct world powers, or industries—are magnified and played out as disputes between the two countries within the island. Furthermore, throughout the last two centuries in particular, homologous yet irreconcilable nationalist projects have been advanced by each side in a constant juxtaposition of mutual threat and codependence. Given this historical situation, the other simultaneously underscores the permeability and fragility of insular space and constitutes the primary obstacle for the appropriate evolution of the nation.

Although the early history of Hispaniola (before and after colonization) coincides with its two neighboring islands (Cuba and Puerto Rico), its status changed significantly in the seventeenth century. Almost from the time of Columbus's first settlement, the French and Spanish battled for control over the island. In fact, the name of the island, La isla española, is often explained as a response to the threat of French domination. The dispute was initially settled in 1697 when the two colonial powers agreed to divide the territory. The relationship between the French and Hispanic colonies was certainly contentious, but the rebellion and establishment of Haiti in the early nineteenth century significantly intensified the opposition between the two sides of Hispaniola. After 1804, Dominican leaders feared that their citizens might follow their neighbor's example and seek independence from Spain. At the same time, they also became increasingly wary of the Haitian government and their plans to further develop the incipient free black nation through the "liberation" of the Dominican half of the island.[4]

Over the course of the following two centuries, both Haiti and the Dominican Republic have claimed the island of Hispaniola as their territorial domain. Despite repeated assurances that they would respect Dominican sovereignty, several Haitian leaders have advocated the rescue of all of Hispaniola from the legacy of colonialism. Jean Pierre Boyer, for example, attempted to fully realize his self-imposed mission to establish a single, free black nation and invaded the newly independent Dominican Republic in 1822. Although they tend to be less messianic in tone, Dominican attitudes towards the western portion of the island have also threatened Haitian sovereignty. The principal source of Haitian immigration in the Dominican Republic has been the subsidized importation of an inexpensive labor force. Despite this economic dependence on Haitian citizens and the periodic decision to "purchase" workers from the other side of the island, the Dominican government has consistently denounced the permeability engendered by contiguity. In one of the most famous incidents of anti-Haitian politics, Rafael Trujillo ordered the massacre of over 25,000 Haitians living along the border in 1937.

These examples reflect the racialized and imperialist beliefs that have engendered prejudice and even extreme violence in the relations between the two countries. Yet they are also representative of a larger nationalistic vision that imagines a reunification of the island. Leaders of both nations have articulated the inherent obligation to recover the neighboring half of the island and reinsert it into its rightful place in national development. They have both advanced nationalist agendas that require the virtual eradication or incorporation of the other portion of the island. In her analysis of the relationship between Haiti and the Dominican Republic, Michele Wucker invokes the metaphor of a cock-fight in which the opposing roosters battle for dominance over the arena: "Like the gamecocks, the two nations of Hispaniola share a history of violence that has been compounded by their confinement. Roosters, after all, fight for territory. It is only when they come into too close quarters that fights break out."[5] Wucker thus characterizes the conflict in terms of a fundamental territorial dispute: both parties fight what they perceive as an invading enemy that challenges their dominant (male) positions.

In this situation of insular subdivision, the battles for political power and for the control of space become conflated. Hence, territorial claims become intensified and the presence of the opponent within the island necessarily constitutes a threat that must be symbolically, if not literally, eliminated. In *La isla al revés*, for example, Joaquín Balaguer—a prominent Dominican intellectual, literary critic, and politician—repeatedly expresses his concerns about the Haitian presence on the island and how it functions as an impediment to the proposed future of the Dominican Republic. Although many of his objections are putatively based on economic concerns, his vision of the island is clearly racialized, and his condemnation of the Haitian influence is often reduced to a purely pejorative derision of the ethnically marked other: "The denationalization of the Dominican part of the borders was no less alarming nor less damaging in terms of the moral aspect. All of the zones near the Haitian territory had been invaded by exotic customs that had conspired not only against the morality of the Dominican people but also against the unity of religious sentiment. Incest and other equally barbarous practices, antithetical to the Christian institution of the family, are common in the lowlands of the Haitian population and constitute a testimony of its tremendous moral deformations."[6] In this description of Haitian culture and its influences (particularly along the border), Balaguer invokes several classic tropes of a derogatory subaltern narrative in which he suggests that the inappropriate presence of Haitians has a destructive effect that must be purged or eliminated in order to preserve the more desirable (and more Christian) society of the Dominican Republic. In this context, Haiti constitutes an infectious element within Hispaniola that must be expelled or eradicated, a disease against which the Dominican Republic must be inoculated or protected.[7]

The specific reference to incest could be viewed simply as a trope frequently evoked in the pejorative denouncement of an inappropriate other. In this case, however, it could also be interpreted as a rhetorical slippage which reveals the underlying drama that is being masked by the excessive anxiety around the Haitian presence. The problem is not necessarily that Haiti and the Dominican Republic are too different but, instead, that they are too similar. The distinction between the two nations therefore must be artificially created and maintained. On one level, Balaguer's denouncement of Haitian barbarism is based on the accusation that incest is common—or rather that is it not uncommon, to reproduce the rhetorical structure of his phrase—within the Haitian community. Yet the specific attention to incest as the principal example of their undesirability may also point to the primary concern that drives this abject depiction: the internal coupling of Haiti and the Dominican Republic threatens to impede appropriate productive national development. By emphasizing this trope as the single most disturbing trait of the Haitian community, he links the sharing of insular territory to the threat of incest.

In this manner, the demarcation of an appropriate, healthy, and productive Dominican nation is expressed in both ethnic and spatial terms. Of course, this anxiety is persistently narrated throughout nineteenth- and twentieth-century cultural and political discourse. Yet the most striking and critically significant dramatization of the conflict and, moreover, the strategies of repression and displacement it engenders can be found in the nineteenth century historical novel, *Enriquillo*. Manuel de Jesús Galván's *Enriquillo* is arguably the most widely read work of Dominican fiction, and the novel is frequently cited as a seminal text in the Dominican canon. Although written and published in the nineteenth century, the narrative takes place in the early colonial period of the island. For the most part, Galvan's novel retells the story of Bartolomé de las Casas's indigienous pupil, Enriquillo, who converts to Christianity. More specifically, the novel traces Enriquillo's attempts to establish himself within Dominican society following his conversion. As with other Latin American colonies, Dominican society was organized around a rigid, ethnically based caste system that severely limited the social mobility of individuals deemed to be of indigenous descent. Consequently, despite his conversion and his adherence to established cultural norms, Enriquillo is not universally accepted as a legitimate colonial subject. Much to his dismay, the protagonist finds that his fellow members of colonial society (especially those that claim Spanish or European descent) resent his relative socioeconomic success. Moreover, the strict demarcations of colonial society prevent Enriquillo from legitimately marrying his beloved Mencía (based on antimiscegenation laws and norms) and making a life for himself with her. At first, the main character is confident that the civilized and Christian ideals he has adopted will allow him to challenge these restrictions and carve out a legitimate place for himself. When his repeated attempts to do so fail, however, Enriquillo finally becomes disillusioned with Dominican society and ultimately leads an indigenous rebellion against colonial authority.

Most of the criticism on Galvan's novel focuses on the protagonist's struggle for justice and on the author's presentation (and rewriting) of national history. Yet the question of insular spatiality—both in terms of how it is alternately emphasized and eschewed—also constitutes a fundamental aspect of the author's literary project. Through its particular staging of incipient Dominican self-fashioning, Galván's novel offers a salient example of the relationship between insularity and nationalism. There is literally no space for Enriquillo on the island, and his repeated displacements—rather than affording him the freedom he seeks—ultimately reproduce the confinement of colonial society. And the most significant and challenging aspects of Galvan's work also reveal a poetics of confinement and excess.

Not only does Galván repeatedly rewrite and relocate national history in *Enriquillo* but he focuses extensively on a love triangle among secondary characters. The elaborate narration of this subplot has been largely dismissed by literary critics as a product of the need for nineteenth century writers to draw out their work in order to earn sufficient income. Yet the progress sought by characters in this section of the novel is also obstructed by the limitations of colonial society, and—as with Enriquillo—they prove unable to find an appropriate space for the realization of their desires within the island. In this sense, Galvan's novel repeatedly retells (and relocates) the principal spatial drama of Dominican national identity: the appropriate development of the nation is persistently thwarted by the lack of sufficient space and the excessive limitations on the available territory.

Of course, one of the most salient and frequently discussed features of *Enriquillo* is the temporal displacement of the narrative. As with many Latin American novels published during the second half of the nineteenth century, *Enriquillo* depicts the struggle to meet the exigencies of appropriate national development. However, rather than focus directly on the problems of the time (as most Latin American national romances did), *Enriquillo* recounts events that take place during the early colonial period. In his novel, Galván narrates the conflicts that arise between members of several sectors of colonial Dominican society. As a free Christian, Enriquillo becomes a prominent member of colonial society, and his success engenders resentment and envy among his compatriots. Privilege at that time was largely based on relative proximity to Europe, and the protagonist's unusual social mobility engendered the hostility of those members of colonial society who could lay claim to European descent.[8] Eventually, two such individuals—Pedro de Mojica and Andrés de Valenzuela—conspire to strip Enrique of both his material possessions and his wife. The protagonist attempts to resolve the conflict through acquiescence and legal protest. However, when these strategies prove unsuccessful, his fight for justice leads to an indigenous rebellion.

Galván does not merely elaborate on existing sources and colonial documents; instead, he actively engages dominant historiographic practices. The novel is presented as a rewriting of Dominican history as documented in earlier sources—most notably, Las Casas's *Historia de las Indias*—and this status is reinforced by frequent references to the novel's textual precursors. Not only does Galván include extensive quotations from Las Casas; he often comments on the need to limit his narration to events documented in existing accounts. In this way, Galván—rather than suggest that his version diverges from those of his predecessors—implies that the work can be inserted into the historical inscription outlined by other texts. *Enriquillo* strives to construct an emancipatory history, but this project is thwarted by preexisting historiographic limitations.

As with most historical fiction, Galván modifies documented data. Citing such fictional deviations in the text, some critics have chastised Galván for his inaccurate portrayal of colonial events.[9] In the case of such accusations, Galván's novel is evaluated through historiographic criteria rather than strictly on the exigencies of verisimilitude. For many critics, however, these apparent inconsistencies constitute an integral part of Galvan's literary project. Doris Sommer, for example, argues that Galván initiated an alternate national history in his novel. According to her, the author invokes the remote colonial past as a response to the excess of historiographic projects in nineteenth-century Dominican Republic: "By the time Galván wrote, he knew that the space of Dominican history had been densely overwritten.... Cunningly, Galván stops the vertigo with a new start, with the irresistible seductiveness of the first beginnings of a country that struggled longer than most to establish some national identity."[10] Sommer proposes that Galván responds to the palimpsest of contemporary Dominican historical writing by returning to a remote past and, thus, reconstituting the origin of national identity. Furthermore, she explains this strategy in terms of Galván's political career: he had advocated reannexation to Spain and had to negotiate an alliance with the new ruling party once reannexation failed. Therefore, according to Sommer, the rewriting of national evolution purportedly allowed the author to liberate himself from the complexities of contemporary national politics.

The problems represented in *Enriquillo*, however, cannot be explained solely in terms of political motivations. The historical displacement allows the author to avoid several issues that subsequently become controversial complexities within Dominican society. Since he narrates events from the early colonial period, Galván is able to reduce racial miscegenation to a binary division between Europeans and Indians. Furthermore, the temporal regression allows him to deal with the island as an integral whole whereas, in a contemporary context, he would have to accommodate the disputed border that divides the island between the Dominican Republic and Haiti. In this fashion, Galván is able to dramatize the insular (re)unification that both Dominican and Haitian nationalisms advocate before and after the publication of his novel. Paradoxically, although this strategy allows him to elide the territorial and racialized dispute of insular subdivision, the problems engendered by this subdivision nonetheless manifest themselves in the novel. That is, even in the apparent absence of the Haitian occupation of a portion of the island, the novel underscores the excesses and limitation that hinder the demarcation of an appropriate space for the productive evolution of Dominican history.

In this sense, the problem Sommer identifies can indeed be traced in his work. Galván attempts to write himself out of the historiographic and demographic overcrowding of Dominican territory; yet, the very problem that he eschews resurfaces through the recurring themes of confinement and displacement in the novel. The principal conflicts in *Enriquillo* arise from the problem of excess: the narrative is driven by a struggle among incompatible versions that compete to occupy the same textual or geographic space. The possibility of the coexistence of competing paradigms, moreover, is thwarted by the limitations of insularity. In fact, Galván ultimately presents both the problem and its solution in terms of physical space. Throughout the novel, insufficient enclosures are repeatedly juxtaposed with the possibility of open spaces. This juxtaposition underscores the need for liberation that is persistently hindered by the limitations of the existing configuration of space in the Caribbean. In *Enriquillo*, the author explores alternative spaces as a possible source of such liberation. However, in the end, the proposed shift fails to resolve the problems of usurped territory or the resulting insufficiency.

This inscription of a layered national history is depicted symbolically through the conversion of indigenous characters and the consequent onomastic structure in which indigenous characters acquire Christian names. Rather than treat this change as a linear evolution, Galván presents it as a simultaneous duality: "Higuemota, o sea Doña Ana de Guevara, como la llamaremos indistintamente en lo sucesivo"[11] [Higuemota, now baptized and known as Doña Ana].[12] The act of conversion does not constitute a stable passage from one identity to another but instead becomes a continual struggle between contradictory subjectivities that are forced to coexist in one person. This dynamic is present in the social structure represented as well. Even those characters who appear willing to shed their indigenous roots find that the former identity is eventually reimposed on them: the indigenous status of Enriquillo and Doña Ana, for example, is invoked in order to negate their acquired prestige and social power. In this way, characters strive to transform themselves, but this movement is impeded by the inevitable coexistence of past and present identities within each subject.

This dynamic is also mirrored in other aspects of the novel. At several points, the narrative focuses on the ruins of a former colonial enterprise or the prior existence of an indigenous settlement that will become the foundation for current colonization. And the novel also presents the literal overcrowding of colonial events. In these instances, Galván narrates a significant event and underscores the inability to accommodate everyone that attends. When Las Casas delivers the first official American mass, the occasion draws a large audience, and Galván comments on this singular gathering:

> Atraídos los unos por amistad o adhesión a las Casas, los otros por la novedad del sagrado espectáculo de una *misa nueva*, que ofrecía la particularidad de ser la primera que iba a celebrarse en el Nuevo Mundo, y otros muchos por la necesidad de aprovechar la época de la fundición y marca de oro extraído de sus minas, jamás se había visto en ningún punto de la isla Española, desde su descubrimiento, tanta gente reunida como la que entonces concurrió a la Vega.[13]

> [Some were drawn by feelings of friendship or loyalty to Las Casas, some by the novelty of a new mass, but most by the need of having their gold ore smelted and assayed. Never since the conquest of the island had so many people congregated in one small town.][14]

Shortly thereafter, the sermons of Father Montesinos also draw substantial public attention. In particular, crowds gather to witness Montensinos's expected retraction of his denouncement of colonial authorities. In this case, the assembly exceeds both predicted attendance and the available space: "La iglesia mayor no podía contener en sus naves el concurso de gente que, estimulada por los soberbios oficiales reales y sus amigos, acudían a solarzarse en la humillación de aquellos humildes religiosos"[15] [the church was again crowded, this time mainly with people who had been encouraged by Pasamonte's party to witness the righting of a wrong done to royal and public authority—and to the rejoice over the humiliation of the Dominicans.][16] In both these cases, the public interest in colonial events threatens to exceed to available physical capacity. This difficulty implies that the coexistence of the diverse components of colonial society is impeded not only by their inherent incompatibility but also by their inability to fit within existing structures.

The love triangle that develops between María de Cuéllar, Juan de Grijalva, and Diego de Velázquez also underscores the problem of colonial insufficiencies—albeit in another register. And, again, the principal conflict is one of excess. As with the cases discussed earlier, this conflict arises because two men desire the same woman, but, in this case, it also acquires a spatial component. Beyond competing desires, the struggle among these three characters specifically becomes the search for a suitable space that will accommodate their desires.

The conflict begins when Juan de Grijalva learns of the planned marriage between Don Diego and his beloved. Although María de Cuéllar is not interested in marrying Diego, she agrees to meet him in the viceroy's garden as part of an elaborate scheme to liberate herself from this planned union. Unfortunately, however, Juan de Grijalva observes this encounter and believes that María has accepted Diego's proposal. Therefore, he agrees to abandon his pursuit of her. In this manner, the initial problem arises from the simultaneous occupation of the garden by all three characters.

In fact, the presence of any of these characters in the garden is rather exceptional. Because the garden is part of the viceroy's residence, it is not generally open to the public and, more importantly, is not a customary location for a clandestine nocturnal rendezvous. Diego de Velázquez affirms the singularity of his presence there when he unexpectedly encounters the viceroy, Diego Colón:

> habiendo recibido los plácemes de vuestra señoría por mi concertado enlace, no he creído faltar el respeto que os tributo, con obedecer la indicación de mi prometida esposa. De otra suerte jamás hubiera puesto los pies en este recinto, que por ser vuestro es un santuario para mí.[17]
>
> [Having already received your Excellency's congratulations on my forthcoming marriage, I cannot think that I saw any lack of respect towards you in obeying the wishes of my betrothed; but for that I should never have set foot in this garden, which I regard almost as sacred ground.][18]

Nevertheless, it is precisely its inevitable association with colonial authority that leads María to invite Diego to meet her in the viceroyal garden. Doña María de Toledo, the Vicereine, believes that the location will encourage Diego de Velázquez to accept the invitation. In this way, María de Cuéllar attempts to use access to this privileged space in order to free herself from an undesirable confinement. However, the occupation of that space by the three characters produces the opposite effect: ultimately, by causing Grijalva to leave, it limits María's ability to construct her own future.

In the end, the unsuccessful pursuit of María de Cuéllar leads both men to leave Hispaniola. The Vicereine Doña María proposes that once Velázquez leaves the island, he will begin to lose interest in María: "Velázquez será encargado de una importantísima empresa, fuera de esta isla; y el tiempo y la ausencia proporcionarán sobradas conyunturas para lo demás; pues he oído decir siempre que el amor se ahoga fácilmente cuando hay mar por medio"[19] [Velázquez will be charged with an important undertaking, far from this island, and time and absence can be counted upon to do their work. I have often heard it said: "Love soon dies when a sea rolls between."][20] The vicereine thereby convinces her friend that removal of one of her suitors from Hispaniola will resolve the problem of excess since his interest will not be strong enough to overcome the physical barriers that will separate them. Unaware of the motivation that inspired the proposed displacement, Diego de Velázquez accepts this assignment and prepares to establish a colony on a neighboring Antillean island. Although he initially considers Jamaica, he opts for Cuba since he believes that he will encounter less resistance from the current occupants. At the same time, a heart-broken Grijalva prefers to distance himself from Doña María and build a future elsewhere, and he leaves to defend the incipient Spanish settlement in Jamaica. In both cases, movement to another island becomes a possible solution given the excess of romantic interest in María. Nevertheless, the strategy does not prove entirely successful for either suitor. The shift to the putatively open, available space of Cuba allows Don Diego to improve his social status and marry his beloved. However, it does not foster a favorable change in María's sentiments, and—although she resigns herself to the proposed union with Don Diego, the marriage is short-lived since María dies not long after the ceremony. After her death, Grijalva learns of her unfailing devotion to him, but he remains nonetheless romantically and geographically displaced by Diego de Velázquez and his relationship with María.

Before accepting her inevitable marriage to Diego, Doña María seeks refuge by retreating to an enclosure. She attempts to insulate herself from the prospect of her future marriage to Diego within the confines of her room: "Tal vez por liberarse del tormento . . . María se esforzó en dominar su angustia, logrando componer el semblante, y pidió a Don Cristóbal permiso para retirarse a su aposento, donde era su deseo permanecer absolutamente sola."[21] [To escape the ordeal of having to hear him out, Doña María with a great effort succeeded in composing her face, after which she asked leave to retire to her room and be left completely alone.][22] As a result, when the strategy of liberating herself by convincing Velázquez to leave the island fails, María begins to internally distance herself from her surroundings. Not only does she isolate herself in her room, but she becomes emotionally detached from events. Doña María de Toledo notices the change in her behavior during a final meeting just before María de Cuéllar leaves for Cuba:

> María de Cuéllar ostentó en esa última visita a sus ineficaces protectores una tranquilidad sorprendente. Parecía perfectamente conforme con su destino. La Virreina lloró abrazándola, la jóven enferma, sin verter una lágrima, con voz firme y segura trató de consolar y serenar el ánimo de su acongojada amiga. Ésta, sorprendida de ver tanta entereza, llegó un instante a persuadirse de que tenía a la vista un milagro de la resignación, aunque la intensa palidez y el melancólico semblante de la pobre víctima desmentía toda su aparente fuerza de alma.[23]

> [Doña María was surprisingly calm on this occasion, and seemed to accept her fate with complete resignation. The Vicereine wept as she embraced her sick friend, who tearlessly, in a firm voice, tried to console and calm her. The surprised Vicereine persuaded herself, for a moment, that the girl with a miraculous strength of mind had decided after all to make the best of her marriage; but this view was belied by the fearful pallor and settled melancholy of her face.][24]

And Doña María's final act of withdrawal is to resolve herself to death. Having obeyed her father, María expresses her freedom to abandon the life that she had struggled unsuccessfully to avoid:

> –Padre mío, os obdecí y no me pesa . . . ¡Adiós!
> Acudió [Velázquez] solícito al lecho . . . y no llegó sino a tiempo de ver la pálida frente de María inclinarse con un lirio tronchado, y sus bellos ojos cerrarse para siempre a la luz de la vida.[25]

> ["Father, I have obeyed you and I do not regret it . . . Good bye!"
> A ray of happiness illumined Velazquez' face when he heard his wife speak . . . but reached her in time only to see her pale brow fall forward like a stricken lily, and her lovely eyes close to the light of the world forever.][26]

In the end, María is not free to pursue her own desires. Nevertheless, she is able to liberate herself through physical separation from the desires imposed on her.

This strategy of shielding oneself from social perils within a domestic structure can also be found in other parts of the novel. The principal conflict of the novel arises from contradictory responses to Enriquillo's evolving social role. His conversion to Christianity, privileged relationship with Las Casas and other powerful members of colonial society, and his eventual marriage to Mencía—a member of the colonial aristocracy with a substantial inheritance—potentially elevate his position far beyond the role conventionally allocated to indigenous subjects during the colonial period. Consequently, he poses a threat to those who wish to preserve existing demarcations of wealth and power. That is, because his relationships allow him to cross established social boundaries, he becomes a transgressive figure. Enriquillo encounters the first major opposition to this destabilizing potential when he plans to marry Mencía. As the two are about to be married, Las Casas receives a letter from royal authorities officially prohibiting the union. According to the letter, Enriquillo and Mencía are legally prevented from marrying unless they obtain a special royal dispensation because of their racial differences: "por la calidad de las contrayentes y muy en especial por ser Doña Mencía de familia castellana y no estar en uso el que tales de su clase se casen con indios, necesitan las reales licencias de la cámara de Su Alteza"[27] [since Doña Mencia is of Castilian family and it is not customary for women of her class to marry Indians, royal licenses will be required from His Majesty's Chamber.][28] Enriquillo and Mencía must overcome significant bureaucratic difficulties because their legal union involves the conjoining of subdivisions of colonial society that are supposed to remain separate.

Although the two are eventually able to marry through Las Casas's intervention, the couple continues to meet with resistance and opposition. Mojica and Andrés de Valenzuela attempt to usurp Enriquillo's power and possessions. In order to shield themselves from the consequences of this persecution, Enriquillo and Mencía repeatedly relocate. With each adjustment, the alternative domestic space offers the possibility of building the existence they desire. In fact, they elect to live in a very modest home in Maguana instead of the multiple alternatives offered to them. Rather than impose on friends or make themselves vulnerable to their enemies, they prefer to resort to the less luxurious surroundings of this marginalized community in order to maintain their autonomy. Nevertheless, none of the spaces the couple occupies can provide protection that would ensure this autonomy. Despite their progressive domestic displacement, Enriquillo and Mencía are not able to successfully negotiate a space for themselves within the existing colonial order. Faced with increasingly restrictions and reductions in his status, Enriquillo eventually flees to the mountains in order to escape this confinement. Once he moves to a less regulated space on the island, he is able—along with the others who faced similar persecution—to fight for indigenous freedom.

In doing so, however, Enrique does not move completely outside the boundaries of colonial society in Hispaniola. He never fully rejects the established order, and his rebellion continues to consist of a fight for the justice to which he believes he is entitled under Spanish imperial law. Furthermore, he insists on controlling the boundaries of the rebellion. Not only does the military success of the rebels depend on their ability to regulate access to the mountains, but the cacique also establishes an organized hierarchy for this subaltern society that—according to Galván's description—closely resembles the social structure that has displaced them:

> Para completar la organización de su pequeña república, Enriquillo creó un concejo de capitanes y caciques, que hacía de senado y ayuntamiento a la vez, antendiendo a las minuciosas necesidades de la errante tribu. Pero el cauteloso caudillo se reservó siempre el dominio y la autoridad suprema para todos los casos. Comprendía que la unidad en el mando era la condición primera y más precisa de la seguridad, del buen orden y de la defensa común, en aquella vida llena de peligrosos azares.[29]

> [Next, Enriquillo appointed a body of captains and caciques to act both as a senate and town council, and attend to the daily needs of his small republic. But he was careful to keep the supreme authority in his own hands, realizing that only so could he secure unity among his scattered people, and that on unity depended their successful defence against the hazards of a perilous situation.][30]

Enrique may be acting as the leader of a band of militant rebels, but he believes firmly in the need to maintain social order. At the same time, he also closely monitors the fighting to ensure that the violence does not exceed appropriate boundaries. He reprimands his former servant, Tamayo, several times for his propensity towards the pursuit of vengeance rather than justice: "Matar a los vencidos ni es propio de los que pelean por la justicia"[31] [It is nor right for those who fight for justice to murder their prisoners.][32] When Tamayo attempts to exterminate a group of soldiers that he has trapped inside a cave by igniting a fire in the entrance, Enriquillo quickly frees them from this unnecessary confinement.

¡Salid de ahí vosotros, los que estáis en la caverna! No temáis; Enriquillo os asegura la vida . . . A estas palabras, los infelices que ya creían ver su sepultura en el lugar que habían escogido como refugio, salieron uno a uno, a tientas, medio ciegos y casi asfixiados por el humo.[33]

[Come out of there, Spaniards! You need have no fear. Enriquillo pledges his word that your lives will be spared. . . . The unfortunate men, who were already convinced that their refuge would prove their sepulchre, came out one by one, choking, and half blinded.][34]

Once again, the strategy of retreating to an enclosure—as with Doña María de Cuéllar, Enriquillo, and Mencía—does not provide the desired protection. Nevertheless, the protection the soldiers seek in this case proves unnecessary. In the end, Enriquillo's goal is not to subvert existing demarcations nor to construct alternative enclosures. Instead, his mission is to regain the access to existing structures to which he believes he is entitled. Given this goal, it is not surprising that Enriquillo happily reenters colonial society at the conclusion of the novel rather than attempt to destabilize it. Enriquillo's movement into a marginalized space allows him to construct an alternative authority. The protagonist uses this authority to reestablish his position within the existing demarcation of colonial space despite his own transgression of its internal boundaries.

Galván's overarching project follows a similar trajectory. The author rewrites Dominican history by appropriating the indigenous past. Hence, Galván's version of the Amerindian legacy might be expected to differ significantly when compared with other accounts, since his historical reconstruction rests on his particular presentation of it. Nevertheless, the author's revisions of existing documents prove relatively minor and subtle. The modifications Galván does introduce do not necessarily produce the expected differentiation either. Mirta Yáñez has analyzed the romantic representation of indigenous figures in *Enriquillo*. She argues that, in Galván's work, the cacique becomes Europeanized and, therefore, less identifiable as Indian.[35] Given this combination of characteristics, Galván's project faces an apparent self-contradiction: the author attempts to reconstruct national history by evincing its indigenous roots on the one hand and diminishing its indigenous component on the other.

The contradiction, however, may not prove irreconcilable. By the nineteenth century, the rhetorical evocation of an indigenous past was an established strategic device that allowed Latin American writers to authorize national discourses. Even in the early colonial period, authorities would significantly alter their portrayal of indigenous subjects in order to advance a specific rhetorical project.[36] Later, in the eighteenth century, Francisco Clavigero constructed a mythical pre-Columbian history through which he challenges the alleged superiority of the Spaniards. Although Clavijero is not genealogically linked to the Aztec legend he presents, the strategy allows him to subvert the existing system in which Latin American autochthony is devalued.

Similarly, Galván's evocation of a legendary indigenous past allows him to construct a particular historiographic authority conducive to his rhetorical situation. In this case, the indigenous hero initiates the inscription of an alternative historiography. This strategy of reconfiguration is especially significant given the canonical status of Galván's work. Not only is *Enriquillo* arguably the principal national romance in Dominican literature, but it constructs national identity in terms of the demarcation of space. The boundaries of the nation are redrawn in a manner that fosters an appropriate coupling which, in turn, historically obviates the subdivision of Hispaniola and obfuscates the racialized opposition associated with this subdivision. Galván positions the foundational fiction of the Dominican Republic not in terms of the relatively prominent African influence, but as the search for the synthesis of European and indigenous components.

This elision, moreover, points to a national and insular reconfiguration as well as a racial one. The principal struggle that is dramatized seemingly reterritorializes the larger spatial conflict engendered by insular subdivision. On the one hand, the intra-insular presence of Haiti is obviated by the temporal displacement of the novel. Yet, on the other, the absent referent is rendered exceptionally present through the anaphoric reiteration of both insufficient and excessively restricted space. Hence, the novel can be understood as a recasting of the Haitian problem. Through the continued—and continually unsuccessful—displacements that the characters confront, Galván persistently dramatizes a fundamentally insular anxiety: there is literally not enough space on the island for its inhabitants. At the same time, their plight metonymically stands in for the essential scenario of Dominican development. The lack of space is not simply a product of scale or purely physical obstacles; instead, Dominicans are blocked in by the occupation of the other half of the island. The excessive displacement and rewriting of the spatial conflict in *Enriquillo* constitutes a failed attempt to compensate for the Haitian presence within the island. In this sense, *Enriquillo* can be understood as an archetypal foundational fiction in Dominican writing: it underscores the problems and possibilities of national development and articulates a discourse of national identity based on the search for an appropriate locus of enunciation.

## Guantánamo and the Strategy of Undesirable Neighbors

Certainly, Hispaniola constitutes the most salient and historically sustained dispute over insular territory in the Hispanic Caribbean: the island has been subdivided into the two countries for several centuries, and each country has articulated a nationalistic vision that depends on the eradication of the other. Yet a homologous dynamic can be traced even when the island is officially occupied by only one country. In the case of the other two Hispanic Antilles, the island is not subdivided but, instead, is principally occupied by a single sovereign (or, at the very least, autonomous) state. Nevertheless, the tensions that are so boldly manifest in Hispaniola can be traced in more subtle instances of territorial occupation. As with Hispaniola, the question of national spatiality can certainly be found in seminal literary texts;[37] in this case, however, I would like to focus instead on how this issue is persistently reinscribed in contemporary cultural production. In particular, the essential conflict that is dramatized in *Enriquillo* becomes especially salient in the complex and problematic relationship that evolves between Cuba and the United States during the latter half of the twentieth century. Although the specific strategies of reterritorialization often prove quite different from those utilized in Galván's novel (even the exact opposite in some cases), the basic rhetorical phenomenon is comparable: the principal threat to spatial sovereignty is elided, yet the presence of the internal enemy can nonetheless be traced through an excessive rewriting or reconfiguration of the conflict.

The United States develops strong economic and cultural interests in Cuba during the second half of the nineteenth century. The ties between the two countries are formalized in 1898 and further reinforced by the conditions of Cuban independence.[38] In the wake of the Cuban Revolution (1959), the U.S. presence on the island was significantly reduced but not eliminated, thus producing a rather paradoxical instance of strange bedfellows. Nonetheless, although direct references to this undesirable coexistence can certainly be found in political discourse, the post-1959 U.S. presence within the confines of the island is rarely mentioned in popular or cultural representations of Cuba's northern neighbor. Instead, once again, the excessive intimacy of these "strange bedfellows" is recast as a proximate threat.

On the *malecón* (the road alongside the sea-wall that runs the length of Havana), a political billboard directly addresses the relationship between Cuba and the United States (figure 1). This billboard is situated on the

**Figure 1. A billboard on the *malecón* in Havana, Cuba. The text reads: "Señores imperialistas, ¡no les tenemos absolutamente ningún miedo! [Mr. Imperialists, we have absolutely no fear of you!]"**

corner of the block where the office of the U.S. Special Interest Section is located.[39] The Special Interest Section is the only official representation of the U.S. government within the national borders of Cuba, and its presence on the malecón is both visually and pragmatically striking: it is a large concrete and glass building surrounded by a tall black fence and armed Cuban guards. The sidewalk alongside the building is closed, and pedestrians must cross the six-lane road to the sidewalk on the other side until they have passed the building. And, although people often gather along the sea wall throughout the city during their leisure time, no one is allowed to sit or stand on the sidewalk directly across from the Special Interest Section (anyone who attempts to do so will be instructed by the guards to move on). Hence, given its location, the billboard is clearly a reference to the unmistakable and imposing presence of the United States that is , quite literally, right next to it and the military "colonization" of the space immediately around it. Curiously, however, the relationship between the two nations is depicted graphically in terms of the more traditional configuration of unfriendly neighbors: the relaxed Cuban (with the machine gun ca-

Figure 2. The stage and seating area facing the building that houses the Special Interest Section.

sually dangling at his side) stands on the edge of a lush, tropical landscape and shouts to the rather agitated but unarmed figure of Uncle Sam located on a barren patch of sand. Moreover, the two figures are separated, not by a fence or heavily guarded border, but by a small stretch of water. Hence, the billboard directly addresses the U.S. presence within Cuba, yet it reterritorializes the spatial relationship of the two nations in terms of the juxtaposed physical borders of the U.S. and Cuban coastlines.

The billboard, furthermore, forms part of a larger system of politically charged reterritorialization. On the other side of the Special Interest Section, a stage and seating area have been constructed. In this manner, the façade of the Special Interest Section is converted (unwittingly) into the backdrop for the political rallies, speeches, and celebrations that are held in this space. At the far end of the triangular area in which chairs are placed for these events, a statue has been erected of the legendary poet and intellectual, José Martí, holding Elián González in his arms.[40] In this sense, the space surrounding the Special Interest Section has been reconfigured in a manner that evokes the menacing proximity of the United States and, at the same time, neutralizes and effaces the more immediate threat of the U.S. presence on the island.

In fact, this example illustrates a significant trend within Cuban rhetoric. The opposition between Cuba and the United States is usually expressed in terms of the ninety miles between the island and the peninsula of Florida. Nevertheless, it can also be found within the island itself: the easternmost region is subdivided between the nation of Cuba and the U.S. military base established before the revolution. To some extent, the cohabitation of the U.S. military and Fidel Castro seems almost incomprehensible.[41] In fact, casual observers sometimes inquire—bewildered—why Castro has allowed the United States to maintain a military base. Whether or not a campaign to force the United States off the island would prove successful, the presence of the military base could be seen as an integral part of Castro's political position. His opponents have sometimes characterized his leadership as an Orwellian corruption of a revolutionary who is unwilling—or, perhaps, unable—to relinquish power and thus compromises the very ideals that had originally brought him into power. Yet this trajectory can also be viewed more generally as a product of the transition between political systems: as Lenin, Althusser, and numerous others have noted, there is an underlying tension between the operating structures of conventional states and the strategies of revolutionary leadership. It is not surprising, therefore, that revolutionary leaders who manage to overthrow the government that they oppose often find it difficult to make the transition from rebel to politician since, in most cases, the very strategies that had allowed them to successfully overthrow their predecessors can undermine their effectiveness once they take control.

Nevertheless, rather than negotiate this volte-face, Castro's solution has been to maintain his position as a revolutionary leader. Hence, in Cuban political rhetoric, the revolution is not merely an event that occurred in 1959, but a continuing process. Officially, Cubans refer to Castro as the "Comandante en jefe," or commander in chief of the revolutionary forces engaged in this process. This title, moreover, is reinforced by the ubiquitous military fatigues. In this way, Castro's position is rhetorically legitimated: as long as he continues to serve as the leader of a revolution that has not yet been fully realized, there is no reason for him to abandon his policies or his rank. In this context, the continuous threat of either a U.S. invasion or capitalist recolonization of the island further justifies Castro's policies.

Given this rhetorical strategy, the U.S. naval base in Guantanamo Bay could be viewed as further evidence of the need for constant military vigilance. Paradoxically, however, the base is rarely cited in mainstream discourses of national identity. Of course, a handful of studies analyzing the significance of the base have been published in communist Cuba. Even these documents, however, offer further evidence of the paradoxical duality of Guantanamo as both a salient threat and a non-space on the island. In the end, the explicit discussion of the naval base and nationalist discourse prove fundamentally incompatible.

In the 1960s, "Guantanamo: A Fence between Two Worlds" insists that the revolution has saved Guantanamo from the untoward influence of the naval base and, at the same time, criticizes the inappropriate threat to that salvation engendered by its continued presence. In this report, Gonzalo Bermejo claims that U.S. cultural values are responsible for the prostitution, gambling, and disease found along the Guantanamo "border," and argues that, although the revolution and the consequent "closing" of this border have improved conditions significantly, only the total removal of the U.S. military from the island will ultimately solve the problem of inappropriate influence. In this text, the author clearly positions himself as a prorevolutionary advocate who condemns U.S. imperialism and praises Castro's government for its redemptive salvation of Cuba. Nevertheless, despite the significant decline in direct and explicit contact after 1959, he continues to denounce Guantanamo Bay as a contaminating influence, condemning the puerile behavior with which the guards on the U.S. side of the fence purportedly torment their Cuban counterparts and criticizing them as ideologically indifferent mercenaries. Paradoxically, therefore, he insists that the revolution has saved Guantanamo from the disruptive influence of the naval base and, at the same time, criticizes the inappropriate threat to that salvation engendered by its continued presence. More importantly, Bermejo's vehement argument for the elimination of the base despite the notable decline in evidence of its undesirable influence points to the rhetorical tension in his argument: if the success of the revolution is measured in terms of the eradication of U.S. cultural influence, the naval base indeed poses a significant threat to the complete and absolute realization of this success. In this manner, the rhetoric of national ideology cannot be fully reconciled with the conterminous occupation of a portion of the island by external and ideologically incompatible forces.

Given the date of publication of this report (1963), these contradictions could be understood as a product of their historical context: that is, the early 1960s constitute a period of transition in which Cuba is both celebrating the triumph of the revolution and condemning the traces of U.S. imperialism that they are still working to eliminate or overcome. In the decades that follow, however, the discourse on Guantanamo Bay remains relatively unchanged. By the end of the twentieth century, there is still comparatively little discussion of the military base in public discourse, and the analyses that are produced echo the assertions of "A Fence between Two Worlds." Olga Miranda Bravo, for example, has published an extensive study of the U.S. Naval presence and its international implications entitled, *Undesirable Neighbors*.[42] She argues that the base is, at best, anachronistic and analyzes several possible strategies for the eventual recovery of the "occupied territory." Miranda Bravo traces the history of the base and its role in U.S.-Cuban relations throughout the twentieth century and asserts that the military presence circumvents the expressed desire of the Cuban people and also violates the right of Cuba as a sovereign nation to complete self-determination. Felipa Suárez Ramos and Pilar Quesada articulate a similar argument in *A escasos metros del enemigo* [A Few Scant Meters from the Enemy]. Their study is one of the few analyses to focus on the extraordinary proximity of the United States and Cuba (as only a few meters rather than ninety miles). As with Miranda Bravo's book, *A escasos metros* highlights the inappropriateness of this relationship and underscores its negative impact on Cubans. In this case, not only do the authors decry the political and sociological implications of the base, but they also pay tribute to the soldiers who have lost their lives on the Guantanamo border.[43]

This type of in-depth analysis of the base and its significance, nevertheless, proves the exception rather than the rule in Cuban cultural production. The fundamental incommensurability of the military occupation of Guantanamo and the Cuban national imaginary is most compellingly evident in the virtual invisibility of the base within Cuban discourse. The naval base is rarely the focal point in discussions of the relationship between the island and its northern neighbor. In fact, even the use of the base to house prisoners from the Middle East has received relatively little attention in the mainstream Cuban press. Numerous articles have been published in *Granma* (the principal Cuban newspaper) that denounce the military actions in Afghanistan and Iraq and the abuse of prisoners at Abu Ghraib. Nevertheless, the majority of these articles either avoid mentioning Guantanamo Bay or downplay its significance. That is, these incidents are cited as further evidence of the excessive and inappropriate imperialism of the United States, but Cuban discourse tends to eschew or marginalize the more local or proximate site of these military operations. The articles that do directly address conditions or operations at the naval base tend to appear in the "foreign language versions" (i.e., Italian, French, English) of *Granma* as major headlines but either appear in the Spanish language version of the paper (the only one generally available for distribution outside of major hotels and other tourist sites) as a small feature on one of the interior pages of the paper or are simply not included at all. In the fall of 2004, the online version of the periodical had included a total of 211 stories on Guantanamo, of which less than half were in Spanish. A search on Abu Ghraib during the same time frame, by contrast, produced more than twice as many stories and a more general search on prisoners and Iraq produced several thousand, many of which appeared in the *Granma Digital-Español* as well as the other language versions. Notably, therefore, even an explicit focus on the war in the Middle East and the treatment of prisoners at U.S. military installations generates a proportionately small number of news items that explicitly address activities at Guantanamo Bay.

This overt attention to the U.S. military presence within the confines of the island is nonetheless exceptional. More frequently, the U.S. military presence on the island is either superficially acknowledged or completely ignored. An instance of this curious duality can be found by juxtaposing scenes from two of Tomás Gutiérrez Alea's films, *Fresa y chocolate—Strawberry and Chocolate—*and *Guantanamera*. In these two popular movies, the director presents the precise physical juxtaposition in rather disparate terms. In the earlier film, two markedly different young Cubans —David and Diego—become friends. By the end of the film, the friendship is genuine and has provoked significant realizations for both characters. Initially, however, their relationship is based on mutual deception and ulterior motives: while Diego attempts to seduce David, David investigates Diego because he suspects him of counterrevolutionary activities. As the two develop a deeper appreciation for one another, David questions his initial assessment and begins to value Diego's ideological position: David realizes that Diego has a strong commitment to the ideals of the revolution (despite his cynicism, irreverence, and apparent decadence) and that his friend's criticism of the system and appreciation of international culture can be assets rather than liabilities.[44] When he attempts to explain these doubts to his roommate, Miguel, the latter reminds David that—given the alarming proximity of the United States—they must remain especially vigilant and suspicious of any possible sedition within Cuba:

DAVID: Miguel, compadre, trata de comprender, chico. A ese tipo [Diego] tenemos que darle una oportunidad.
MIGUEL: ¡No me digas, chico! ¿Qué cosa es ésta? ¿Comunismo francés? ¿Primavera de Praga? Mira David, ahí mismo, a 90 millas está el enemigo. Y todos los flojos, los que critican están de ese lado.
DAVID: Pero yo estoy aquí. Y él también está aquí. ¿Por qué no puede ser revolucionario?
MIGUEL: ¡Porque la revolución no entra por el culo, chico!⁴⁵
[DAVID: Miguel, try to understand! We have to give that guy a chance.

MIGUEL: You don't say! What's this? French communism? Prague Spring?
Look, David, right there, 90 miles away, is the enemy! And the weak, those who criticize, are on that side.

DAVID: But I'm here. And he's here, too. So, why can't he be a revolutionary?

MIGUEL: Because revolution doesn't enter through the ass!][46]

In this exchange, David tries to convince Miguel that in order to be successful and live up to its own ideals the revolution must be more open and accepting of difference. Nevertheless, Miguel insists that the threat on the other side of the ocean forces them to be stricter and protect themselves from the danger of outside influences that could destroy what they are striving to create. Hence, Miguel invokes the rhetoric of international politics both to justify intolerance and to reinforce the necessity of strategic isolationism.[47] Of course, the even greater proximity of the enemy could readily be cited as a justification for extreme vigilance. Nevertheless, in this case, Miguel insists on an absolute division between interiority and exteriority: the nation must be protected from invading forces, and inappropriate apertures must be carefully guarded against the ever-present threat of the enemy lurking a short distance beyond the island's shores.

The latter of the two films, *Guantanamera*, is Gutiérrez Alea's final production and is a parodic representation of romance and bureaucracy in contemporary Cuba.[48] Yoyita returns to her hometown for a visit after fifty years as a successful singer living in Havana. Just as she is finally reunited with her childhood love, Cándido, Yoyita suddenly dies in his arms. Consequently, Cándido, Yoyita's niece (Georgina), and her husband (Adolfo) all accompany the corpse to Havana where Yoyita will be buried as the inaugural test of a new funereal transportation program that Adolfo has devised. Among the many obstacles and delays the trio encounters in the trip across the island, the group is forced to backtrack in order to transport a pregnant woman who has gone into labor to the nearest hospital. When the driver calls ahead to alert the hospital of their imminent arrival, a comical confusion is produced by the ambiguous reference to their point of origin:

DRIVER: S.O.S. [...] Cambio.

VOICE ON RADIO: Aquí patrulla. Aquí patrulla. Identifíquese. Cambio.

DRIVER: Tenemos una emergencia. Una mujer que está de parto. Es el carro de sevicio especial número 13 de la base de Guantánamo.

3 / DANCING WITH THE ENEMY     133

| | |
|---|---|
| VOICE: | ¿De la base de Guantánamo de los americanos? Cambio. |
| DRIVER: | No, no. De la cuidad de Guántanamo. De la base de taxis de servicio especial número 13.⁴⁹ |
| [DRIVER: | S.O.S. Can you hear me? Over. |
| VOICE ON RADIO: | Patrol here. Identify yourself. Over. |
| DRIVER: | We have an emergency. A woman in labor. This is special service car number 13 from the base in Guantánamo. |
| VOICE ON RADIO: | From the American naval base in Guantánamo? Over. |
| DRIVER: | No, from the City of Guantánamo . . . From the special service taxi base number 13.]⁵⁰ |

In the context of the scene quoted, the unusual coincidence of the phrase "base de Guantánamo" referring to something other than the U.S. naval base and the ensuing misunderstanding become part of a farcical escalation of unexpected detours in the principal trajectory of the film. This moment of comic relief becomes more significant, however, given the title of the film and the repeated use of the eponymous song. Of course, in the filmic narrative, "Guantanamera" refers to the female protagonists. At the same time, nevertheless, it inevitably invokes the significance that the song has acquired as a critique of the threat to Cuban folklore and culture posed by capitalist and U.S. forces.⁵¹

The juxtaposition of the scenes from the two films points to the contradictory status of the U.S. military presence. On the one hand, the base is rendered insignificant by its virtual invisibility in Cuban discourse: the distance between the United States and Cuba is expressed more traditionally in terms of the width of the Florida Straits than in terms of the small stretch of land that separates Cuba from "Gitmo" on the eastern end of the island.⁵² On the other, however, the more immediate proximity cannot be completely erased from Cuban consciousness or quotidian existence. The intersection of practical experience and a rhetorical insistence on a particular spatialization of the U.S.-Cuban relationship engenders curious paradoxes in which the base is both omnipresent and utterly absent. The continued existence of the base is fundamentally irreconcilable with the fetishistic attachment to the ninety-mile separation. Nevertheless, the extraordinary proximity of the base cannot be fully eradicated by the persistent (re)territorialization of the relationship. As the examples discussed earlier have demonstrated, Cuban discourse tends to minimize direct contact with the base. It is cited as an inappropriate presence, but the practical consequences in daily life are presented as, at most, limited. Yet curious manifestations in popular culture suggest that the separation is not so absolute. Furthermore, alternative perspectives on the region point to an even more complicated imbrication of the base and its neighboring province.

The Aaron Sorkin play and subsequent film, *A Few Good Men*, fictionalize events that occurred on the Naval Base. In fact, Sorkin's older sister had recently become an attorney within the Judge Advocate General's core when she was assigned to the court martial on which his play is based. In the play/film, two marines are tried for killing a fellow member of their unit. They admit to having killed the deceased marine, but claim that it was an accident that resulted from an attack ordered by their superiors. According to Sorkin, this aspect is drawn directly from his sister's account of the facts: in the court martial, ten marines were accused of killing a private in their company during a disciplinary action intended to punish the deceased for inappropriate conduct. Although such actions were officially condemned, the accused claimed that they were acting on the orders of their commanding officer.

Hence, although many of the specific details and characters in the film are fictional, they underscore the complicated physical reality of Guantanamo. That is, the military base is literally yards from Cuba and, in that location, the two nations are separated by a small area of terrain densely populated by land mines and patrolled by soldiers along a fence on either side. The members of the U.S. military indeed coexist with Cubans on the opposite side, as Colonel Jessep claims in Sorkin's script: "I eat breakfast seventy yards away from 3,000 Cubans who are trained to kill me."[53] Not only does this statement reflect a curious reality, but it is used as a justification for exceptionality in *A Few Good Men*: the officers argue that, given their rather unique location, marines at Guantanamo cannot be expected to fully conform to norms established outside of Cuba.

This situation is further complicated, moreover, by the presence of Cubans who have been employed as daily workers on the base. As Mary Ellen Chenevey McCoy explains in her analysis of the relationship between the military base and its neighboring communities, these individuals would make daily round trips between Guantanamo and Gitmo via a small path that had been demarcated for safe passage through the mine field. In both cases, given their lack of investment in insularity as a defining condition of national identity, these authors attend to the specific consequences of cohabitation that are either marginalized or effaced in Cuban cultural discourse.[54]

Even when these complexities are directly addressed by Cuban writers, however, the contradictory status of the base is ultimately reinforced. The specific conditions of the base highlight its location within the insular boundaries of Cuba, yet the extraordinary obstacles render the Guantanamo border impenetrable, even for those individuals that potentially value its existence. As a dissident émigré, the protagonist in Reinaldo Arenas's autobiographical novel *Antes que anochezca* has a distinct attitude toward the U.S. presence in Cuba. At one point in the novel, Reinaldo, the protagonist, tries to reach the naval base in order to escape persecution and seek asylum in the United States. The description of this endeavor underscores the extraordinary militarization of the narrow separation between Cuba and the base. His efforts are thwarted by the overwhelming presence of geographical barriers, land mines, alligators, armed guards, and trained dogs. He recounts how he narrowly escaped from these perils during his failed attempt to reach the base:

> Durante toda mi travesía por la orilla del río había sentido unos ruidos que eran como chasquidos. No se por qué, pero me pareció que la luna me decía que no entrara en aquellas aguas. Seguí caminando hasta encontrar un lugar donde no se escuchasen aquellos chasquidos para lanzarme al río. En aquellos momentos empezaron a aparecer por los matorrales extrañas luces verdes. . . . A los pocos instantes, sonó el estruendo de una ametralladora; era una balacera que pasaba rozándome. Más tarde me enteré de que aquellas luces verdes eran una señal; eran rayos infarrojos. Se habían percatado de que alguien quería cruzar la frontera y trataban de localizarlo y, naturalmente, aniquilarlo. Corrí y me trepé a un árbol frondoso, abrazándome a su tronco todo lo más alto que pude. Carros llenos de soldados con perros se lanzaron a mi búsqueda; toda la noche estuvieron buscándome muy cerca de donde yo me encontraba. Finalmente, se marcharon.[55]

> [While walking next to the river I kept hearing crackling sounds. I do not know why, but it seemed to me that the Moon was telling me not to go into those waters. I continued walking until I got to a place where I did not hear those crackling sounds anymore, and looked for a good spot to enter the river. Suddenly, strange green lights began appearing . . . A few seconds later I heard machine-gun fire; the bullets seemed to be grazing me. I later found out that those green lights were signals; they were infrared lights. The guards had discovered that someone was trying to cross the border; they were trying to locate and, of course, to exterminate the intruder. I ran to a tree with a dense canopy and climbed as high as I could, hugging the trunk. Cars came, full of soldiers with dogs, looking for me. All night they searched, at times rather close to my hiding place. At last, they left.][56]

Although the geography of the area contains obstacles such as the river that impede Reinaldo's progress and facilitate the control of movement, the landscape also protects him from the technological and human mechanisms of this control. In retrospect, Reinaldo realizes how fortunate he was to escape his attempted crossing unharmed: "En la terminal de trenes de Guantánamo me encontré con el negro. Me miró asustado . . . me dijo que, después de todo había tenido mucha suerte, porque una cajas que yo le dije haber visto, eran minas que de haber sido pisados me hubiera hecho volar en pedazos."[57] ["At the Guantánamo train terminal I came across the black guy. He looked scared . . . he told me I had been very lucky after all, because some boxes that I mentioned having seen were mines, and if I had stepped on one, it would have blown me to bits."][58] In the end, Reinaldo abandons this strategy and eventually travels to the United States by concealing his identity and leaving Cuba via the Mariel boatlift. Arenas's novel thus renders the distance between Cuban national territory and the naval base more insuperable that the separation between the island and the Florida peninsula.

In each of these cases, the relationship between Cuba and Guantanamo Bay is presented as dysfunctional or as an inappropriate coexistence but not as the principal juxtaposition between the two nations. The contentious presence of the military base within the confines of the island seemingly legitimates the need for relentless vigilance against the ever-present threat of invasion. That is, supporters of the revolution cite the occupation of the base as inappropriate and illegal. At the same time, however, mainstream discourses of Cuban identity cite isolation as the defining characteristic of their insular existence and generally eschew references to the occupied territory within the island itself. Hence, the relationship with the United States is characterized in terms of the very proximate threat of invasion from the outside. The enemy that is already contained within the space of the island is externalized and expelled. In this instance, moreover, the process of differentiation is simultaneously expressed in terms of cultural ideology and spatiality: the corrupting influence of capitalist excess—or, conversely, the promise of escape from the repressive limitations of Castro's communism—are always already located outside the insular national space of Cuba.

Given the relationship between Cuba and the United States and the rhetorical positions so frequently adopted by the Communist Party in Cuba, the relative invisibility of Guantanamo Bay is, at best, curious. That is, political leaders, analysts, scholars, and journalists frequently level strong anti-imperialist critiques against the United States and denounce tactics such as the embargo as nothing short of strong-arm colonialism and international crimes. These critiques, moreover, are often linked to official internal policy in Cuba; that is, given the bellicose and imperialist tendencies of the only remaining world superpower, Cubans must be willing to sacrifice or endure certain hardships. In this context, Guantanamo would be a logical target of condemnation and could be invoked in order to legitimate the purportedly inevitable implementation of vigilance, restrictions, and intolerance (even when these infringe on communist ideals or civil liberties). Consequently, we might expect the base to be cited regularly as evidence of the imminent threat posed by the United States. Nevertheless, as I have argued here, the military base is rarely invoked in this manner. In fact, even when it is the implicit referent—as in the case of torture and abuse of prisoners—it is hardly ever named explicitly in the anti-U.S. calumny that is repeatedly recited in public discourse; the activities themselves are denounced, but their specific location is often elided. Hence, despite its obvious relevance to contemporary policy and political rhetoric, Guantanamo becomes the trace of the ongoing interdepedence between Cuba and its northern neighbor—its *pareja de baile*—that must be both both embraced and negated.

## Vieques Libre: The Paradoxical Spatiality of a "Free Associated State"

As a U.S. territorial possession, Puerto Rico's formal relationship with its northern neighbor is almost diametrically opposed to the separation that evolves in the wake of the Cuban Revolution. Not surprisingly, therefore, the formal presence of the U.S. government in Puerto Rico tends to be received more favorably than in Cuba. Nevertheless, in this case as well, the allocation of a portion of Puerto Rican territory to the U.S. military and the resulting consequences have incited debates on the political and international status of the island. Although the majority of Puerto Ricans living on the island officially support a formal affiliation with the United States, many of these supporters have expressed resentment for what they perceive as cultural imperialism. That is, the U.S. presence is often seen as the principal obstacle in the (continued) development of Puerto Rican identity. In this context, anti-Americanism can be equated with nationalism.

Paradoxically, therefore, an array of individuals who disagree vehemently about the exact political status of Puerto Rico can be brought together in the unified cause of resisting the excessive influence of the U.S. presence on the island. Not surprisingly, therefore, U.S. military bases in Puerto Rico have been the site of political protests and controversy over the years.[59] For the most part, however, this type of formal opposition has been limited to small groups that actively seek to eliminate existing ties to the United States and the removal of all affiliated government institutions. The U.S. naval bases in Culebra and Vieques, however, have become the focus of widespread national and international attention.

Over the course of the century following the transfer of Puerto Rico from Spanish colony to U.S. territorial possession at the conclusion of the Spanish American War (1898), there have been several major changes in the precise structure of the island's government.[60] The United States has maintained its status as the principal political power on the island, yet the exact role of local government and its relationship with federal authority has been repeatedly reevaluated, altered, and challenged over the years. Along with this larger political relationship, the position of the U.S. armed forces in Puerto Rico has also changed. The military presence on the island diminished significantly in 1900 with the abolition of the transitional government, but there has been a subsequent gradual increase over the last century. When Puerto Ricans were granted U.S. citizenship in 1917, they also became eligible for the draft; subsequently, many residents of the island were trained and sent into combat during WWII and the wars in Korea and Vietnam. The change of status in 1952, moreover, was directly connected to the island's role in post-WWII global politics. The plebiscite and ensuing creation of the Free Associated State was negotiated primarily by two individuals: Luis Muñoz Marín—a prominent politician who advocated modified interdependence between Puerto Rico and the United States through "industrialization by invitation"—and Rexford Guy Tugwell, who was appointed by President Roosevelt to help design New Deal policies and later named governor of Puerto Rico in 1940 and 1945.[61]

According to Tugwell, officials in Washington, D.C. were anxious to maintain stability in the Caribbean, and they viewed Puerto Rico as a principal mechanism in the realization of this goal. Therefore, as James L. Dietz and other historians have argued, the willingness of U.S. politicians to consider granting increased control to the Puerto Rican government was largely based on the strategic significance of the island as a potential guardian of the Caribbean, the Panama Canal and, by extension, the hemisphere.

In this way, two of the principal changes in Puerto Rico's status are connected to the island's role in U.S. military policy. Therefore, the increasing military presence on the island since 1900 is not merely a product of the sustained political relationship with the United States but can be understood as a significant coadjuvant in how that relationship is defined and redefined. It should not be surprising, therefore, that the U.S. military bases in Puerto Rico have been the site of political protests and controversy over the years. The U.S. naval bases in Culebra and Vieques, however, have transcended the traditional parameters of such protests. The particular staging of opposition in and about Vieques, moreover, has dramatized the contradictory spatiality of the island as both a clearly demarcated nation and a territorial possession of the United States.

Culebra and Vieques are both small islands off the eastern coast of the main island of Puerto Rico. They are home to approximately 3,000 and 9,000 residents respectively, and each serves as the site of a major U.S. naval base. When the size and activities of the base on Culebra increased significantly in the early 1970s, numerous protests were staged. As a result, in 1971, the Navy agreed to discontinue live artillery testing, withdraw from a portion of the island and establish a wildlife preserve. Ironically, however, they replaced the lost terrain on Culebra by expanding their operations on the neighboring island of Vieques.

Following this strategic shift, the naval base on Vieques has consistently engendered controversy and opposition by the civilian residents and Puerto Ricans outside the "isla nena."[62] Critics of the base have repeatedly cited the destruction of the island's economy and natural resources, the failure of the base to produce the socioeconomic development that the military had promised and the inherent danger to the civilians residing in such extreme proximity to live artillery testing. Yet the portrayal of Vieques is not limited to this type of pragmatic accusation. Because of the particular issues raised and the strategies utilized by activists who support or oppose the base on Vieques, the debate surrounding it has transcended the specific discussions and concerns addressed to become one of national territoriality. In fact, Vieques has been characterized as a symbolic topos that underscores Puerto Rico's paradoxical spatiality as a "free associated state."

In Puerto Rican literature, for example, the small island is depicted in terms of a vexed relationship with the U.S. presence. Jaime Carrero's epic poem "Vieques del Caribe" presents it as the site of the mythical genesis of Puerto Rico. The earlier sections of the poem recount how the Puerto Rican people are created through the fusion of Spanish, Indian, and Black populations on Vieques. This process, however, is disrupted by the expropriation and corruption of Puerto Rican territory by the U.S. Navy. In this sense, Vieques becomes the metonymic incarnation of Puerto Rico; hence, the "invasion" of the island by the U.S. military interrupts Puerto Rico's natural evolution.

One of the most famous works of Puerto Rican literature set in this location is Pedro Juan Soto's *Usmaíl*. The novel focuses on a Puerto Rican family living in Vieques and their problematic relationship with the United States. This tension is reflected in the protagonist's desire to define himself and the conflicts engendered by a necessary dependence on the United States. In fact, the title of the novel itself encapsulates this tension since it can be read alternately as the name *Usmaíl*, as a reference to the postal service—U.S. mail—and as a codification of the struggle of the protagonist to determine his status as a U.S. male.

Similarly, Esmeralda Santiago's novel *America's Dream* situates Vieques as the point of departure of an impossible journey. The title character, América, moves from work as a hotel housekeeper on the small island to a position in childcare in the United States. The novel does not focus on the naval base or the controversies it has engendered. Nevertheless, the protagonist is directly affected by the demographic complexities of Vieques: not only does she work in a hotel that caters to foreign tourists but she is also in a long-term relationship with a man (the father of her fourteen-year-old daughter) who has a family on another part of the tiny island. Hence, América faces excessive and inappropriate occupants in Vieques that, paradoxically, both threaten and facilitate the realization of her desires. In this sense, the naval base is elided yet the crises it has provoked are reconfigured in alternate terms. Consequently, as with *Usmaíl*, the title of Santiago's novel alludes to the problematic status of national identity on the island: because of the incursion by undesired and disruptive elements, a tension develops between the two meanings of the title—the dream of the protagonist and the "American dream" of limitless possibilities.

In this manner, the military base on Vieques is portrayed as a disruptive presence in Puerto Rican cultural discourse. Nonetheless, criticism of the base intensified dramatically when Puerto Rican security guard David Sanes Rodríguez was killed by a misdirected bomb in April 1999. In the wake of this accident, the military was forced to interrupt normal training exercises, and the firing range was physically occupied by protesters while the military attempted to renegotiate its role on Vieques with officials in San Juan and Washington, D.C. This political activism not only brings increased international attention to Vieques, but it also connects a wider array of individuals and locations to the island. International political figures regularly visit the activists who occupy the firing range and "invade" the surrounding waters in small boats. In addition to this civil disobedience, marches and demonstrations are organized throughout Puerto Rico and the United States. In this fashion, the discussion and demonstrations in the years following the death of Sanes Rodríguez provoke a territorial dispute that repeatedly (re)enacts a larger national debate that is never fully realized.

Similarly, protesters demonstrating in Washington, D.C. denounce the imperialist policies of the United States in Vieques; at the same time, however, they locate their critique in a manner that evades the issue of the island's political status. Many of the participants in such demonstrations carry flags (either Puerto Rican or the official flag of Vieques) and banners. In one case, a group of protesters display a large flag that simultaneously functions as a banner. They hold a large Puerto Rican flag with the words "Pa'fuera la Maria de/U.S. Navy out of Vieques" superimposed on the alternating red and white stripes. In the context of a march in Washington, D.C. culminating in a demonstration in front of the White House, both the more general accusation of the United States—as opposed to the more specific exhortation of "Pa'fuera la marina de/U.S. Navy Out of Vieques"— and the implied solidarity with other affected areas are logical modifications. Nevertheless, this banner also codifies the problem in a manner that cannot be explained solely by the location of the event: although it underscores the international relevance of the situation and attacks the imperialist policies of the U.S. government, the banner avoids explicitly denouncing the political status of Puerto Rico. By moving from Vieques to the world as the sites of an inappropriate (and excessive) U.S. presence, the text notably elides any reference to U.S. imperialism in Puerto Rico per se. At the same time, however, the absent referent is evoked by the inscription of the message on the Puerto Rican flag. In this manner, the banner draws on larger questions of political status and national identity, but also suppresses these issues by focusing explicitly on the more localized territorial dispute.

In fact, comparable rhetorical strategies can be traced throughout the protests that evolve following Sanes Rodríguez's death. The documents that record these events point to a performative battle of contested space(s) that repeatedly reinscribes the paradoxical spatiality of Puerto Rican national identity. The newspaper articles and essays written about the controversy interpret the dispute as a rejection of the U.S. presence that nevertheless eschews the larger political change that this position would imply. Several of the essays included in the volume, *Victoria de un pueblo* [Victory of a People], underscore the symbolic value of Vieques.[63] Juan García Passalacqua, one of the contributers to the collection, avers the performative function of Vieques as a unique site of postcolonial resistance: "Vieques is a symbol for national affirmation against the Unites States . . . people have found a way to express their rejection of colonialism without having to choose between the options for political status."[64] This contradictory acceptance of the current political relationship with the United States on the one hand and the opposition to the naval base on the other has led several analysts to question what precisely makes the latter so distinct from the former. Raymond Hernández, a reporter with the *New York Times*, attributes the widespread opposition to Vieques to the combination of causes that it conjoins. In short, Hernández argues, Vieques has something for everyone:

> Vieques, simply is an activist's dream . . . It has the destruction of an ecological system, along with claims that people are being exposed to toxic chemicals, which environmentalists are seizing upon. It has the specter of American colonialism that human rights advocates and Puerto Rican nationalists are pointing to. It has the suggestion of racism that civil rights activists and Hispanic leaders are up in arms over. . . . To top it all off, the issue has an ideal boogeyman in the United States military, which has been relatively quiet about making its case for the bombing exercises.[65]

In addition to this combination of factors, the unprecedented opposition to Vieques (both in quantity and the unusual alliances among erstwhile political rivals) could also be attributed to its rhetorical significance. The military occupation of Vieques has provoked a fundamental crisis in the discourse of Puerto Rican identity. That is, Vieques has become increasingly controversial because it calls into question the postulation of insularity on which Puerto Rican writers traditionally have based discourses of identity.

Similar themes of invasion and territorial battles can also be traced in the staging of political protests about Vieques and the subsequent narrative reconfigurations of these protests. In this way, the protests themselves mirror the issue being opposed: they become a symbolic battle for control of land in nationalist terms. In fact, many of the complaints that denounce the effect of the naval base also focus on the question of territorial possession. In these cases, however, the issue becomes one of control over both the island and its surrounding waters. One of the greatest criticisms leveled against the Navy is that their occupation of the island has compromised the fishing industry. Ironically, however, many of the conditions that allowed the fishing industry to thrive (i.e., relatively deep waters close to the coastline with no interference from commercial marine traffic) are the very characteristics that make the island suitable for naval training. Hence, the incompatible uses of the maritime conditions are juxtaposed, and the local fishing industry becomes the symbol of a utopian past that was sacrificed to the militaristic needs of the postindustrial invaders. In his statement to the Military Readiness Subcommittee, the resident commissioner in Washington, Carlos Romero Barceló, repeatedly refers to Vieques as a "tropical island paradise" that has been destroyed by naval activities conducted on the island and beyond its shores:[66] "[W]e are convinced that the accumulated damage of bombing operations has damaged and poisoned the environment, has damaged historic and archeological sites, has damaged and poisoned endangered species, the flora and fauna and the surrounding sea."[67] Similarly, residents of Vieques characterize the island before the establishment of the naval base as an idyllic, rural community with a self-sustaining economy based on the cultivation of natural resources. Nazario Cruz Viera, whose family had opposed the Navy's presence for years describes the destructive force of the base on the island: "I can tell you the history of this island from beginning to end, and it was better before the Navy came here. . . . Before, there were farms and the landowners needed many people to work them. They even gave you a place to live. We had everything. We lacked nothing."[68] Not only is the arrival of the Navy thus depicted as a disruption in the natural development of Vieques, but the removal of the base also promises the recuperation of the idealized past. In these terms, Culebra is seen as a model. Although his claims could easily be challenged, the comments of one resident, William Miró, demonstrate this portrayal of Culebra as a standard to be emulated: "Culebra has accomplished a lot, and they removed the Navy. . . . They are the example."[69] In both cases, this historical trajectory points to a desire to claim the lost island of Vieques. The past is cited as an example of what the relationship between the island and the surrounding waters should be, and the present circumstances constitute an unacceptable aberration of those conditions. In this case, therefore, the island's residents are not forced into isolation by what Pedreira has depicted in *Insularismo* as an allegorical fear of the Dutchman lurking beyond their shores.[70] Instead, the invading enemy is already inside the island and must be removed in order to restore a prosperous existence.

During one incident in particular, the protest was enacted and reenacted in multiply symbolic terms. After several activists were imprisoned for trespassing on military property, large groups took over a tiny piece of land outside the prison where these individuals were being held. The land was occupied by both opponents and supporters of the naval base. Although the two groups occasionally shouted competing slogans at one another, there was no direct conflict or confrontation between them. According to several observers, the opposition between them was expressed most clearly through a display of flags. González described this symbolic competition: "A United States Flag, planted by supporters of Puerto Rican statehood and guarded by police officers, is by the highway, set off by a buffer zone ringed by yellow police tape. An enormous Puerto Rican flag stands in front of the prison, near a small platform decorated with yellow ribbons.... Although there have been some incidents of flag stealing, the police said that there were no serious disturbances at the camps."[71] Of course, flags are inherently charged as symbols of patriotism and frequently become (re)signified as the assertion or rejection of national identity. At the same time, the protocols surrounding flags in Puerto Rico mirror the complex political status of the island. The regulations concerning the flag adopted in Puerto Rico after the Spanish American War are comparable to the restrictions placed on the fifty state flags and their required subordinate position to the federal one: with few exceptions, the Puerto Rican flag must be accompanied by a U.S. flag, and the U.S. counterpart must be above the local one. One verse of a controversial version of the popular song, "Que bonita bandera" (What a Beautiful Flag) specifically addresses the undesirable hierarchy created by this regulation: "No quiero verla flotando / al lado de una extranjera / yo quiero verla solita / sobre mi Borinquen bella [I don't want to see it floating / alongside a foreign one / I want to see alone / above my beautiful Borinquen]."[72] Hence, the protest in this case becomes a doubly metaphoric claiming of the disputed territory. The description of the scene indicates that officials who were present had some concern for the potentially incendiary nature of the competition and the consequent need for protection—i.e., the guarded and buffered U.S. flag. Nevertheless, the incidents are characterized as relatively harmless and are not seen as violent manifestations of the differences between the groups. In this way, the symbolic battle between the U.S. Navy and the residents of Vieques is recast as the struggle over whose flag will lay claim to yet another contested space. As with the billboard on the malecón in Havana, this game of "capture the flag" playfully reterritorializes a serious situation of national spatiality.

Given the controversy and the responses to it, the circumstances of Vieques can be viewed as a microcosm of the Puerto Rican situation that has been displaced and intensified. The persistence of the military presence despite widespread opposition underscores the complex status of Puerto Ricans as U.S. citizens: as Romero Barceló repeatedly asserts, the use of Vieques without serious regard for the rights of its residents marks a disenfranchisement of the people of Puerto Rico. In a sense, the Puerto Rican community has resisted the interpellation of them as invisible or dispensable. At the same time, however, this resistance has taken the form of postulating an opposing yet rhetorically equivalent claim to territoriality. In other words, the space of the nation is defended against the undesired presence of an enemy that is, at the same time, claiming the contested space in order to defend itself against being invaded or, at the very least, overpowered by its own enemies. Instead of being resolved or reconfigured, therefore, the territorial battle between the United States and Puerto Rico is repeatedly displaced—both literally and symbolically—and reenacted in terms of an alternate line of demarcation. In this way, the claim to insular space becomes a rhetorical mechanism that allows the Puerto Rican community to differentiate itself from the nation that governs it but to which it does not fully belong.

As with Guantanamo and Hispaniola, the larger conflict with the purportedly extranational enemy is elided through the precise circumscription of Vieques and thus is never explicitly staged. The excessive presence of the enemy within the confines of the peripheral space of Vieques constitutes an unwelcome manifestation (and reminder) of the internal other that is inherently embedded within the Free Associated State. The desired distance from the enemy that is fundamentally absent or lacking in Puerto Rico must be repeatedly reenacted in order to performatively create the political separation or distinction that is always already absent in Puerto Rico.

## Insularity and Contested Spaces in the Hispanic Caribbean

Each of these instances underscores a fundamental tension between the idea of national space on the one hand and the experience of political borders on the other, and these contradictions can be traced through representations of contested terrain. In the three cases examined here, the quotidian reality in which the nation and its other are intimately connected and—more importantly—inevitably interact within the boundaries of the island is refuted by the insistence on binary opposition. Conversely, national rhetoric asserts that the island and nation are fully conterminous and, therefore, situates the enemy beyond the coextensive borders of both, yet this vision is repeatedly disrupted by evidence of the putatively external enemy within the island.

As I have argued here, this paradox provokes a crisis of identity since it overtly challenges foundational notions of Hispanic Caribbean spatiality. And the precise responses to this crisis reveal both the shared attachment to insularity, on the one hand, and the divergent political status of the islands on the other. Dominican cultural discourse alternately denounces the inappropriate contiguity of Haiti and articulates a vision of the island-nation that erases this coexistence. The U.S. presence within the island's boundaries is suppressed in Cuban cultural discourse through the repeated insistence on the political and geographic relationship between the two nations. In Puerto Rico, however, the national question is elided through the focus on the territorial dispute in Vieques and the carnavalesque performativity of the protests it incites. In all three cases, the embedded other cannot be directly acknowledged or accepted in its entirety because this internal presence belies the foundational claims of insular self-fashioning. Under these circumstances, the rhetoric of self-definition depends on a condition that cannot be fully achieved or sustained. Nevertheless, these disruptions to the insular logic do not completely dislodge its rhetorical role. Instead, the false dichotomy is repeatedly reinscribed through a palimpsestic reinscription of national space.

In *Thirdspace*, Edward Soja examines the problems of spatialized dichotomies in which the collective self is located in opposition to a differentiated other. He argues that divisions are constructed in terms of privilege and power on one side and subordination and disenfranchisement on the other:

> Hegemonic power, wielded by those in a position of authority, does not merely manipulate naively given differences between individuals and social groups, it actively *produces and reproduces difference* as a key strategy to create and maintain modes of social and spatial division that are advantageous to its continued empowerment and authority. "We" and "they" are dichotomously spatialized and enclosed in an imposed territoriality of apartheids, ghettos, barrios, reservations, colonies, fortresses, metropoles, citadels and other trappings that emanate from the center-periphery relation. In this sense, hegemonic power universalizes and *contains* difference in real and imagined places and spaces.[73]

Hence, not only is power enacted by and through the demarcation of territory, but spatial division also engenders a particular cosmogony and epistemology in which knowledge, self-understanding, and relationships are mediated by location. Similarly, insular dichotomies produce and reproduce difference in the Hispanic Caribbean, despite incompatible geopolitical circumstances. In doing so, moreover, the rhetoric of insularity repeatedly reenacts the power of the nation by reinscribing the space of the island.

The physical and rhetorical situations of the Dominican Republic, Guantanamo, and Vieques constitute an exacerbation of the intersection of spatial and national politics. As I have suggested earlier, the title of this chapter, "Dancing with the Enemy" refers to the process of self-fashioning in which the nation is defined through a perpetual process of differentiation, opposition and conflict. Despite the complex specificity of international relations in each case, the "enemy" becomes the photographic negative of the national "I," the inverted reflection that both defines and threatens its opposing entity. Hence, the nation and the enemy it claims are inextricably tied to one another in this rhetorical operation: the national "we" is entirely dependent on a separation from a "them" that must be, by definition, outside the nation. Paradoxically, therefore, this rhetorical situation simultaneously necessitates a connection with and a separation from the opposing other.

As Wucker proposes in her study of Hispaniola, the problems engendered by such spatialized discourses of identity are further intensified in the case of the Caribbean by the strong identification with a particular geographic circumstance and its concomitant concept of space. What is significant about the three instances examined here, moreover, is that they expose the false dichotomy on which the nation is always already defined by a literal and symbolic separation from outside forces. In the Hispanic Caribbean, the nation is defined in opposition to a putative other that is purportedly located beyond the nation's boundaries. In these cases, however, the manifestation of the enemy's presence within the demarcated national space highlights the underlying paradoxical relationship with this other and therefore constitutes a crisis of identity that must be overcome.

To some extent, the phrase, "dancing with the enemy" might be seen as excessively playful and celebratory given the nature of the conflicts that I have analyzed. I use the phrase nonetheless to characterize how the fundamental conflict of insularity is often encoded in a manner that can deceptively intensify particular aspects of the territorial dispute while effacing others. The complex dynamics of the dance with the putatively proximate adversary metaphorically dramatize the essential dynamic that is at work in the discourse machine of Hispanic Caribbean insularity: it repeatedly reterritorializes the extranational in a manner that both reaffirms the ontological insular binary and reinscribes the very contradiction that this binary must negate. Understood in these terms, the (dis)placement of the enemy is playful and productive in that it "plays into" the underlying tension that the rhetoric of insularity must perpetually (and excessively) renarrate.

# 4
## Out of Place: Insular Topographies in the Diaspora

> RUBY: Is this anything like Cuba?
> RAFAEL: No . . . It doesn't feel like an island.
> —*Dance with Me*

RANDA HAINES'S FILM, *DANCE WITH ME*, TELLS THE STORY OF TWO CHARacters, Ruby Sinclair (Vanessa L. Williams) and Rafael Infante (Chayanne), who fall in love and eventually come to understand one another despite significant cultural and personal differences. The evolution of this relationship is traced through their respective interactions with music and their (in)ability to dance with one another. The exchange quoted above takes place outside the home of an individual who sells car parts, where Rafael—who has recently emigrated from Cuba to Houston—has arranged to purchase a part for an old truck that he is restoring. When they first arrive, it appears that no one is home, so they decide to wait. As they soon discover, however, the man that they are looking for is indeed there; he is simply in the backyard with his family celebrating the engagement of his daughter. Once the two men meet and discover that they are both from Cuba, Ruby and Rafael are invited to join the celebration. The man leads them through the house/shop into a small oasis of Cuban culture in the backyard. The characters' brief access to this cultural oasis becomes especially significant in the evolution of the plot since it is here that Ruby has the opportunity to briefly enter Rafael's world and the two are able to dance together successfully for the first time.

This scene demonstrates how the space of the diaspora is often reterritorialized in insular terms. Not only do Caribbean communities recreate aspects of their culture and countries of origin when they migrate, but this process is often rhetorically linked to insularity. The juxtaposition of the two exchanges between Rafael and Ruby suggests a direct link between the space of the island and of the backyard: Houston may not feel like an island, but the spatiality of Cuba can be reproduced in a manner that allows Rafael to be more at home there.

As I have argued earlier, insularity is always constructed in rhetorical terms; it articulates an absolute dichotomy between the interior and exterior of the nation that will never coincide perfectly with geopolitical or demographic conditions. Nevertheless, the close approximation that has existed historically between the island and the nation has engendered a tradition of self-fashioning that presupposes an underlying equation between insular boundaries and political borders. Throughout most of late nineteenth- and early twentieth-century Caribbean literature, writers tend to assume that the Antilles constitute the primary—or even exclusive—locus of enunciation for all discourses of national and regional identity. During the twentieth century, however, a sustained and increasing migration has been produced that would presumably call this supposition into question. Currently, both Caribbean people and their cultures are linked to multiple geographic locations.[1] Hence, we might expect to see a concomitant shift in rhetorical self-fashioning among Hispanic Caribbean communities. That is, as the diaspora becomes an increasingly significant place of cultural production, the rhetoric of insularity should be rendered less relevant or be radically reconfigured to accommodate this change. Instead, the centrality of the island is enhanced rather than displaced by this shift. Recent trends in the commodification and marketing of Latino cultural production in the United States have reinforced preexisting tropes of self-definition. Consequently, a tension develops between the desire to generate forms of cultural expression that codify the current circumstances of the Latino community and the persistence of earlier tropes that cannot readily reflect those circumstances.

Contemporary developments in U.S. Latino music and literature offer paradigmatic examples of this tension. In particular, the Latin music explosion that occurred during the second half of 1999 is a concise manifestation of how certain characteristics of *latinidad* are emphasized and mechanically reproduced. The marketing trends and resulting consequences are not limited to the music industry however. Latino literature has also become increasingly "trendy," both in academic contexts and in the commercial publishing market; therefore, the production and packaging of Latino texts is often subject to the same processes that can be traced within the musical phenomenon. More specifically, in the case of U.S.-Caribbean literature and cultures, marketing trends tend to reinforce the rhetoric of insularity as a defining characteristic of *caribeñidad*, yet the excessive emphasis on this rhetorical tradition can undermine the project of self-expression being articulated. In both the musical and literary cases, the parameters of commodification delimit the discursive possibilities of innovation: the appeal of Latino cultural production depends on its distinctiveness, but this distinctiveness must be framed in highly familiar and reproducible forms. Of course, this situation tends to emphasize readily comprehensible aspects of Latin American specificity. At the same time, however, the cultural elements that are reinforced by this process can be fundamentally incompatible with the search for an autochthonous discourse in the United States: that is, Latino performers and authors often strive to develop a mode of self-expression that reflects the specific circumstances of the U.S. Latino communities, yet the commodification of Latino culture simultaneously insists on the reproduction of expressive modes that are only relevant in the Latin American context. Consequently, a fundamental contradiction emerges between the specific content of cultural production and the limitations of form that are often imposed on its expression by the exigencies of commercialism.

## From Cultural Stereotypes to "Latinos, Inc.": Images of *Latinidad* in U.S. Media[2]

As the twentieth century drew to a close, the growing Latino population in the United States took center stage in the arena of popular culture. In fact, during the first half of 1999, almost every major national news source in the United States reported on the development of the Latino community, or communities, and their contributions to the "mainstream." These articles, moreover, do not simply underscore the increased visibility of Latinos; the journalists also attempt to define the relationship between this group and purported demarcations of dominant U.S. culture. Therefore, a tension develops between the emphasis on ethnic specificity and the insistence on an inherent compatibility between this subgroup and the general population. In his analysis of the representation of Latinos in film, Charles Ramírez Berg argues that stereotypes often mediate the alterity of Latino culture and, in doing so, render it comprehensible. The ontological imperative in the *fin de siècle* discussions of emergent Latino culture points to a homologous desire to maintain its exotic quality and innovative otherness yet, at the same time, stabilize that difference enough to ensure its facile interpretation. The journalists must aver simultaneously the uniqueness and the translatability of their subject, even though the two arguments often prove incompatible.

In his study, *Strangers among Us*, Roberto Suro analyzes the complex patterns of cultural development among Latino populations in the United States. He argues that the identity of immigrant groups is traditionally forged through opposition to the mainstream. In the case of Latinos, however, factors such as diversity, the continual influx of recent immigrants into established communities and a lack of successful political leadership have hindered this type of cohesion. Suro examines the evolution of Latino populations in specific urban areas and underscores the unique patterns of development in each case. Furthermore, the author argues that because it does not fully conform to existing models, Latino immigration ultimately transforms the role of ethnic diversity and cultural assimilation. According to Suro, the construction of a successful Latino community "will require a new approach to the interplay of political rights, group identity and social eligibility."[3]

Conversely, Oscar Hijuelos proposes that Latino experiences do follow a well established pattern of translocation and discursive tradition within U.S. culture. Citing changing demographics, Hijuelos argues that the role of Latinos has shifted from marginal to mainstream: "Once upon a time ... exposure to [Latino] culture depended on where you lived, whom you knew and talked to, and what you read in Spanish language newspapers.... I'm glad to report that times have changed. Thanks to the influence of the newly arrived and the children of the once newly arrived, a Latino presence is being felt in all areas of American life."[4] Although Hijuelos affirms the singularity of the Latino cultural influence, he also compares its role to that of previous immigrant populations that have redefined national culture. Furthermore, the title of the piece, "North to Home," can be interpreted as a reference to an established tradition of essays that examine geographic and cultural displacement. Hijuelos's title evokes, for example, the seminal work published by Carey McWilliams, *North From Mexico*. In the 1990 edition of the work, McWilliams comments on his title. The author describes his struggle to articulate the project in a way that did not oversimplify or reduce the diversity of the subject matter. Rather than identifying them as Mexican, Mexican-American or Chicano, he chose a title that reflected the relative geographic position and common trajectory of the peoples of Mexican descent in the United States: "[I]n the end, I was driven to the conclusion that the title would have to refer to a process, a movement, a point on the compass. For it is the direction in which the people have moved that has given unity to their lives; it is the point on the compass that has remained fixed and constant."[5] Of course, this choice allows McWilliams to avoid terms that privilege a specific ethnic, ideological, or class-based identification. Nevertheless, both the title and the explanation shift the terms of identity from fixed geographical limits to the experience of movement.[6]

Furthermore, Hijuelos's title does not merely evoke significant predecessors within the Latino canon. In fact, "North to Home" more closely parallels the title of Willie Morris's autobiographical essay, "North toward Home." In his essay, Morris traces the process of self-discovery through displacement and expounds upon his cultural identity by contrasting experiences in New York with his Southern background.[7] This intertextuality indicates that translocation is an established strategy in the construction of cultural discourse: not only have immigrant groups contributed significantly to mainstream culture in the past, but the narration of migratory experiences is depicted as a seminal foundation of cultural rhetoric in the United States.

In this sense, these texts grapple with fundamental questions of self-definition among minority and immigrant populations and attempt to identify the unique characteristics of the Latino population. More importantly, the authors suggest that the presence and contributions of these groups has fundamentally altered mainstream culture. Yet, at the same time, both Suro and Hijuelos draw comparisons with other groups and highlight how contemporary Latino populations have followed established models of development.

The duality between similarity and difference is enhanced further in the case of commercial marketing. Corporations that want to take advantage of the sudden visibility of Latino culture must maintain a delicate balance between these poles in order to appeal to both a minority and a mainstream consumer. It is not surprising therefore that advertisers and market analysts tend to alternately assert the uniqueness of Latino culture and its universal translatability. In an article entitled "Generación Latino," Helene Stapinski proposes that the mainstream is conforming to the margin. She argues that the demographic impact of Latinos is particularly acute among adolescents: "Hispanic teens are the fastest growing youth segment in the U.S. and they're redefining mainstream culture."[8] According to Stapinski, not only have Hispanic teenagers become an important consumer base that is provoking visible changes in commercial marketing, but their prevalence has also generated trends that extend beyond the minority population. In the article, she examines instances of non-Hispanic youth who have embraced and adopted specific aspects of Latino culture. She cites, for example, New York promoter John Rivera who has observed the impact of this trend on local dining habits: "Latin food has always been popular in the United States, but now it's ultra-trendy. Latinos and Latino wannabes alike can be found washing down their fancy $14 lobster-filled *empanadas* with expensive tequilas and the newest round of imported beers."[9] Stapinski, nevertheless, also points out the inherent difficulty in taking advantage of such increases in popularity. The diversity of Latino populations may contribute to the mass appeal of its products, but it also makes marketing strategies less manageable. As Angelo Figueroa, a former editor of *People en Español*, explains: "It's hard to capture the essence of Hispanic teens in one product. . . . Hispanic teens are culturally all very, very different, unlike African American teens in the U.S. who are basically listening to the same kind of music. You have to walk this fine line to make sure it appeals equally to all these groups."[10] Of course, it should be noted that Figueroa contrasts the apparent diversity of Hispanic youth and the putative homogeneity of African American adolescents. His claim that African American consumers are relatively uniform points to an overly simplistic racialization of African American teens. Yet it is nonetheless significant that he posits them as the monolithic other against which the demographic profile of Latinos is defined. In this sense, he suggests that Latinos do not conform to existing models of minority cultural practices but instead introduce an element of diversity that distinguishes them from their more homogeneous counterparts.

This balancing act between distinctiveness and universal comprehensibility may constitute a dilemma for advertisers, but the music industry seemingly resolves the potential conflict through formulaic reproduction. In their focus on the so-called Latin music explosion, the same duality between singularity and commonality can be traced. On the one hand, writers, artists, and record executives emphasize the diversity of Latin music and the unique innovations of each singer or group. On the other, however, these unique innovations are packaged in astoundingly similar ways. In fact, some critics have reduced the Latin music phenomenon to the success of one singer: Ricky Martin. They argue that his sudden commercial triumph called attention to other artists rather than being representative of a genre that was already acquiring mainstream appeal.

Nevertheless, whether Martin generated the wave of Latin music or rode it, his case can be seen as paradigmatic. Through the success of his English-language debut and performances at awards shows, he gained widespread attention and became the face of the phenomenon.[11] It should also be noted that this surge in popularity follows a dramatic transformation in the singer's appearance as well as a shift in his musical style. By the time he appeared at the Grammy Awards ceremony in 1999, his hair was shorter and blonder than in earlier years, he dressed primarily in dark, tailored Armani outfits, and the song he performed offered a linguistic and rhythmic fusion.[12] In the wake of the media attention that follows, reporters cite both his Latin influences and his similarity to North American teen idols, ranging from Elvis Presley to Michael Jackson. In his chapter, "Latino Dolls," José Quiroga cogently analyzes Ricky's ability to repeatedly transform himself into the commodity that suits a particular demographic desire without ever fully conforming to or becoming permanently associated with a reified identity. In fact, Quiroga argues that Ricky's extraordinary popularity can be attributed to this elusiveness. In this sense—whether queer or straight, Latino or mainstream—Ricky manages to maintain a fluid identity that engenders mass appeal across traditionally insuperable divisions. In other words, Martin appears to have mastered the "fine line" Figueroa refers to and thus manages to appeal equally to all groups.

And this paradigm is repeatedly reproduced in the wake of Martin's universal success. Consequently, despite the avowed diversity within Latin music, conformity is created among ostensibly distinct artists. For Enrique Iglesias's debut in the Anglophone market, "Bailamos," two separate videos are filmed. The first of these reflects the inclusion of the song on the soundtrack for the film, *Wild, Wild West* and features frontier themes and images. Since it is unusual for two videos to be filmed for the same single, the appearance of the second video is itself surprising. Furthermore, the themes, images and style of the video are almost identical to those of Martin's "Livin' La Vida Loca." Both videos feature a crowd of dancers, dressed (often scantily) in brightly colored outfits, gyrating in a night club (also decorated in bright colors and luminescent—although not necessarily well lit—fabrics) while the singer performs on stage. Both videos also intercalate the club scene and images of a more intimate exchange between the star and one of the female dancers. Given these similarities, the seemingly superfluous production of a second video for "Bailamos" facilitates a comparison—and possibly a conflation—of the two artists and reinforces the idea of a constructed continuity. Iglesias's music is both touted as markedly different from Martin's and, at the same time, presented as virtually identical.

In the case of Marc Anthony's English-language debut, a similar recasting occurs. Although Marc Anthony is best known as a performer of salsa, he began his musical career singing hip-hop and R&B in English. In fact, he recorded an album in English, *When the Night is Over*, before releasing his salsa albums. Therefore, as the singer himself points out, the supposed crossover into English is actually a return to his professional and personal roots: "I was born and raised in New York; English is my first language. . . . I just worked backwards."[13] The release of his self-titled album in 1999 marks not only a return to English but to his original style of music. Nevertheless, the first single from the album, "I Need to Know," is perhaps the most Latin-influenced track, incorporating more prominent brass instruments and Latin rhythms. And, again, the video for the single is noticeably similar to Martin's (and, of course, Iglesias's): it features Marc Anthony performing on stage while surrounded by brightly-attired dancers in a night club. These scenes, moreover, are also interwoven with images of a more intimate relationship, although in this case the exchanges trace a romantic relationship rather than more explicit instances of sexual encounters. Hence, although Marc Anthony is cited as a decidedly different type of Latin performer, the initial marketing of his mainstream debut underscores his similarity to established artists rather than his distinctiveness.

As with the phenomenon examined by Stapinski, the most striking example of the formulaic status achieved within the popularity of Latin music can be found in its extension beyond the Latino artists themselves. Although, notably, his popularity seems to have proven even more ephemeral than the other examples, Lou Bega's initial success underscores the ability of the Latin music phenomenon to transcend the ethnic specificity from which it emerged. Unlike the mainstream reterritorialization that often occurs with the rising popularity of ethnically specific phenomena, the singer does not simply coopt particular attributes or styles; instead, he mimics the practice of performing latinidad itself. On the one hand, Bega reinforces the cultural traditions that the phenomenon draws upon. His version of fusion underscores the heritage: "Mambo No. 5" is a remake of Dámaso Pérez Prado's recording, and Bega's appearance and style are reminiscent of classic Latin singers. As with earlier examples, the central image featured in the corresponding video is of the artist performing the song. Although the performance in this case does not feature an audience or large group of people dancing in front of the singer. Nevertheless, he is depicted on stage with a microphone, singing to the female dancers that surround and interact with him throughout the song.

Paradoxically, however, Bega is the first non-Hispanic artist that emerges from the fin de siècle Latin music explosion. His heritage has been described as a mixture of Ugandan, Sicilian, and German.[14] At first glance, "Bega" may appear to be an alternative spelling of "Vega," a relatively common Spanish family name. Nevertheless, Lou Bega is, in fact, a sobriquet derived through a reconfiguration of the singer's surname, Loubega. In this manner, a minor adjustment in the conventional marks of identity allows for a misinterpretation that suits both the performer's style and the current trends in popular music. Furthermore, the construction of his name, his image and his music exemplify the ability to recreate the established paradigm in the absence of the ethnic identity that purportedly generates it.

Bega's success, moreover, is attributed to his ability to both adhere to and deviate from traditional Latin models. On the one hand, he successfully reproduces the classic style of performers such as Prado: "Bega, 24, is setting fashion trends not just with his music but with his nostalgic Havana look. He dresses to reflect his songs' age, wearing a pinstriped suit, gaiters, and a borsalino hat."[15] At the same time, however, Bega is also praised for his ability to set himself apart from the competition through his individuality. Goar Biesenkamp, a record executive who worked with the artist at BMG, argues that: "We have proven that a strong song, a charismatic and ambitious artist, and effective and committed management can beat the international competition."[16] According to Biesenkamp, the purported superiority in this case can be attributed to an effective combination of specific elements of musical production rather than to an inherent connection with the cultural legacy he enacts. In this manner, the non-Latino artist manages to out-perform his Latino counterparts. Bega's success, therefore, is ostensibly the result of the simultaneous capacity to approximate other performers and to differentiate himself from them.

In fact, each of these cases presents a particular negotiation or reconfiguration of cultural identities. Not only is the possibility of applying the same adjective to describe the ethnicity of artists whose roots are traced to New York, Miami, San Juan, the Philippines, Spain and Germany, in and of itself, rather surprising, but it also calls into question what exactly it means to be Latino. One could also argue that the descriptor may refer to the music rather than the individual performers; nevertheless, the musical styles of these and other artists identified as Latin prove equally diverse. The commercial explosion of Latin music thus creates a discursive environment in which performers of ostensibly varied cultural and musical backgrounds are indiscriminately placed under the same rubric.

Of course, such phenomena are common within the entertainment industries. When a current trend proves successful, subsequent marketing often extends the trend far beyond its initial context. Therefore, it is not surprising that purportedly diverse components become interchangeable in the promotional rhetoric. At the same time, however, the simultaneous insistence on originality and continuity and the consistent maintenance of a careful balance between the two create a complex discursive situation. And the vocabulary used to describe the trend reflects this complexity. Reviews and articles that focus on individual artists or the Latin music trend itself often use words such as "explosion" to characterize the phenomenon and describe it as an inevitable and irreversible development of contemporary adolescent culture. Furthermore, the writers tend to imitate the music they examine in their occasional incorporation of Spanish lexicon: the music is "caliente" and the performers are described as "hot tamales" or even as a "corazón-throbs." The interweaving of Spanish and the generation of such bilingual neologisms also underscore the supposed distinctiveness of the trend: the use of a new vocabulary suggests that the phenomenon cannot be characterized adequately by existing terminology. Nevertheless, the contributions of this putative cultural revolution are easily represented and apprehended through the demarcation of stable and reproducible parameters. In fact, the term "corazón-throb" is entirely emblematic of this phenomenon.[17] That is, on the one hand, the phrase conjoins Spanish and English lexicon (mediated, of course, by the multicultural hyphen) in a single, new term. At the same time, however, the Spanish half of the word is only comprehensible to a mainstream (and not necessarily Spanish-speaking) audience through its insertion into an existing English language expression (heart-throb). In this way, the innovative Latino influence is clearly visible in the neologism, but its meaning relies on the maintenance of a preexisting linguistic paradigm. Therefore, in the end, the changing role of Latin music in the United States indeed reflects a demographic shift that, in turn, introduces a new element into cultural commodification. The commercial representation and reception of the phenomenon, however, ultimately recreates the very paradigms its novelty supposedly displaces. In this way, the so-called Latino music explosion strikes a delicate—and commercially effective—balance by introducing discrete innovations into recognizable (and reproducible) patterns of cultural production.

Along with this discursive demarcation of Latino culture, a homologous spatiality of latinidad can be traced through these cultural representations. In each case, the principal location featured in the videos is a stage from which the singer performs and entertains his audience. According to Jameson's analysis of the logic of late capitalism, places of entertainment and consumption seemingly exist outside of normal time and space, effacing the quotidian and allowing for the perpetual pursuit of pleasure. Even the specific geographic or cultural references that are reproduced in these locations become part of a simulacrum of place that reduces (or even eliminates) the limits that would inevitably exist in the context of the referent.[18] The corazón-throbs in this case are all represented in strikingly similar spaces of perpetual night, cosmopolitanism, pleasure, and disposable income. Martin, Iglesias, and Marc Anthony quite literally perform for a highly sexualized, intradiegetic audience and all three of the singers are pursued by at least one of the female characters depicted. Furthermore, through the shared lexicon of setting, the object of desire being offered to the viewer is framed by a spatialized iconography of readily recognizable markers of location-specific identity that are rendered universal and, therefore, mobile. The visual narratives present (or, at the very least, evoke) eroticized scenes of Latin-themed, night clubs through the use of lighting, interior design, costumes, and choreography. In this manner, the locus of Caribbean cultural production is commodified through its repeated insertion into an ur-space of contemporary Latin music.

In this fashion, the phenomenon of the Latino music explosion exemplifies the impact of marketing on the construction of latinidad and underscores a general interaction between place and cultural production. As this interaction evolves and becomes increasingly transnational, it is inevitably altered by shifting systems of power and value. Although her analysis focuses on sexual rather than transcultural identity, Rosemary Hennessy examines a comparable problem in *Profit and Pleasure*. She asserts that the logic of late capitalism commodifies sexual subjects in a manner that inappropriately divorces them from the material contexts that had originally engendered them. Hence, the transnational flow of capital in a globalized world produces a particular configuration that favors certain characteristics and obfuscates others. Hennessy traces how profit has been an excessive influence in recent constructions of sexuality, and she argues for the development of sexual subjects based on more appropriate traits such as desire and affect: "[M]aking visible the connections between forms of identity and capital's historical processes can change the frame through which we might imagine the horizon for change and can perhaps enable us to forge new forms of subjectivity and political alliance that might target for transformation the exploitative, oppressive, and acquisitive relationship neoliberalism protects."[19] According to Hennessy, therefore, a counter-productive tension develops between the forces of capitalist production and the expression of sexual subjectivity, and this tension marginalizes forms of self-definition that might call into question the hegemony of profit. At the same time, however, she also suggests that the recognition of this problematic relationship and its implications could engender a more appropriate reconfiguration of sexual identity.

As Arlene Dávila cogently argues in *Latinos, Inc.*, a similar tension develops between the representation of Latino cultural identity and strategies of mass marketing. The commodification of latinidad reinforces recognizable tropes of identification that are drawn from the country or region of origin. This tendency can be traced throughout constructions of latinidad, yet it becomes highly significant and even contradictory in representations of caribeñidad since it intersects with issues of spatiality. These constructions reinforce preexisting tropes of self-definition and thereby engender an intense and consistent identification with the island as a defining characteristic. That is, the particular traits emphasized by commodification are directly linked to the geography of the Caribbean; therefore, they are not only decontextualized but quite literally *out of place* in constructions of U.S.-Caribbean identity. On the one hand, this perpetuation of insularity outside of the Antilles facilitates a continuity between cultural production in the Caribbean and in the diaspora and fosters the (re)production of a highly recognizable signs of caribeñidad. On the other, however, it privileges the spatiality of the homeland in a manner that is not easily adapted to the circumstances of Hispanic Caribbean communities in the diaspora. In this way, the commodification of Latino culture in the U.S. market engenders a fundamental contradiction: U.S.-Caribbean authors and artists must negotiate their cultural expression in terms of a geographic circumstance that is no longer relevant or central to their experiences of caribeñidad.

## Home Again? Return Migration and Self-Fashioning in Contemporary U.S.-Caribbean Literature

The insistence on recognizable and reproducible tropes is not necessarily limited to marketing strategies and the commodification of Latino cultures. A similar desire to introduce innovation into existing paradigms can also be traced in the configuration of positionality and spatiality. Given the prevalence and significance of insularity in Hispanic Caribbean discourse, authors located outside of the region must inevitably situate their narratives of self-definition in terms of this tradition. In the case of authors in the United States, however, this relationship with rhetorical traditions often undermines the attempt to produce innovative forms of cultural expression. In fact, this shift within the discourse of national identity based on geographic movement often becomes the focus of works by contemporary U.S.-Caribbean authors: these narratives present the struggle of an individual character or family to negotiate their own subjectivity within a changing geographic and cultural landscapes. That is, the author presents the search for identity of characters who are immigrants or children of immigrants. Such works can take the form of a *bildungsroman* or a *künstlerroman* that culminates in a trip to the island of the protagonist's ancestors.

In Edward Rivera's *Family Installments*, for example, the protagonist's struggle for self-definition leads him back to the Caribbean. At the close of the novel, Santos stands over the graves of his relatives in Puerto Rico and contemplates their legacy. Furthermore, in response to this experience, he draws upon fragments of literature that he has studied but can only partially recall. The novel concludes with his embryonic attempt to formulate an appropriate articulation: " 'turned to bones, I should wish to be laid to rest.' Was that it? Somebody's 'Brown Burial'? 'Earned burial'? Maybe 'Bourne Aerial.' . . . I'd brood about it on the flight back home."[20]

For Santos, the trip to Puerto Rico constitutes the final "installment" in his coming of age. The visit to the graveyard affords closure, the completion of a cycle. Furthermore, this ending suggests that Santos's development will now enable him to construct his own narrative. The visit is a necessary step through which he finalizes his artistic formation. Hence, beyond experiences involving education, racism, sexuality, and relationships with friends and relatives, it is a voyage to the Caribbean that constitutes the final rite of passage in the protagonist's formation. In the end, it is the return to this seminal insular space that engenders the full realization of his individual—and authorial—subjectivity.

A similar trajectory can also be found in other novels by contemporary U.S.-Caribbean authors. In *How the García Girls Lost Their Accents*, Julia Álvarez narrates the struggle of the García sisters to reconcile their desire to be American, to fit in, with the traditions and values embraced by their parents. As with Santos, Yoyo's sense of self is closely connected to her relationship with language. Her journey of self-discovery, moreover, traces her evolution as a writer. This process is most strikingly and poignantly articulated in a chapter entitled "Daughter of Invention," in which she confronts competing ideas about appropriate language and begins to establish her own voice as a developing writer.

The title of the chapter refers, most explicitly, to her mother's idiosyncrasies. Along with the malapropisms often produced by her broken English (i.e., necessity is the *daughter* of invention), Yoyo's mother is repeatedly frustrated by her inability to successfully realize any of her innovations. When she spots an advertisement for a suitcase with wheels—an idea that she had conceived of previously, inspired by the large quantities of items that immigrant families transport to and from the Caribbean—she admits defeat: even when she has a successful idea, the *yanquis* beat her to it. In this sense, the title of the chapter ironically points to her unfulfilled desire to be the mother of invention.

Yet the title also has a deeper significance. Along with these anecdotes about her mother, Yoyo recounts an incident that occurred when she was asked to deliver a speech honoring her teachers. Reveling in the opportunity, she prepared a draft that extolled the virtues of students who surpass their teachers. Much to her dismay, however, Yoyo's father is horrified by the apparent irreverence of this approach. When she reads the draft to her parents, he promptly rips the paper from her hands and destroys it. Later, Yoyo's mother quietly enters her room and helps Yoyo to write an alternative version of the speech. According to Yoyo, this collaboration was her mother's final attempt at invention. From that point on, Yoyo's writing took the place of the innovations that her mother was never able to create. Hence, Yoyo's mother helps her to reconcile the tension between the exigencies of (trans)cultural tradition and the search for an appropriate means of self-expression in the diaspora. Through this generational shift, Yoyo is able to realize the desires that her mother was unable to fulfill.

This (re)writing of the speech constitutes a key moment in the künstlerroman of *García Girls*. As such, this incident evokes a typical trope of immigrant literature: the scene enacts the complex relationship between the dreams of the parents and the possibilities available to the children. The novel, moreover, repeatedly underscores the contradictory status of cultural shifts between generations of immigrants. In fact, the title of the novel, *How the García Girls Lost Their Accents,* points to this contradictory status: although the title is ambiguous, the novel suggests that the "loss" is both negative and positive. The García sisters must come to terms with the need to preserve their heritage and to develop a superior command of the U.S. code (literally and figuratively) in order to succeed and, in doing so, justify the sacrifices that their parents have made. And Yoyo is able to manipulate that code through her writing.

Of course, similar themes and tensions can be traced throughout immigrant narratives. What is significant in the case of Álvarez's work, however, is the roles that movement and a sense of place play in Yoyo's formation. In the end, it is a trip back to the island that allows her to truly become the "daughter of invention." The space of the island affords a particular understanding of the past, which, in turn, enables Yoyo to fully and legitimately assume her role as the producer of Dominican American discourse and culture. As with *Family Installments,* Alvarez's novel traces a journey of self-discovery that draws on the transcultural knowledge of the protagonist. At the same time, however, this evolution culminates in an expressive ability that can only be fully articulated once the space of the island has been reclaimed.

In this manner, return migration functions as a rite of passage that affords closure, privileged knowledge, and enlightenment. The protagonists in both novels are thus, literally and figuratively, able to insert themselves in the insular tradition. This ritual, moreover, constitutes a crucial step in their progression towards transcultural identity and discursive authority. Through this narrative structure, the pilgrimage to the Caribbean becomes a necessary coadjuvant for the self-formation of the protagonist. The island itself affords an essential element that presumably cannot be obtained beyond its borders, and the main character's search for identity therefore becomes an attempt to recover this missing element. That is, the displacement created through migration has engendered a loss that the principal character must overcome in order to achieve complete maturation.

## *Dreaming in Cuban*: The Role of Insularity in Contemporary *Caribeña* Fictions

This relationship with the island proves especially complex (and often problematic) in contemporary Cuban American writing. Unlike their Puerto Rican and Dominican counterparts, the island constitutes a relatively inaccessible homeland from which Cuban American writers are displaced both temporally and spatially.[21] As Ruth Behar clearly demonstrates in her edited volume *Bridges to Cuba/Puentes a Cuba*, contemporary Cuban American culture is always already constructed in terms that strive to overcome the insurmountable division between the space and place of discursive production.

As several of the essays and works in the volume demonstrate, however, this condition is not necessarily a negative or counter-productive one. Similarly, Gustavo Pérez Firmat explores the potential value of this interstice as a site of self-definition in *Life on the Hyphen*. At the same time, however, Cuban American authors often engage with or reproduce a sustained bond to the island, which privileges a foundational geographic experience that inevitably proves unattainable. Hence, as Silvia Spitta has argued in her essay on transculturation and the Cuban-American imaginary, the island becomes fetishized in a melancholic relationship and its primordial loss can never be fully overcome. In other instances, geographic displacement has lead to the construction of a translocality that codifies both a desired connection to the homeland and, at the same time, the necessary mobility of the diasporic community. In both cases, nonetheless, the relocation of cultural production engenders a rhetorical crisis in that the existing archetypal tropes of self-definition can not simply be preserved and reproduced in the diaspora.

In her first novel, *Dreaming in Cuban*, Cristina García takes the poetics of translocal insularity to its furthest consequences. In fact, the novel constitutes an extraordinarily striking example of the conflict between innovative self-expression and conventional tropes of Caribbean spatiality. García presents several characters who fight to preserve connections despite obstacles that impede them. Throughout the novel, the three generations of del Pino women rebel against the boundaries that confine them and, in doing so, struggle to transcend the geographic circumstances that prevent the full realization of their desires. Consequently, the content, themes and structure of *Dreaming* stunningly dramatize the problems and possibilities of translocal insularity.

One objective shared by the three women is to achieve successful communication in spite of the obstacles that thwart their efforts. Throughout the novel, Celia, the matriarch, writes and receives letters from Cuba—several of which are included in the text—and she frequently reflects on the significance of her correspondence in the narrative. Nevertheless, her epistolary communication ultimately proves unsatisfying since it underscores the very distance it is intended to diminish. The most poignant case of this paradoxical function is perhaps the last letter Celia receives from her estranged husband; it arrives the very day that she learns that he has died. As she struggles to comprehend it, Celia notes the multiple ways the letter marks their separation:

> Celia fingers the sheet of onion parchment in her pocket, reads the words again, one by one, like a blind woman. Jorge's letter arrived that morning, as if his prescience extended even to the irregular postal service between the United States and Cuba. Celia is astonished by the words, by the disquieting ardor of her husband's last letters. They seemed written by a younger, more passionate Jorge, a man she never knew well. But his handwriting, an ornate script he learned in another century, revealed his decay. When he wrote this last missive, Jorge must have known he would die before she received it.[22]

Ironically, even though Jorge's letter does manage to traverse the expanses dividing the couple, its singular ability to simultaneously overcome and reinforce this division renders the communication unsettling.

To a certain extent, this epistolary exchange is evocative of the critical debates surrounding "The Purloined Letter": The timing of the letter's arrival constitutes either the inevitable fulfillment of its function—however uncanny that function may prove—or an unintentional change in its meaning. Yet, at the same time, it also points to the questions that Rey Chow has raised regarding the translatability of writing systems. In her analysis of *Of Grammatology* and Derrida's use of examples from other linguistic and cultural systems of codification, Chow suggests that he recontextualizes signs in a manner that affords them with a particular meaning but that also erases preexisting processes of signification.[23] In García's novel, a curious tension develops between the meaning of Jorge's letter and the semiotics of a particular place and time. His words are able to facilitate communication across a seemingly insuperable divide and thus form part of a writing system that links disparate locations, yet the letter cannot effectively conjoin these locations. In this manner, Jorge's letter ultimately codifies the incommensurability of sender and recipient: it inscribes, not their connection, but their very separation as significant and—if not fully comprehensible—legible.

In fact, throughout the novel, García calls attention to how language and systems of codification negotiate distance and spatiotemporal divisions. Although Celia's correspondence with her granddaughter initially proves more satisfying, she again confronts a semiotic disjuncture that is reinforced rather than transcended by the letters. Celia comments, for example, on the alienated quality of her granddaughter's Spanish: "Pilar, her first grandchild, writes to her from Brooklyn, in a Spanish that is no longer hers. She speaks the hard-edged lexicon of bygone tourists itchy to throw dice on green felt or asphalt."[24] In each of these cases, the letters underscore geographic and temporal displacements. The two interlocutors are separated because of distinct locations in both time and space. The role of letters for Celia is particularly ironic, since one of the principal motivations for this correspondence is to temporarily erase such separations. Furthermore, the capacity of Celia's letters to highlight both connection and insuperable division suggests that the desired effectiveness of this expressive mechanism has been compromised.[25]

Letters, however, are not the only device the characters in *Dreaming* employ in order to achieve long-distance communication. Celia and Pilar also meet through visions. In fact, Celia enacts this ability in order to compensate for the failed epistolary exchange: "She closes her eyes and speaks to her granddaughter, imagines her words as slivers of light piercing the murky night."[26] Through this description of the telepathic connection,

Celia's words are imbued with a penetrative ability that her written discourse lacks. In this way, she hopes to recover the lost connection. Nevertheless, this mechanism also proves susceptible to the divisive forces between the two characters, and the separation persists until they eventually reunite in person: "For many years, Celia spoke to Pilar during the darkest part of the night, but then their connection suddenly died. Celia understands now that a cycle between them had ended, and a new one had not yet begun."[27] Additionally, both Celia and her daughters, Lourdes and Felicia, experience visions that allow them to interact with characters after they have died. In this case as well, the desired communication is not always realized. Unlike letters, however, the connection is not characterized as fundamentally flawed. In fact, Lourdes expresses ambivalence towards her father's posthumous apparitions precisely because she perceives them as successful. At one point, she attempts to dissuade him from confiding in her about the family history: "I know too much already."[28] Presumably, the potential threat resides in the veracity of the information her father shares with her. Therefore, the problem with this connection is not its lack of completion but, instead, the fact that it potentially affords an inappropriate or undesired connection.[29] Nonetheless, through this connection, Lourdes has access to an alternative discourse or expressive mode that transcends the usual boundaries of space and time. As with Jorge's letter, her visions constitute a form of communication that is unhindered by the geotemporal obstacles that divide the del Pino family. Yet, once again, this extraordinary communicative mechanism proves problematic and unsettling.

García's characters also explore their ability to manipulate more conventional modes of communication. Several characters comment on the role of language as a tool of expression and self-definition. Of course, the lack of a common linguistic system constitutes the most serious impediment for interpersonal connection.[30] For this reason, Celia is particularly concerned with the generational changes that she perceives in her grandchildren. Not only is she distressed by the apparent anachronism of Pilar's Spanish, but she worries that the inability to communicate with her son's children will prevent her from imparting her cultural legacy: "Javier writes that he has a Czech wife now and a baby girl. Celia wonders how she will speak to this granddaughter, show her how to catch crickets and avoid the beak of the tortoise."[31] Felicia also experiences a similar generational gap when her mental state interferes with her linguistic comprehension. As she listens to her son, Ivanito, she discovers that she cannot readily understand him: "What is he saying? Each word is a code she must decipher, a foreign language, a streak of gunshot."[32] In this case, therefore, the characters' ability to transcend boundaries engenders a communicative loss that cannot be readily overcome by genealogical bonds.

As with most transcultural literature, the cycles of loss and recovery of language in the novel underscore its function as a mechanism for constructing and preserving identity. In *Dreaming*, moreover, not only is language tied to a particular place but, instead, the space of the island itself is linguistically coded. When they travel to Cuba at the end of the novel, Lourdes and Pilar experience a recovery of their native tongue. For both characters this resurgence of their native language represents a recuperation of their past, but this recuperation has distinct implications and value in each case. For Lourdes, this reconnection represents the dreaded return of the trauma that she had sought to escape: "Old sentences lurk beneath the mattress, in the rusted coils beneath her back."[33] For Pilar, however, it constitutes a welcome discovery of a missing expressive ability: "I've started dreaming in Spanish, which has never happened before. I wake up feeling different, like something inside me is changing, something chemical and irreversible. There's a magic here working its way through my veins."[34] According to these characterizations, the geography, architecture, and inanimate objects in Cuba speak a particular language, a code that can only be experienced or through a direct corporeal and spiritual connection to the landscape of their ancestral homeland. The island thus engenders what Kristeva has identified as the function of poetic language: it allows meaning to be rendered in both a semantic and a semiotic register.

Pilar's delight in her recovered ability is not surprising, since she spends most of the novel searching for a satisfying mode of self-expression. She is closely identified with her painting, and it plays a pivotal role in her development. Furthermore, this activity becomes the catalyst for a redefinition of her relationship with her family. Lourdes does not truly understand her daughter's work, and, at times, is distressed by Pilar's artistic tendencies. She discourages Pilar from pursuing a scholarship, since she does not believe that a career in art is an appropriate future for her daughter. Nevertheless, in spite of Lourdes's fundamental inability to empathize with her daughter, her maternal pride eventually leads her to support Pilar. For the opening of her second bakery, Lourdes commissions her daughter to paint a mural to commemorate the U.S. Bicentennial. Although she fears her mother will be displeased, Pilar cannot fully restrain her artistic instincts, and she paints a rather irreverent portrait of the Statue of Liberty. Lourdes detests the painting but refuses to allow anyone to criticize her daughter's work. Pilar describes her reaction when the painting is first revealed at the opening of the bakery: "The blood has drained from my mother's face and her lips are moving as if she wants to say something but can't find the words. She stands there, immobile...when someone yells in raucous Brooklynese, 'Gaaahbage!'. . . . Before anyone can react, Mom swings her new handbag and clubs the guy cold inches from the painting. Then, as if in slow motion, she tumbles forward, a thrashing avalanche of patriotism and motherhood, crushing three spectators and a table of apple tartlets. . . . And I, I love my mother very much at that moment."[35] In this way, Pilar's painting fosters a bond between the two even if it does not generate a tangible increase in their respective capacity to fully comprehend one another's chosen forms of self-expression.

Through her painting, Pilar also postulates an alternative semiotic system. She asserts that painting provides a more felicitous means of expression than conventional language since it is capable of transcending acknowledged limitations: "I mean, who needs words when colors and lines conjure up their own language? That's what I do with my paintings, find a unique language, obliterate the clichés."[36] Pilar, nevertheless, is not the only character to imbue artistic elements with semantic potential. At one point, Felicia describes the ability to speak in colors with her children. When she speaks with Ivanito in a particular color, for example, they are able to achieve a level of communication that she finds extremely gratifying. And when she discovers that they no longer share this ability, she laments the separation that this loss underscores. For mother and son, color had constituted an expressive mode through which they could connect in a way that more traditional forms of communication presumably did not allow.

Given this context, it is not surprising that Pilar's recovery of Spanish is accompanied by the development of a more extensive artistic palette when she returns to Cuba. Through this visit, she discovers new shades that she incorporates into her work: "Mostly I paint [Abuela] in blue. Until I returned to Cuba, I never realized how many blues exist."[37] In this way, not only does Pilar expand her artistic repertoire, but the nature of island affords an expressive tool that she had sought unsuccessfully outside it. The renewed connection with Cuba engenders the acquisition of an ability that had been dormant or completely inaccessible. Through this connection, as with the previous generations of del Pino women, she is able to develop a mode of signification that lies outside of the normal parameters of (inter)personal communication. Once again, moreover, it is direct contact with the landscape and the privileged spatiality of the island that fosters this ability.

García presents her characters' struggle to overcome a sense of lack or incompleteness. In fact, most of the narrative traces the attempts of the principal characters to recover from the damaging effects of personal loss. The recuperative process, more importantly, engenders the need to restructure confined spaces. The characters in *Dreaming* repeatedly confront physical restrictions that inhibit the realization of their goals. The most obvious limitation the characters encounter is the absolute separation between Cuba and the United States. For Pilar, the inability to gain access to the island becomes the source of a debilitating loss. She finds the experience so destructive that—as a young adolescent—she embarks on a journey that she hopes will lead her back to her lost roots. For other women in the family, the island both nurtures and suffocates them. Lourdes describes it as an island-prison but also acknowledges that she cannot exist without her homeland. In this way, Cuba simultaneously provides necessary connections and severs others.

This contradictory dynamic, moreover, is also reproduced in other registers in the novel. In some instances, containment is presented as a protective shelter from an external threat. Celia uses the house as a shield against external danger, even if she is not convinced the supposed danger truly exists: "Although Celia was not a believer, she was wary of powers she didn't understand. She locked her children in the house on December 4, the feast day of Changó, god of fire and lightening and warned them that they'd be kidnapped and sacrificed to the black people's god if they wandered the streets alone."[38] Pilar thrives on the ability to shut herself in the small studio constructed in the back of her mother's warehouse. This afforded protection, however, requires sacrifice. Pilar's sanctuary is created through the displacement of the items that had been stored in the space previously—an absence Pilar regrets. Moreover, given the choice, both Pilar and her relatives prefer the risks of expansion. Although confinement may afford certain luxuries, the realization of their respective desires requires freedom of movement.

In the end, nevertheless, this desired mobility can also prove destructive. Lourdes's corporeal boundaries, for example, shift dramatically over the course of the novel. In her role as owner of a bakery in New York, she gains substantial weight. Later, she starves herself and sheds the additional pounds, and then promptly regains them once she resumes eating. In this way, Lourdes's body becomes a confined space with unstable boundaries. As she experiences the oscillations between excess and extreme deprivation, Lourdes struggles to demarcate and preserve a treacherous balance between the two states. Her sister wages a similar battle on a different plane. The deterioration in Felicia's mental state is described as the eradication of boundaries. Felicia experiences a need to escape from reality, but her withdrawal becomes excessive and she temporarily severs her connection with the world beyond her. In this fashion, both sisters initiate an upheaval of their own boundaries in order to rectify a perceived problem. Unfortunately, however, the resulting shifts themselves become a problem, and fixed boundaries must then be reinstated. Given the critical significance of both of these issues, the struggles depicted transcend the personal battles of the characters and become a fundamental negotiation of feminine subjectivity.[39]

From the perspective of the characters in Cuba, as well, the potential of destabilized borders constitutes a threat for both the island and its inhabitants. On the one hand, Cuba is repeatedly defined in terms of its opposition to the sea. Throughout the novel, the characters comment on the juxtaposition of these two elements. Celia spends extended periods of time on her front porch, staring at the ocean and reflecting on her life. When Pilar is found at her relatives' house in Miami, her mother flies to Florida to retrieve her. As soon as Lourdes arrives in Miami, the contiguous Caribbean waters underscore the proximity of Cuba and her mother's island: "Lourdes could smell the air before she breathed it, the air of her mother's ocean nearby."[40] Through the identification of Celia with the sea, Lourdes unexpectedly encounters the possibility of realizing the journey that Pilar has failed to complete.

At the same time, however, the ocean constitutes a destructive force that must be detained. The del Pino's house in Santa Teresa del Mar is almost destroyed by a tidal wave, and Celia describes her extended vigilance of the sea as protecting the island against other types of invasion. Nevertheless, these potential threats of attack are not enough to deter Celia from occasionally immersing herself in the water. At times, during her late-night vigils, Jorge appears to Celia and beckons for her to follow him into the sea. She is enticed by the prospect of reaching her late husband, but she only manages to alarm her daughter, who fears that her mother will drown in the violent currents.

In this way, the discourse of Cuban identity requires both a reification and a destabilization of insular boundaries. Each of the characters in *Dreaming* occasionally elects to cross boundaries in order to access the solution that ostensibly lies just beyond them. They continuously confront the need to surpass existing demarcations of space but must also face the inherent dangers engendered by such transgressions. Hence, García constructs an apparently irreconcilable conflict: the narrative traces the characters' need to eliminate the boundaries on which their subjectivity is fundamentally based.

The narrative structure of the novel, moreover, reinforces this conflict. As even a cursory glance at the novel reveals, both the division of sections and the titles assigned to chapters and subsections of chapters underscore the role of fixed boundaries in the structure of the text in a manner that is incommensurate with the fluid movement evoked by its content.[41] The novel is comprised of episodes that are either narrated by or that focus on individual characters. Throughout the novel, episodes devoted to the three generations of the del Pino family are repeatedly intercalated. This interweaving creates a dialogue between characters and events that are separated in time and space. The apparent fluidity of the narrative between the various temporal and geographic locations of the characters facilitates the desired transcendence for which the characters strive.

Nevertheless, the organization of the chapters and sections of the novel contradicts this suggestion and reifies instead more traditional boundaries. The novel is divided into three sections, each of which is subdivided into chapters. Through the use of titles and dates, García establishes fixed temporal boundaries. Many chapters are devoted to a single character or event. Furthermore, when a chapter moves between settings, each episode is subdivided. Not only are these subdivided episodes identified, but the author uses the names of the characters and dates to identify them. The chapter entitled, "Enough Attitude," for example contains the sections, "(1975)" and "Pilar (1976)." The narration of each framed episode, moreover, both adheres to and underscores Aristotelian unities of time and space. Therefore, although the individual episodes are not ordered in accordance with a chronological progression, the linear narrative is maintained since the novel is ultimately comprised of a succession of linear episodes.

The placement of the letters in the novel also frames the narrative. Five of the chapters in *Dreaming* are entitled "Celia's Letters" and include the correspondence between Celia and her Spanish lover during particular years.[42] More importantly, each of the three sections of the novel ends with these letters, and the first two sections are also subdivided by an additional epistolary chapter. Each of the individual letters is dated, and the years corresponding to these dates are included in the chapter's title. Within each grouping, furthermore, the dated correspondence progresses chronologically, and the epistolary chapters also appear in ascending order throughout the novel: the first one introduced is, "Celia's Letters: 1935-1940"—which includes letters dated from March 11, 1935 to September 11, 1940—and the final chapter is, "Celia's Letter: 1959."[43] Therefore, the linear progression of the letters is maintained and also reinforced by the repeated references to their respective dates.

The culmination of the novel with the chapter "Celia's Letter: 1959," is itself significant. The reduction of the established pattern of the preceding epistolary chapters to a single letter points to the end of the progression they traced. This closure is reflected in the content of the letter as well. In it Celia informs her lover that she will no longer write to him. The letter's date clearly historicizes it, and its content points to the personal changes in Celia's life, changes which coincide with national events, that lead her to abandon her correspondence: "The revolution is eleven days old. My granddaughter, Pilar Puente del Pino, was born today. I am fifty years old. I will no longer write to you, *mi amor*. She will remember everything."[44] By ending the novel with this letter, García underscores a clear demarcation between a pre- and post-Revolutionary narrative and between Celia's and Pilar's narration of their histories.

This concluding chapter, moreover, collapses the temporal progression of the novel into a singularity. As Said has suggested, the beginning and conclusion of a history jointly demarcate the historical narrative they frame. This gesture thus inscribes the subsequent story of the del Pino women in a post revolutionary Cuba that can only be narrated by Pilar. The systems of signification and communication that the characters cultivate over the course of the novel strive to transcend conventional boundaries and establish connections among the three generations of the family. In the final chapter, however, García invokes a more conventional relationship between genealogy and historiography. At the conclusion of the novel, historical memory is neatly inserted into a legacy that will be inherited by the next generation. This shift, moreover, is directly linked to a reduction—a cessation even—of discursive production. Not only is the erstwhile sequence of letters diminished to a single missive, but the content of that letter announces the conclusion of this form of communication and inscription.

Of course, to a certain extent, this gesture points proleptically to the discursive role that will be taken up by Pilar. As Rocío G. Davis has suggested in her analysis of the novel, García's text moves toward a final reconciliation and conjoining of the voices of the principal female characters. "At the center of the novel is Pilar Puente, born in Cuba and raised in Brooklyn, who must deal with her antipathetic relationship with her mother, Lourdes, and her longing for her grandmother, Celia. Similarly, Lourdes and Felicia, Celia's two daughters, struggle to unravel their complex ties with their mother as well as those with their own daughters. The novel thus presents a composite portrait of diverse mother-daughter relationships, offering a multiperspective vision of the possibilities for division and unity, adaptation and adjustment, separation and bonding."[45] Consequently, the conclusion of the novel could be viewed as a final reconciliation that will allow Pilar to take the place of the matriarch and effectively narrate the (feminine) family history in a manner that the previous generations were never able to fully realize. That is, as with "Daughter of Invention," Celia's self-imposed silence facilitates the development of Pilar's expressive or authorial role. Nevertheless, the final chapter does not truly function as a mise en scène for the narrative that textually precedes it. More importantly, perhaps, it inserts the potential new beginning into a highly confined location and historical moment. Structurally, this conclusion suggests that if the del Pino women ultimately achieve intergenerational communication, it is only because their entire history can be contained with the temporal rupture or perpetual suspension of revolutionary promise in Cuba.

In the end, García produces incompatible temporal dynamics in *Dreaming*. On the one hand, she attempts to subvert a conventional linear temporality and allows her characters to connect despite such divisions. On the other, however, the narrative is consistently circumscribed by an overarching structure that reaffirms traditional chronological and genealogical progression. Even though the narrative episodes included in each section are not bound to a linear progression, this temporal fluidity is consistently shaped by an overt chronological structure. Hence, the continuous reaffirmation of a conventional progression reinforces the temporality that García's characters ostensibly seek to overcome. Furthermore, this contradiction is not limited to temporality but is engendered by the paradoxical treatment of other boundaries as well. In her novel, García attempts to transcend the limitations of Cuban identity through transgression. At the same time, however, the recuperative project leads to a reaffirmation of existing paradigms. Therefore, *Dreaming* ultimately reinscribes the boundaries of national discourse rather than destabilize them.

Because of the unique status of Cuba, Cuban literature is often interpreted as a response to or a reflection of its sociopolitical context. According to this interpretation, García's recuperative project becomes an attempt to reduce the anxiety produced by the forced abandonment of the island. Joseph Martin Viera, for example, asserts that García creates a compelling revision of history through her realistic examination of the struggles of Cuban immigrants. Arturo Arango does not specifically discuss *Dreaming*, but he argues that the realism of Cuban American literature is compromised by its psychological undercurrents: "[F]or those who have chosen exile and continue to be bitterly opposed to the Revolution, whatever is Cuban remains a nearly pathological obsession; for those of us on the inside, however, their works increasingly seem to lack the nutrients of their native soil, to have become mired in the always treacherous sands of nostalgia."[46] Despite their diverging arguments, both authors insist that the representation of Cuban American writers is determined by their immigrant status; that is, the literature produced by these authors purportedly reconstructs Cuba in order to overcome the fragmentation of geographic displacement.

As with the culminating chapter of García's novel, "Celia's Letter: 1959," the Cuban Revolution has a clear influence on many texts produced in both Cuba and the diaspora during the second half of this century. Hence, the historicized reading of pre- and postrevolutionary literature can prove both legitimate and productive. Nevertheless, this approach has developed into a dominant hermenuetic that pervades Cuban Studies, and the concomitant periodization (pre- vs. post-1959) and geographic demarcation (the island vs. the United States) becomes an almost inevitable binary in the analysis of contemporary cultural production. Within this critical context, the insular themes can certainly be read as a direct response to the Cuban communties' current relationship to both space and time. The role of insularity in Cuban cultural production, however, transcends the specific context of the postrevolutionary diaspora. In fact, María Cristina Saavedra proposes that Cuban authors continuously reconstruct the island in order to resolve a particular crisis of national identity. The rhetorical project of reconciling disparate visions of Cuba thus constitutes a defining element of national discourse rather than a strategic response to specific circumstances. Saavedra outlines a tradition in which authors construct utopian representations in order to realize this project. In this way, the mythical island becomes the principal foundation of national discourse that must be perpetually reconstituted, both irrespective and in spite of historical shifts.

In the context of Cuban American—and, to some extent, caribeña—fictions, the persistence of insular tropes can produce an even greater contradiction. On the one hand, these authors such as García strive to transcend conventional boundaries and paradigms in order to more appropriately codify the Latina experience. On the other, however, their fetishistic attachment to the island and to the legacy of insularity privileges the homeland and repeatedly reinserts their writing into an encumbered nostalgia that thwarts the development of an innovative mode of diasporic (self)expression.

## Shifting Topographies and the Space(s) of Hispanic Caribbean Cultural Production

Through this contradictory relationship between content and form, *Dreaming in Cuban* delivers a stable and highly recognizable vision of translocal Cuban identity. As with the emblematic significance of corazón-throb cited earlier, the title of the novel points to the underlying dynamic of the project itself: it alludes to a familiar process of self-expression (dreaming) that is articulated in a distinct and culturally specific code.[47] Nevertheless, the novel successfully conforms to the exigencies of commercialism and presents a comprehensible, familiar, and even predictable tale of transcultural self-discovery. The specific struggle of Cuban American genealogy is thus neatly contained within the parameters of conventional narrative structure.

It is not surprising, therefore, that García's novel has been one of the more successful examples of recent U.S.-Latino literary production. In fact, García herself has attributed the success of her novel—and, to some extent, other Latino fiction—to its ability to establish connections among distinct historical moments, locations, and experiences. According to the author, the increased recognition of Latino writers is directly connected to demographic increases. More specifically, however, she also suggests that the positive reception of these narratives is based on their capacity to mediate traditional divisions of language and culture: "Those of us who kind of straddle both cultures are in a unique position to tell our stories, to tell our family stories. We're still very close to the immigration, we're in the wake of that immigration, and yet we weren't as directly affected by its as our parents and grandparents were. So we are truly bilingual, truly bicultural, in a way the previous generations were not."[48] García thus ascribes the commercial success of her work to an expressive mode that effectively codifies transcultural (and transgenerational) experiences.

Although the relative success of the novel can be attributed to the circumscription of a (trans)cultural shift, it does not imply that *Dreaming* constitutes a unique example of Latino literary production. In fact, García's work epitomizes a prevalent trend in U.S.-Caribbean cultural production. As with *Family Installments* and *García Girls*, her novel questions the structures that potentially disenfranchise the diaspora but never truly dislodges them as the principal pillars of cultural discourse. In this approach to the insular discourse of Caribbean identity, the island is reinforced as the lost home that must be mourned, but that cannot be recovered. Hence, although the diaspora is claimed as the space of transnational mobility, the foundational space of the island is reified as the principal location of self-definition. The island thus functions as what Foucault has called a heterotopia of crisis, a physical location outside the traditional parameters of normal existence.[49] This alternative space, furthermore, is imbued with sacred qualities and becomes tied to a rite of passage through which members of the society, who are compelled to travel through this space, are transformed and become able to assume a more privileged position once they reenter the quotidian social space. According to Foucault, however, this practice is associated with more primitive societies and heterotopias of crisis are eventually replaced with heterotopias of divergence.

Although heterotopias of divergence can certainly be found within Caribbean societies, the preservation of this ritualistic return as a right of passage that must be achieved in order to reach full self-realization perpetuates the role of the island as a sacred space of crisis. More importantly, perhaps, within diasporic communities the homeland is ,by definition, located elsewhere in this configuration of diaspora. Hence, this sacred space of crisis is rendered fundamentally inaccessible. The reproduction of insularity traced in the works examined here, enacts a particular representation of otherness while still maintaining an inextricable attachment to the structures of identity that precede migration and diaspora. This Janus-like duality, moreover, engenders an irreconcilable discursive contradiction: Hispanic Caribbean cultures cannot look backward toward former modes of self-definition that have become inaccessible and simultaneously move forward toward the formulation of new models of cultural production.

The continuity of insularity in Caribbean cultural discourse thus engenders a fundamental paradox within the process of self-fashioning. The desire to preserve cultural distinctiveness, however, does not hinder productive development. The obstacle resides instead in the particular situation of that distinctiveness in a geographically bound insularity that is firmly located in the Antillean archipelago. As in the case of the rhetorical framing of Latino culture in the United States, the representation of the island in Álvarez, Rivera, and García's novels is presented as a new phenomenon that is a direct consequence of recent migration. In these cases, however, identity formation is articulated in terms of a teleological pilgrimage that must lead back the homeland before moving forward. Therefore, although the novels indeed codify a significant demographic change, the processes are linked to a spatiality that is not easily reterritorialized in the diaspora without substantial reconfiguration.

At the same time, however, this complex negotiation does not necessarily constitute an insurmountable obstacle. In fact, the proleptic and often utopian nature of nationalisms frequently postulates the discrepancy between the current location and status of the nation against a more idealized vision of what it should become. In postcolonial discourses of self-definition, moreover, the conventional paradigms are not always uncritically reproduced but are often presented in terms of a counter-hegemonic contestation. Hence, the persistence of insular tropes, in and of itself, does not necessarily signal a backward intransigence. Historically, in fact, insularity has proven surprisingly malleable and able to adapt to major changes in the socio-political and cultural circumstances of Caribbean nations. In order to perpetuate this tradition and remain equally flexible in the current context, insularity must be reconfigured in a way that allows for the concomitant shifts in topographical discourses that inevitably accompany diasporic mobility. In other words, the island should be represented not as a sacred space of self-realization but, instead, in a manner that problematizes the very system that privileges the island as the primary location of caribeñidad.

I do not mean to suggest the insular paradigm established in the Antilles is the only source of self-definition for a writer in the diaspora or that the rhetoric of insularity is always deployed uncritically.[50] My aim has been instead to underscore a predominant trend within U.S.-Caribbean discourses of identity. The particular intersections of rhetorical and commercial forces that I have traced favors the transplanting of a reified configuration of Hispanic Caribbean spatiality—a reification that, paradoxically, Hispanic Caribbean discourse perpetually seeks to destablilize. Consequently, the significance of insularity in contemporary Caribbean cultural production does not merely reflect an attachment to anachronistic rhetorical traditions; insularity is also reinforced by the stable paradigms of identity (and identification) on which the commodification and marketing of latinidad fundamentally depend. García's novel, therefore, constitutes a paradigmatic case of a larger tendency: it reinscribes the subject within parameters that contradict the very fluidity that the narrative strives for or even celebrates.

In this sense, the examples analyzed here trace the shifting topographies of contemporary caribeña cultures: the principal spaces of Hispanic cultural production have clearly been reconfigured as a result of demographic changes, yet the spatiality of caribeñidad has not fully moved away from rhetorical tropes that construct the Antilles as the hegemonic epicenter of cultural production. Contemporary caribeña spatiality is therefore "out of place" in the diaspora both in the sense that it emerges from the insistence of a particular demarcation of Caribbean places and spaces and because it does not fit easily into the new (and changing) context of U.S. Hispanic Caribbean cultural production. In the end, both the space and spatiality of Hispanic Caribbean cultural production must be reterritorialized to better accommodate the changing demographic circumstances of caribeña communities and thus transcend the fundamental contradiction of insularity in the diaspora.

# 5
# Virtual Islands: The Negotiation of Translocal Spatiality

> Estamos en otra isla. New York es otra isla.
> He querido evadir
> el determinismo geográfico, pero estamos en
> otra isla: ustedes y nosotros.
>
> [We are on another island. New York is another island. I wanted to avoid geographic determinism, but we are on another island—you and us.]
> —Manuel Ramos Otero,
> "La otra isla de Puerto Rico"

THE LATIN AMERICAN STUDIES ASSOCIATION (LASA) HOLDS ITS CONvention once every eighteen months. In order to accommodate the transhemispheric membership of the organization, the location of the convention has traditionally alternated between major U.S. and Latin American cities. Accordingly, following the previous meeting in Chicago, the March 2000 conference was expected to be held in Latin America. The announcement that the conference would take place in Miami elicited mild amusement from several members of the organization. On the one hand, the selection made perfect sense given the logic of the alternating structure: current flight patterns make Miami a relatively accessible destination for most Latin American residents. On the other, however, the choice seemed to reflect the commonly held belief that Miami had become as Latin American as Buenos Aires or Mexico City.

To a certain extent, this incident is representative of a larger trend. As scholars such as Arlene Dávila, Agustín Laó-Montes, and Raúl Villa have aptly noted, major U.S. cities are increasingly marked by Latin American influences. That is, not only are major metropolitan areas such as Chicago, Los Angeles, Miami, and New York home to significant Latino populations, but the spatial and cultural ethos of these cities has been fundamentally "latinized." Hence, as in the case of the LASA convention in Miami, these urban centers can be viewed as interstitial spaces in which the real-and-imagined places of diasporic, migrant, and Latin American experiences coexist with mainstream U.S. society.

At the same time, however, the lived experience and perception of transformed space cannot be immediately absorbed or codified within existing structures of Caribbean identification. Given the nature of insularity and its inherent attachment to fixed geographic borders, translocal paradigms of identity engender a fundamental paradox in the Caribbean context. New York and Miami may indeed be increasingly Caribbean cities, yet they are not readily apprehensible as the topos of insular self-fashioning. Consequently, in order to function as an appropriate locus of enunciation for discourses of Caribbean self-fashioning, the spatiality of these locations must be reimagined in Antillean terms or the concept of insularity must be reconfigured in order to accommodate the translocal.

In the preceding chapter, I have underscored how U.S.-Caribbean literary and cultural production can excessively privilege the island and, in doing so, positions itself as always already out of place. Nevertheless, despite this tendency, the rhetoric of insularity and the spatiality of the diaspora are not necessarily incompatible. In order to be rendered productively, insularity must be reconfigured counter-hegemonically. At times, insularity is imagined in a manner that actively (re)negotiates its historical attachment to geographic specificity. In these cases, Hispanic Caribbean writers and artists can deploy insular tropes in a manner that invokes the traditional attachment to geography without fully subscribing to its ontological centrality. Under these circumstances, they advance a critical discourse that fundamentally problematizes the primacy of the Antilles as the principal locus of cultural production and self-formation.

As a result, these reconfigurations of insular tropes—whether produced in the Antilles or in the diaspora—dialogue with the established discursive tradition but also dynamically reterritorialize it in accordance with the shifting circumstances of Hispanic Caribbean communities. In this fashion, not only does U.S.-Caribbean culture move beyond the conventional boundaries of the Antillean homeland, but it also reimagines the avowed role of the island as a defining trope of Caribbean subjectivities.

## Translocal Caribeñidad

Given the increased interconnectedness of the Antilles and the world beyond its borders, the conventional space and spatiality of the Caribbean cannot be taken for granted; instead, it must be actively negotiated. Recently, Caribbean communities have redefined themselves in more geographically inclusive terms. The defining tropes of identity are rendered, not according to fixed and bound geographic specificity, but along more fluid and inherently mobile lines. Certainly, the most salient instances of translocal insularity emerge in the diapora itself. Nevertheless, the self-expression that is produced within the Hispanic Antilles also responds to this shift. The tension between the conventional spatiality of caribeñidad on the one hand and the shifting loci of enunciation on the other is also codified within the literary and cultural production of Cuba, the Dominican Republic, and Puerto Rico. That is, even within the forms of cultural expression that are clearly identifiable as island-based, the impact of the diaspora cannot be ignored. Moreover, not only do Antillean texts increasingly refer to and represent the diversity of Caribbean locations, but they often critically engage with the challenges that the diaspora inherently poses to insular self-fashioning.

Given its relative isolation, the critical engagement of contemporary Cuban cultural expression with questions of the diaspora proves especially striking. Literary critics and intellectuals have devoted considerable attention to comparative analyses of Cuban and Cuban-American textual production. Similarly, numerous studies have focused on the effects of relative isolation and the lack of mutual comprehension or productive dialogue between the two groups. In his analysis of Cuban cultural production, Ambrosio Fornet cites the problematic relationship between the island and the United States: "Certainly, the first half of the twentieth century (not to mention, the second) in Cuba would be completely incomprehensible if we did not bear in mind, on the one hand, the profound conviction of many Americans that Cuba has never been anything more than an appendage to Florida and, on the other, most Cubans' long standing love/hate relationship with the United States."[1] According to Fornet, Cuba is constructed in terms relevant to the conflicts of international politics. In this manner, the stark division between the island and the diaspora is often embedded in twentieth century cultural discourse, yet it does not tend to be the explicit focus of the texts produced in Cuba. Consequently, Fornet and other intellectuals and scholars have struggled to comprehend the underlying influence of this relationship with the Cuban American community.

Although this relationship tends to be underrepresented in Cuban literary and cultural production, it has occasionally constituted a prominent theme of narratives generated in Cuba. In fact, Juan Carlos Tabío's recent film *Aunque estés lejos* (2002), negotiates the complexities of the interactions between Cuba and the exterior. More importantly, perhaps, the film critically engages the difficulties that emerge from the unwillingness to fully acknowledge these interactions or their impact on cultural discourse. *Aunque estés lejos* presents the struggle of Mercedes and Pedro, two characters who are trying to produce a film in Cuba. Their proposed film centers on a romance that develops between a local man and a Cuban American woman who visits the island. Although the man initially dreams of seducing her in order to be able to immigrate to the United States, a genuine affection develops between them, and the film concludes with her returning to the island to be with him.

On the hand, this proposed plot could simply be understood as thinly veiled antiemigration propaganda. The initial subterfuge is abandoned, and the romance concludes, not with a departure to the United States, but with the successful reincorporation of the Cuban American woman through the union of the two characters. In this fashion, Cuba becomes the site of the "happily ever after" ending and the divided community (i.e., Cuban/Cuban American) is reunited. The plot that they initially envision therefore rewrites the more conventional scheme that regards connections with tourists and with the Cuban American community as a potential source of escape. At the same time, it also reconfigures the anxieties around the possibility of return migration: rather than attempt to reclaim ancestral resources or fundamentally alter the socioeconomic conditions, the Cuban American immigrant is reincorporated through the romantic pairing.

On the other hand, however, this vision becomes increasingly complicated as *Aunque estés lejos* unfolds. Mercedes and Pedro are forced to seek international funding in order to make their film, and they present the proposed project to Alberto—an established figure in the Spanish film industry. Alberto, however, has his own ideas for the movie and proposes significant changes: he suggests a romantic thriller in which a Spanish man becomes involved in the problems of a beautiful, mulata musician from Cuba. Mercedes and Pedro initially dismiss Alberto's alternative as excessively stereotypical. Alberto subsequently reveals, however, that the plot is pseudo-autobiographical, based largely on his own complicated relationship with his place of birth (Cuba) and his estranged past.

In this manner, *Aunque estés lejos* underscores the complexities of interdependence. On one level, it highlights the problem of finance and competing interests that become particularly prevalent during the Special Period.[2] On another, it calls into question the very demarcations that privilege the island as the primary or exclusive location of Cuban culture and expression. Tabio's film does not merely present the conflict between opposing interior and exterior views that must be negotiated in the case of international cosponsorship. Instead, the film suggests that the relationship between Cuba and the diaspora does not fit neatly into established paradigms of stereotypes and mutual misrecognition. It stages a complex set of multidirectional interactions that inevitably disrupt the conventional plots and modes of self-representation. In this sense, the film dramatizes the very problem that Fornet had identified. Moreover, it points toward the incommensurability of stark division and points toward the need for a dynamic engagement between cultural discourse produced on the island and that generated beyond its borders.

Given the relative prevalence of circulatory migration and frequent travel between the Dominican Republic and the United Sates, the impact of the diasporic community on the island is even more apparent than in the Cuban context. Nevertheless, the engagement with the role of the diaspora and the challenge it poses to traditional paradigms of self-definition does not tend to constitute the explicit focus of texts produced on the island. As in the case of *Aunque estés lejos*, recent cinematographic production offers a vision of migration and its implications for island-based culture. Ángel Muñiz's *Nueba Yol* (1995) presents the adventures of Balbuena, who moves to New York in search of better economic opportunities and a better life. As he quickly discovers, however, New York is not the extraordinary land of opportunity that he had hoped. Instead, he encounters linguistic, cultural, and economic difficulties that he had not anticipated. Through his sense of humor and charm, he manages to overcome these obstacles. Nevertheless, his encounters with other residents of the city—including fellow immigrants—ultimately convince him that New York does not truly offer a better life. In the end, he decides to return to the Caribbean. Moreover, he persuades his compatriot—with whom he has fallen in love—to return to the Dominican Republic with him.

As with the original film proposed by Mercedes and Pedro in *Aunque*, *Nueba Yol* can be seen as a simple demystification of the myth of migratory success and the opportunities for a better life in the United States. It presents many of the (stereo)typical tropes of the migrant experience and celebrates the ingenuity of the protagonist and his ability to overcome these obstacles. At the same time, however, Balbuena rejects the alternatives available in New York and opts instead to struggle for a better life in

Santo Domingo. And, once again, the romantic coupling leads to a return migration and a reincorporation of the diasporic subject.

In this manner, Muñiz's film seemingly debunks the notion of the American dream and suggests that Dominicans would be better served by struggling for a better life at home. Although Muñiz does not utilize the same structural or metanarrative devices that Tabio employs, he does complicate this antiemigration vision through his oeuvre. In *Nueba Yol*, the portrayal of the immigrant experience is not limited to Balbuena's personal trajectory. The diverse Dominican characters he encounters embody an array of circumstances, motivations, and sentiments regarding migration. In the end, these additional characters do little to challenge Balbuena's decision to return to the island; nevertheless, they place his choices in the wider context of demographic conditions that transcend the specific mobility and desires of the main character(s).

More importantly, perhaps, the apparent resolution at the conclusion of the film is displaced in the sequel. In *Nueba Yol III* (1998), Muñiz depicts Balbuena's continuing struggle for a better life and his attempts to overcome the changing legal regulations that restrict immigrant benefits.[3] Despite his decision to return to Santo Domingo, Balbuena finds himself, once again, turning to the opportunities of the diaspora in order to realize his dreams of a better life. In this sense, the combination of the two films, underscores the inevitable interdependence between the two loci. Balbuena may not find the utopian fantasy that he had hoped for in the northern metropolis, but he cannot successfully exist in isolation in either location. In the end, a better life is not tied solely to either place but relies instead on a more unified Dominican community.

Given the long-standing and, in some cases, highly systematized role of migration in Puerto Rico along with the sustained political ties to the United States, it is not surprising that Puerto Rican literary and cultural production has addressed the relationship between the island and diasporic communities in an even more thorough and consistent manner.[4] Moreover, the impact of the diaspora has been intensified in the Puerto Rican case by the relative proportionality of populations on and off the island: unlike the Cuban and Dominican cases, the extra-insular population has closely approximated the internal one for several decades.[5] Consequently, the textual production of the last several decades explores how historical paradigms of self-definition are challenged and influenced by the relationship between the island and the diaspora. Recent scholarship in Puerto Rican studies reflects an acute awareness of the contradiction that emerges from this relationship and the mobility of circular migration. Titles such as *Island Para-*

*dox* and *Puerto Rico: The Commuter Nation* suggest that, not only does the Puerto Rican community extend beyond the geographic boundaries of the island, but the very notion of *puertorriqueñidad* has been fundamentally altered by this reterritorialization of the community.

Similarly, the work of contemporary Puerto Rican authors frequently addresses the impact of the diaspora and the expanding terrain of the Puerto Rican community. In some cases, moreover, the texts narrate the very process of spatial reconfiguration that these demographic shifts incite. Luis Rafael Sánchez's "La guagua aérea" ("The Airbus") for example, chronicles the voyage of a flight from San Juan to New York. As the title suggests, the route has been repeatedly traveled by several of the passengers, who are described collectively as, "boricuas que viajan, a diario, entre el eliseo desacreditado que ha pasado a ser Nueva York y el edén inhabitable que se ha vuelto Puerto Rico"[6] [a thousand and one travelers moving between that precarious and discredited paradise that is New York and that eroded and inhabitable paradise that is Puerto Rico.][7] One passenger in particular is systematically transferring the contents of his home in Puerto Rico to his residence in New York: "Si no puedo vivir en Puerto Rico, porque allí no hay vida buena para mí, me lo traigo poco a poco. En este viaje traigo cuatro jueyes de Vacía Talega. En el anterior un gallo castado. En el próximo traeré cuanto disco grabó el artista Cortijo."[8] [If I can't live in Puerto Rico because I just can't make it there I'll take it all with me bit by bit, this time I've got four crabs from Vacía Telega, last time I brought over a purebred fighting cock and next time it will be every single ever recorded by Cortijo.][9]

Although his personal relocation project may prove an adequate resolution of this character's circumstances, it also causes some difficulty for the fellow occupants of his flight. The crabs escape from their temporary confinement and begin to wander throughout the cabin. A flight attendant is apparently unprepared for the event and becomes noticeably alarmed. The passengers, in turn, misinterpret her reaction as a indication of terrorist activities and also become distressed. The discovery of the actual cause, however, incites communal relief, and the shared experience unifies the passengers.

Through this episode, Sánchez constructs a definition of the Puerto Rican migration experience. The fugitive crustaceans momentarily embody the combination of confinement and freedom the passengers must also navigate. The "airbus" affords a necessary liberty that allows identity to be sustained in spite of geographic movement. At the same time, however, this identity is based on a cultural specificity that must be reconstructed in a wholly foreign context. The *mise en abyme* generated also demarcates the divisions within the plane: the passengers are contrasted to the "tripulación particularmente gringa" (uniformly gringo crew) and, at the same time, are united by their shared cultural experience. In this way, cultural differences both disrupt and solidify the traveling community.

As with most literature that addresses community displacement and movement, Sánchez examines the strategies that individual characters utilize in order to adjust to their changing circumstances. Moreover, he also underscores the shift in parameters of identity engendered by migratory patterns. This discursive reconfiguration is exemplified in a humorous exchange between two passengers. Toward the end of the narrative, a passenger initiates a conversation with the narrator by inquiring, "¿De dónde es usted?"[10] ["And where are you from?"][11] The narrator explains that he is from Puerto Rico, but this response proves both self-evident and unsatisfactory to his interlocutor, and he specifies that he is from Humacao. In order to meet her expectations, the narrator reciprocates and repeats his neighbor's inquiry. With her rather playful response, the fellow passenger mimics the narrator's earlier answer and, thereby, generates an unexpected demarcation of national boundaries:

> Unos ojos rientes y una fuga de bonitos sonrojos le administran el rostro cuando me contesta—*De Puerto Rico*. Lo que me obliga a decirle, razonablemente espiritista—*Eso lo ve hasta un ciego.* Como me insatisface la malicia inocente que le abunda el mirar... añado, copiándole el patrón interrogador—*Pero, ¿de qué pueblo de Puerto Rico?* Con una naturalidad que asusta, equivalente la sonrisa a la más triunfal de las marchas, la vecina del asiento me contesta—*De Nueva York.*[12]

> [With a coquettish twinkle in her eye and a shameless blush in her cheek she replies "I'm from Puerto Rico," forcing me to say, just slightly psychic, "Even the blind can see that much," adding "From which town in Puerto Rico?" And she specifies "From New York."][13]

Through the detailed description of this paradigmatic flight, "La guagua aérea" narrates this process of national transfer and extension. Not only does Sánchez construct "[e]l espacio de una nación flotante entre dos puertos de contrabandear esperanzas,"[14] [in its pursuit of a new space, furiously conquered. It is the course of a nation afloat between two ports where the contraband is hope].[15] but he also presents a vision of Puerto Rican identity that is based on the movement between these two national epicenters. In this way, the interstice created by constant migration becomes the foundation for a discourse of national identity rather than threaten or destabilize it.

"La guagua aérea" presents a relatively salient discussion of the phenomenon of migration; but Sánchez is not the only Puerto Rican author to explore the discursive implications of this demographic shift within a narrative context. Manuel Ramos Otero's "La otra isla de Puerto Rico" ("The Other Island of Puerto Rico"), the short story quoted in the epigraph at the beginning of this chapter, explores the furthest consequences of this perpetual island-hopping. In this story, Ramos Otero traces the complicated last testament of an individual from Puerto Rico who has died while on vacation in Athens. Through the development of this plot, the author constructs a definition of national identity that is not based simply on the oscillation between two epicenters but instead on the conjoining of various insular spaces. The story begins with the death of the Don José Usbaldo Olmo Olmo, and almost all of the events narrated take place after his death. The plot, therefore, centers on the attempt to trace the history of Don José and his family. The narrator gains access to Don José's library and attempts to reconstruct the familial history through the multiple volumes of his memoirs and the other volumes "que don Don José Usbaldo Olmo Olmo había 'amasado,'" [that don Don José Usbaldo Olmo Olmo had 'amassed'"].[16]

Within this reconstructive project, the narrative continuously focuses on islands and the role of insularity. Through repeated references to Greek mythology and Homer's epic, moreover, the project is characterized as an odyssey that will transport its hero back to the point of origin. In tracing this odyssey, the narrator encounters references to various insular spaces, including Martinique, Haiti, Iceland, the Canary Islands, Japan, and Robinson Crusoe's island. Although he underscores the affinity among these locations, he also asserts the need to maintain the singularity of each: "La voluntad es otra cuando es otra la isla y otro el canto de las sirenas cuando el tablero es el mar y los peones somos nosotros," [The will is another when the island is another, and another the chant of the Sirens when the chess table is the sea and the pawns are us].[17] In this way, Ramos Otero creates a connection among the islands that neither conflates them nor constructs a single, monolithic definition of insularity.

The author also problematizes the location of the other island he refers to in the title. On the one hand, this alterity is engendered by the juxtaposition of distinct insular spaces. As Yolanda Martínez-San Miguel notes in her analysis, however, this juxtaposition also leads to a (con)fusion among the islands through multiple repetitions of the term: "Estamos en otra isla.

New York es otra isla. He querido evitar el determinismo geográfico, pero estamos en otra isla: ustedes y nosotros," [We are on another island. New York is another island. I wanted to avoid geographic determinism, but we are on another island—you and us].[18] Although the narrative clearly asserts that New York constitutes another island, the referent also becomes ambiguous, and it is unclear whether New York is the only other island or whether the "you" and the "we" he refers to are on the same (other) island or different ones.

In addition to this ambiguity, Ramos Otero also introduces the possibility of encountering other islands within Puerto Rico. Not only does he suggest that satellites such as Vieques may constitute such other islands, but he also uses the term to refer to different visions of the nation: "José Ariosto le contaba del otro Puerto Rico, de la otra isla a la que estaban destinados, como si estuviera haciendo trenzas negras con el tiempo y entre los dos todo empezaba," ["José Ariosto spoke to him about the other Puerto Rico and the other island for which they were destined"].[19] The term is also further expanded through the equation of the island and other spaces within it:

> Como si la isla, el caserón y la biblioteca flotaran sobre pilotes de pino, a su vez enterrados en archipiélagos de arena, tejidos por hilos de agua dulce y corrientes de agua salada, para que la posición de esa otra isla constantemente se alterara a sí mismo su cielo.
>
> [As if the island, the mansion and the library were floating on piles of pine needles, buried at the same time in archipelagoes of sand, woven through threads of fresh water and currents of salt water, so that the position of that other island were constantly altering the sky to itself. ][20]

In his analysis, Rubén Ríos Ávila argues that the shifting signifier of "la otra isla" underscores the impossibility of locating Puerto Rican history: Finally, it becomes increasingly impossible to locate the author of the memoir or the place of the memoir. Therein lies the basic assumption of the story: Puerto Rico can only be conceived as an *otra isla*, ever shifting from the focus of the narrative to the same extent that the subject of the narrative shifts as well. 'La otra isla de Puerto Rico' is about the impossibility of assigning ultimate authority for the writing of national memoir, or national memory."[21] According to Ríos Ávila, the construction of insular history is displaced by the repeated dislocations of the island. Through this allegorical function that postulates the island itself as other, insular alterity extends beyond geography and becomes a defining characteristic of perpetually shifting entities.

"La otra isla" exemplifies the persistence of the rhetoric of insularity within definitions of Caribbean identity. The need to incorporate multiple loci does not foster a rhetorical shift; instead, the rhetoric is modified in order to accommodate this topographic expansion. Through its ambiguous and flexible use, the phrase "la otra isla" ceases to refer to a single specific, island and becomes a term that could denote the diverse landscape of national identity. In this manner, Ramos Otero constructs a discourse of national identity based on movement through distinct insular topographies.

These works undoubtedly underscore the increasing importance of migration and the extra-insular population, yet they also reflect a sustained engagement with the diaspora as a legitimate space of Caribbean self-fashioning. More importantly, they do not merely establish a "separate but equal" parity between the two loci: beyond recognizing the legitimacy of diasporic cultural expression alongside that of the Antilles, they interrogate the impact of expanding terrain on Caribbean cultural production. The increasing translocality of contemporary communities destabilizes conventional plot and structures. These works therefore point to the need to develop new narrative paradigms that are better suited to the changing landscape of Caribbean spatiality. Consequently, these authors stress the need to rethink the demarcation of cultural spaces and to redefine insularity, not strictly in accordance with the geographic borders of the Antilles, but in more appropriately flexible—and, perhaps, mobile—terms. They point towards the possibility of resituating insularity in an inherently translocal cultural landscape.

Of course, the emergence of this trend within Antillean cultural production is particularly striking. That is, in addition to diasporic writers who are intrinsically motivated to challenge the primacy of the island as the locus of self-fashioning, the recognition of this shift by Caribbean authors and artists offers compelling evidence of its impact. Not surprisingly, however, the dynamic reworking of insularity proves even more significant in the diaspora. As I argued in the preceding chapter, insular modes of self-definition are often reproduced in an excessively fixed and limiting manner in U.S.-Caribbean cultural production. Nevertheless, insularity can also be reimagined in terms that allow it to be productively mobilized in the diasporic context.

Over the past half century, the extensive political and demographic ties between Puerto Rico and the United States have fostered conditions that fundamentally challenge the historical demarcation of national space. Given the particular intensity of the paradoxical relationship between the space and places of cultural identity, therefore, Puerto Rican discursive production offers acute and significant examples of insular reterritorialization. The processes of translocal insular self-fashioning, in and of themselves, are codified in an exceptionally striking manner on Web sites that address the current circumstances of the Puerto Rican community. Hence, I would like to turn to a in-depth examination of how traditional models of Puerto Rican identity are reconfigured in the diaspora in general and in cyber-space in particular.

## The Coquí Controversy: A Case Study in Globalized Reterritorialization

There is, perhaps, no better symbol of the contemporary paradox of translocal insularity than the coquí. As almost anyone who has ever visited or lived in Puerto Rico can readily affirm, the coquí is a prevalent inhabitant of the island. This small native frog makes its presence known through the distinctive nocturnal calls that have become closely associated with the landscape in Puerto Rico. Even when they remain concealed—either by foliage and natural camouflage or within the interstices of urban density—their daily ritual of vocalizing at dusk makes their ubiquitous presence undeniable. The coquí is not merely a natural phenomenon; the frog is also a symbol of Puerto Rican identity. The close link between the coquí and the Puerto Rican habitat has afforded it a privileged status as a cultural icon. Hence, not only is the coquí avowedly Puerto Rican, but it also is evocative of the specific locality of the island.

Its iconic status is manifested by a wide array of representations of the frog on the island. Shops in Old San Juan and near other tourist attractions usually offer a variety of anthropomorphized renditions of the coquí engaging in activities such as playing traditional local instruments, dancing, or simply reclining in a hammock. Although certain representations faithfully imitate the appearance of the frog, many of the reproductions bear little resemble to the biological referent. In fact, a particular iconography of the coquí has developed: it is most commonly depicted as a bright, green frog with a relatively small head and seemingly uncharacteristic features such as directly forward–facing eyes and small ears. The marketing of both the more realistic and the primarily cartoon-like figures appeals to a foreign desire for transportable souvenirs of the purportedly exotic destination that visitors tend to seek:[22] they codify a rarified local specificity through a representation that is both charming and readily comprehensible.[23]

Interestingly, the consumers of these figures are not only foreign tourists. The coquís also appeal to Puerto Rican consumers.[24] Local consumption of the imagery occurs because the coquí offers a particular representation of puertorriqueñidad.[25] The coquí is a symbol traditionally associated with Puerto Rico and Puerto Rican identity. Moreover, this symbolism is directly connected to the putative biological and/or mythological autochthony of the frog. Certainly, the pervasive presence of the animal throughout the island reinforces its association with the Puerto Rican landscape. More importantly, traditional cultural folklore asserts that the species is utterly incapable of surviving in any other environment. According to popular lore, the coquí will simply die if transported to a different ecological environment such as, for example, New York. But Puerto Ricans also insist that the tiny frog is equally unable to withstand a shift to (an ostensibly equivalent biological setting in) neighboring islands such as St. Thomas or Hispaniola. In other words, although no clear scientific evidence has been offered to support such claims or explain why the animal would be affected by biologically irrelevant political borders, many local residents assert that the coquí will undoubtedly perish if removed from the territory of Puerto Rico. Hence, according to these claims, the coquí is Puerto Rican to an extreme: it thrives in Puerto Rico and perishes anywhere else. According to this mythology, therefore, the production of locality takes precedence over ecological habitat and ultimately constitutes the true basis for (symbolic) cultural survival.

Recently, this myth has been empirically refuted by an unexpected population explosion of coquís in Hawai'i.[26] Although it is unclear precisely how or why the original progenitors were transported to this other insular environment, the coquí, rather than perishing, has thrived in its new location. Ironically, however, its new human neighbors are less than thrilled with the unexpected survival skills of the frog. The Hawai'ians, who have no reason to cherish the coquí as a cultural symbol, view its sudden proliferation as a troublesome infestation that threatens both ecological sustainability and tourism. The coquí is decried as an alien frog that endangers the existence of the more legitimate inhabitants of the island. The HEAR (Hawaiian Ecosystems at Risk) Project describes the escalating "anthropocentric concerns" associated with the coquí's inappropriate and disturbing vocalizations: [27]

> *E. coqui* has a *loud, piercing call* that often disturbs people's sleep (calls are typically measured at **90–100 decibels** at a distance of 0.5m [1.5'] from the frog). This same problem has been noted for other species of *Eleutherodactylus* introduced to areas outside their native ranges. Several populations of frogs have come to our attention as complaints from disturbed residents, visitors, or hotel managers. All of these have been for

small choruses of frogs. Large choruses can be deafening but are restricted so far to a couple of nurseries and a few residential areas.[28]

In this manner, the very characteristic that had been considered euphonic in Puerto Rico becomes strident and inappropriate in the Hawai'in setting. Paradoxically, the mythology of the coquí is reproduced by the Hawai'ians through this hostile rejection of it as an unwelcome immigrant: the coquí is viewed as being *out of place*, not part of the more autochthonous—and, by extension, more appropriate—ecosystem, and it is therefore characterized as an invading element that must be eliminated. Rather than being sold in iconographic form to locals or tourists as a charming representation of local folklore, the coquí becomes a pernicious pest when reterritorialized in the Hawai'ian context, and this transformation does indeed threaten its continued survival.[29]

In addition to being represented, examined, and discussed in its respective habitats, the role of the coquí is also reconstructed in cyberspace. The coquí often adorns Puerto Rican Web sites, where it is used as a symbol of cultural identity, although it is not usually explained or identified per se. In this context, the coquí forms part of an iconography of puertorriqueñidad (along with depictions of the shape of the island, silhouettes of the gun turrets and bastions of the El Morro fortress and other images that would presumably be readily recognizable as culturally specific markers of identity). On these sites, whether the coquí is depicted in a more realistic form or drawn in a manner similar to the cartoon-like figures, it is almost always presented as a symbol of cultural pride or nostalgia. On Web sites that address the presence of the coquí in Hawai'i, however, this same frog is shown in graphic technical photographs and narrated by definitions of its biological classification along with characterizations of the frog as a "threat" and a "pest."

In equally stark contrast, the auditory components of these territorialized representations offer rather distinct characterizations of the coquí. Puerto Rican sites often feature a few seconds of coquí sounds that play as the page opens. One site in particular offers visitors the opportunity to open an audio file and listen to an extended sample of the typical "chorus" of coquís that can be heard after sunset in language evoking nostalgia and the intimate domestication of the tropical island. One of the sites dedicated to the coquí *problem* in Hawai'i also allows visitors to open files containing either a single coquí or the more typical concatenation of calls. But, in the latter case, the link to open the auditory component is accompanied by an editorial comment that exclaims: "If you enjoy peace & quiet, just imagine trying to sleep through *this* every night!!"[30]

Of course, the story of the coquí in Hawai'i is not entirely unprecedented. In fact, the transplanting of Puerto Rican inhabitants to these other islands had occurred long before the coquí ever made its first documented appearance in the Pacific. According to James L. Dietz, Hawai'i was identified as a logical destination for Puerto Rican workers who were being encouraged by government-sponsored organizations to emigrate during the first half of the twentieth century. Not only would the developing political link to the United States presumably facilitate this redistribution of labor, but the strategy was based on the belief that the similarities in geographic and agricultural circumstances would make Puerto Rican workers ideally suited to the Hawai'ian labor environment and allow them to adapt readily to conditions there. Given the significant cultural differences, however, the transition between the islands was not necessarily as easy as the economic strategists imagined. In fact, the relocation of Puerto Rican workers to the South Pacific engendered tensions homologous to those raised by the subsequent arrival of the coquí. In a sense, these concerns could conceivably be paraphrased as questions of adaptability that would apply in both cases: would they thrive or perish in the new environment? Would their arrival and propagation threaten the (more) native inhabitants of the island? Were they viewed as an excessively disturbing presence that would upset the natural tranquility of their new insular environment? The question of this group's status and their ability to survive in spite of this uneasy displacement continues to be an important issue among scholars long after the initial wave of immigrants. In fact, Arturo Morales Carrión cites the Puerto Rican community in Hawai'i as an exemplary case of puertorriqueñidad in the diaspora: "Hawaii has a very important Puerto Rican community that has grown through several generations without losing its identity."[31]

Hence, the coquí functions as a cultural symbol that (re)enacts the very processes of increasing translocation that the Puerto Rican community has experienced over the last century. As a national symbol, the coquí is inextricably bound to a particular location and locality. Through processes of globalization such as migratory patterns that are inexorably linked to accelerating mechanisms of international trade, it becomes disconnected from this locality and is reterritorialized in terms of an evolving system of international capital and power. Moreover, the sudden mobility of the autochthonous icon by means of the Internet engenders problematic reinterpretations of an already complex cultural commodity. Both the problem of multiple (re)interpretations itself and the representation of the coquí's translocal transformation on the Web point to a phenomenon through which erstwhile location-specific identities are reconfigured via the Internet. The particular spatiality of the World Wide Web allows for formerly noncontiguous spaces to be brought together without *necessarily* compromising their position or geographic specificity. The cyber-construction of puertorriqueñidad underscores the mechanisms through which the structures of self-definition are alternately reinforced and radically alerted by demographic shifts in the community.

In order to fully contextualize the significance of this cyber-construction, I will now briefly turn to a discussion of the rhetoric of insularity and its historical role in Puerto Rican discourse. Drawing upon this rhetorical tradition, I will then more closely examine how this spatiality is reconstituted on contemporary Puerto Rican Web site through the reterritorialization of both the coquí and insular iconography in a manner that simultaneously reifies and reconfigures previous constructions of insular spatiality.

## Insular Topographies and Puerto Rican Spatiality

In *The Production of Space*, Henri Lefebvre argues that space acquires meaning through the interpretation and signification of particular natural or physical characteristics. Hence, according to this understanding of spatial codification, islands become legible or comprehensible as they are defined and potentially reinvented in a series of new sociopolitical contexts.[32] At the same time, a semantics of insularity emerges over time through the discursive association between the specific geographic circumstances of islands and particular signifying characteristics. As I have asserted earlier, islands become a repeating trope through which authors offer a vision of societal definition.

In 1516, for example, Thomas More published the first edition of *Utopia*. Following in the tradition established by works such as Plato's *Republic*, More depicts a fictitious society that becomes a heuristic device through which he comments on and critiques his own. Nevertheless, More does not reproduce Plato's "disclaimer" in which he explicitly declares that he will describe a nonexistent republic in order to construct an *exemplum* of an ideal society; instead, More methodically examines every detail of his imagined island. Perhaps because of the extraordinary detail and style of the descriptions, More's depiction of the hypothetical island acquires an intensely visual quality. Beyond a description that alludes to or evokes physicality, his text produces the very spatiality of utopia.

Nevertheless, regardless of how "real" More's utopia becomes as a representational space, the author onomastically negates the possibility of a specific extratextual referent or location for the island: utopia literally means nonplace or nowhere. Although, for the most part, the intelligentsia among More's readers interpreted the island's name as a clear indication of its fictionality, many believed that the specific place More described could be located in the physical world. As Carlo Ginzburg points out, the publication of early editions of *Utopia* sparked fierce debates among certain scholars regarding its precise location.[33] Given this confusion, Ginzburg questions the ambiguity in More's text. Of course, there are any number of reasons why this strategy may have appealed to More at the time. Ginzburg's analysis, however, does not point to an explanation of More's particular historical situation or his authorial intent. He focuses instead on the implications of the ekphrastic production of an island. That is, More creates a separate, distinct world that, because of its spatiality, becomes as "significant" as the natural one. Furthermore, since the textual spatiality both builds on and dialogues with existing codification of physical space, the island is inevitably juxtaposed with the space inhabited by More and his readers. In this way, the fully realized spatiality of utopia enhances its function as a heuristic device for critical commentary. I would argue, therefore, that More's utopia constitutes both a precursor to and a paradigmatic case of the *virtual* island. It is a representational space in which insularity is the defining characteristic. Nonetheless, the precise signification of this insularity is not predetermined but constructed and reconstructed rhetorically within the text.

As I have argued in the preceding chapters, depicted islands often realize a similar function in Puerto Rican literature: they act as a heuristic device that highlights the current social and cultural conditions and, whenever appropriate, point to possible improvements. Of course, Pedreira's *Insularismo* is the most salient and explicit example of this trend. Unlike More's text, however, the island that Pedreira diagnoses in his text is not a fictional place that lies outside the quotidian social reality. Instead, the island he depicts represents both the current status of the nation and the idealized vision of what it should become.

In the U.S. context, however, this simultaneity does not exist in precisely the same way. Insular landscapes do not conjure the current location of the community, but rather invoke the originary space of the lost homeland. In this sense, islands symbolize absence, distance, and displacement. Nonetheless, the deployment of insular tropes in Puerto Rican literature and culture also marks a shift in spatiality: rather than the fixity traditionally associated with the bound demarcation of the Antilles, these fictional and artistic representations highlight fluidity as a defining characteristic.

As Ramos Otero's short story demonstrates, the move to another island does not simply signal the substitution of one insular setting for another; in fact, the "otherness" of the island is identified with mobility and change.

This dual role of islands as symbols of both displacement and progress becomes particularly apparent in the iconography of Puerto Rican Web sites. The nature of cyberspace facilitates the construction of alternative communities: it allows for the formation of associations that would not be readily available in the physical world. As Juana María Rodríguez cogently argues, in the face of the anxieties produced by the apparent fluidity of the Internet, innovative practices are deployed in order to regulate movement and identity. These practices reveal both the new possibilities afforded by technological innovation and the desire to maintain preexisting boundaries of communication and interaction. A careful examination of contemporary Puerto Rican Web pages illustrates how emergent communities are formed, negotiated, and regulated. More importantly, perhaps, the graphic and textual components of the virtual world allow these communities to develop their own spatiality. In this context, the island comes to represent both a specifically local icon tied to the Antilles and a more ubiquitous symbol of the mobile, global community of the diaspora. This combination is evidenced in phrases such as "de Puerto Rico pal mundo" (from Puerto Rico to the world) and "el boricua mundial" (the worldly Rican) found on several Web pages.[34]

In some cases, more importantly, a paradoxical simultaneity of the insular and the global can be found. The Internet disrupts conventional terrestrial space and constructs an alternative spatiality. According to *The History of the Internet*, the technology developed out of the need and desire for more efficient and secure communication and exchange of information.[35] It allowed data to be transferred directly between computers via remote servers without the need for translation or the physical movement of information by means of intermediary devices. In its initial incarnations, therefore, movement between and among related sources of information was facilitated, but the physicality of this movement was not codified or represented in highly visible or recognizable terms. That is, although early *intranet* and *Internet* communication already facilitated the digital conjoining of geographically noncontiguous locations, this reorganization of space was not directly represented in the medium itself.[36] Although it was originally employed in the development of video games and other technological interfaces, virtual reality involved a graphic representation that established a mimetic relationship with physical space: the virtual environment that was constructed both reproduced and reconfigured the physical world. The development of the World Wide Web and Web browsers brought these two technologies together; the spatiality of the Internet became a highly visible and integral component of its usage. The potential movement and connections of the Internet are currently represented in terms of spatial metaphors: the Web itself acts as a symbol for the interweaving and multidirectional connections, and language such as "home," "back," and "forward" reinforce this representation of cyberspace as a more fluid physical reality.

The spatial metaphorical characterization certainly affects the use of the Internet and makes it more suitable for certain types of content; yet it also extends to the function of the medium in social interactions. As Donna Haraway has argued, the very structures of identity and community formation are transformed by the coevalness of cyberspace. Groups are clearly brought together in time and space across previously insuperable boundaries. At the same time, however, the cohesiveness of these groups relies on relatively stable mechanisms of identification such as gender, race, ethnicity, occupation, class, and nationality.[37] Through this experience of virtual space and movement, moreover, the simultaneous conjoining of multiple locations has become more apparent and, at the same time, forms part of the codification of cyberspace through which digital data is interpreted.

In addition to reproducing existing markers of community identity, the spatiality of Puerto Rican Web sites also codifies the processes of virtual self-fashioning. That is, it fosters communication among users and, at the same time, underscores the ways in which traditional locations of puertorriqueñidad are transformed in cyberspace. In a personal web page entitled, "Mi bohio nuyorkino," (My Puerto Rican Hut) the bohio of the title is superimposed on the center of a map of Puerto Rico.[38] Just behind the island, the New York City skyline occupies most of the horizon with open ocean and sky on either side. Similarly, in a site called "New York Boricua," the main page features a frame in the upper portion which includes the time and temperature in San Juan and Spanish Harlem (as identified in an animated caption beneath each) on either side of the frame, flanking a small oval in the center (figure 3). The left half of the oval features the edge of El Morro and is thus clearly identified as San Juan. As in the case of "Mi bohio nuyorkino," the right half includes the buildings from the Manhattan skyline. The resulting synthesis, furthermore, constitutes a new spatiality that could not be found in the physical world. At the same time, however, both sites rely on a system of iconographic symbolism: the juxtaposition of New York and Puerto Rico can only be apprehended through the recognition of specific buildings and representations of these places. This use of referentiality and the demarcation of space also

**Figure 3. The header that appears on the main page of** *nyboricua.com*

point to the specifically virtual nature of this spatiality. The images depend on an implied visitor who is already familiar with the architectural and geographic landscapes depicted. Meaning is thus transmitted and interpreted through this common familiarity: both the creator of the page and its visitor share an iconographic literacy that can only be understood by having traveled to the places themselves or having accessed sufficient images of them previously.

At the same time, the alternate mode of juxtaposition in each case is also a significant component. The layering of the images in "Mi bohio nuyorkino" establishes a particular movement from the bohio situated on Puerto Rico in the foreground and New York in the background.[39] Through this movement and the specific representation of each space, the image also creates a temporality in which the folkloric past of Puerto Rico is conjoined with the modern urban landscape of New York. In this sense, despite their apparent coeval and conterminous juxtaposition, the relative position and imagery of each situates Puerto Rico in New York's past.[40] The representation of the Antillean space in "Mi bohio nuyorkino" is also both individual and universal since it contains a single person or familial dwelling yet also depicts the space of the entire island; the diaspora on the other hand is expressed through the skyscrapers of the very specific location of the other island that is incorporated in the image: Manhattan. Although the skyline has a comparable iconographic function to the bohio, the scale in this case has shifted from the representation of a single dwelling to a collective architectural portrayal that can only be perceived from a vantage point that is outside the island. The image creates a virtual island in which the past and present, individual and collective, local and universal are conjoined in a single location but are not completely equated or fused. In this manner, not only does the artist create a space that could not exist outside of cyberspace, but the image also codifies the experience of the Puerto Rican diaspora itself.

The alternative juxtaposition of insular Puerto Rican places found in "New York boricua" also codifies this experience, yet the compositional analysis in this case is notably different. Rather than layer the spaces or reference them through distinct iconographies, the representation of each space points to a parallel equation. Although the exterior wall of El Morro appears in the foreground of the image, the edges of the two islands are juxtaposed through a hyperbole in which the coast of Puerto Rico is separated from lower Manhattan by only a small canal. The rectangles on either side of the oval, which alternate between displays of the current time and temperature in the two locations—San Juan and Spanish Harlem—identified in the scrolling caption, characterize each space as equally present and dynamic. Hence, as with "Mi bohio newyorkino," the two principal islands associated with the Puerto Rican experience are joined but not fused; nevertheless, in this case, the juxtaposition is not depicted in terms of temporal or spatial movement but instead as the conjoining of culturally significant locations. In fact, given the linguistic ambiguity of the term boricua, the title could be interpreted alternately as "Puerto Rican New York" or "New York Puerto Rican."[41] This ambiguity destabilizes even the grammatical hierarchy in which either the place or the individual would be subordinated to the other in the articulation of identity. The experience of the diaspora in this case is expressed as one that is constantly produced and reproduced in the present and that relies on a fluid interaction between space and its inhabitants.

The virtual island constructed in "New York boricua" codifies the experience of the diaspora, but it also points to the function of the Internet itself. As George Landow has pointed out in *Hypertext 2.0*, the popularity of the Internet has been based largely on its ability to provide access to places and activities that would otherwise remain outside the purview of daily existence. In most of the cases he examines, the "access" provided is directly linked to commercial interest and non-normative activities such as gambling and pornography. Nevertheless, in their relatively explicit commercialism, these sites underscore an underlying function of the Web: they allow users to temporarily enter a world that they might otherwise not be able or want to inhabit outside of virtual reality and, at the same time, potentially maintain the stability and anonymity of a private or familiar location.[42] On the one hand, the small oval containing El Morro and part of the Manhattan skyline that appears at the top of the page alludes to and reconfigures the space of the two islands. On the other, however, it also functions as a window that points to the voyeuristic component of Internet access through which visitors may peer into and, to some extent, virtually enter the space of the diasporic experience.

The capacity of the Web to accommodate this production of space becomes perhaps even more apparent in sites entitled, "Growing Up Nuyorican" and "boricuadesterrao." On the center of the principal page of "Growing Up," designed by Samuel García, a small island with a single palm tree appears floating on a very thin horizon.

Unlike the cases analyzed above, this island is not geographically specific. It contains no structures or recognizable landmarks; instead, it contains only the palm tree at its center and, in fact, is not much larger than that object (i.e., the diameter of the island closely approximates the height of the tree). Rather than depict Puerto Rico, Manhattan, or any other specific insular location, the image is evocative of the trope of the deserted island. The background of the entire page, against which the insular scene is set, is a panoramic view of the night sky filled with stars and celestial objects. Hence, the small insular icon and its ocean horizon appear to float in outer space. This image, furthermore, serves as a repeating border that appears between sections of the page containing content such as a picture of García's mother, favorite song lyrics, recent news, and announcements. In this sense, the virtual island underscores the power of the internet to overcome traditional separations: the imagery of the deserted island floating in the cosmos suggests isolation, disconnectedness, and the loss of the homeland. Yet through its function as a border that frames the content of the page, the island has been reterritorialized as a mechanism that demarcates—and thus creates—spaces of personal identity, communication, and connection.

Similar imagery is used in boricuadesterrao.com. In this case, the site is not a personal Web page but a virtual catalog featuring items of Puerto Rican folklore. The logo on the top of the page also features a small island containing two palm trees but no other distinguishing. The themes of disconnectedness and loss are reinforced by the title of the company: Boricua Desterrao refers to a displaced Puerto Rican who has been removed from his homeland. The company's current purpose, according to the Web site, is to provide access to cultural crafts and folklore for those individuals residing outside the island who might otherwise not have access to such items:

> Boricua Desterrao began operations in 1999 as a catalog operation, selling miscellaneous home decoration items by local artisans. As some of our catalogs began making their way overseas via family members . . . we began to receive inquiries from the United States . . . We then realized the need of

Puertorricans [*sic*] abroad to get affordable Puertorrican goods, not easily obtained outside Puerto Rico. We do not sell $1500 paintings, $500 carvings or anything remotely over-priced or exclusive. The publication of a catalog is very expensive, time consuming, inflexible and non-interactive. Hence, our evolution into an Internet Store with its instant feedback and very attractive pricing.[43]

As a result, despite their distinct purposes, both "Growing Up" and "boricuadesterrao" present cyberspace as a means to overcome the isolation and disconnection that are potentially engendered by diasporic displacement.

I do not mean to suggest, however, that the difference in purpose between these two sites is insignificant. With the exception of "boricuadesterrao," the examples discussed thus far are personal Web pages designed primarily for networking and sharing information with other individuals. In each case, the virtual island represents an amalgam of the various sites and places that the page's owner claims as personally significant. Hence, the owners are able to construct a personal homeland that conjoins various real and imagined locations. Although these sites are not designed to generate significant profit, they certainly depend on a commercial economy. The proposed exchange—even if it is only on a personal level—requires that both parties have the necessary access to the Web. The sites themselves exist, moreover, thanks to corporate sponsorship that supports secondary advertising: the source of the page is maintained by a server that profits through subscriptions and advertising that appear on several of the pages. In this way, the exchange of information presupposes that both parties have the capability and desire to function as consumers.

In the case of more commercial sites, the consumerist role of the visitors is more explicit. In these instances, the raison d'être of the site is to appeal to the needs of visitors as clients. According to the description cited above, Boricua Desterrao altered its corporate structure in order to meet the needs of its customers more efficiently, and its current incarnation as an internet store is designed to maximize the selling potential of the web and thus appeal to a mass consumer who is specifically seeking moderately priced goods.[44] A particularly poignant example of the evolving packaging of culture to maximize its allure for Puerto Rican consumers can be found on "coqui.net." As with the Hawai'ian controversy discussed earlier, the iconography of the autochthonous creature codifies the complex function of highly local(ized) cultural symbols in cyberspace. Unlike the Web sites discussed thus far, coqui.net is a commercial portal that features information about and links to various companies and services located in Puerto Rico. Of course, the name of the site itself is significant since it invokes the coquí and, by extension, the cultural mythology and symbolism connected to the tiny frog. In this context, the concept of a coquí-net is significant because it suggests that the site constructs a space on the Internet in which the coquí's domain is extended beyond the physical boundaries of the island. The welcome page of the site serves as the default home page for coqui.net subscribers and as the primary entry to the services offered for users from outside the network who access the service via the Web. It features a coquí inside a small square in the form of a central processing unit that is wired to a series of buttons that function as links to the various content areas offered—i.e., news, help, information, user's manual, search, and so on. In this sense, the technology of the computer is used metaphorically to represent the movement enabled by coquí.net. Navigation through coquí.net mimics the service being provided: the coquí is enclosed within a particular finite domain, and it is able to gain access to other spaces through the electronic connections without having to fully abandon its current surroundings, just as Puerto Ricans can move around the world without abandoning their cultural home. The problems and possibilities of the coquí's movement through cyberspace are repeatedly codified in the images found throughout the site. In fact, in a former incarnation, the principal page of coqui.net depicted a large specimen (relative to the scale of the illustration, that is, since its body obscured approximately half the represented island of Puerto Rico) leaping vertically into the air from the island depicted on a globe.[45] In this way, the World Wide Web provides a conduit through which the exclusively autochthonous creature can travel freely without threatening its purportedly site-specific existence.

As the home page of an Internet service provider, the imagery on the site is constantly changing to reflect new developments in corporate sponsors and within the services provided directly by coqui.net. Throughout these changes, however, the expanding domain of the coquí—that is, the ability of this inherently local inhabitant to move freely beyond its traditional boundaries—is a recurring theme. When coqui.net first introduced high-speed Internet access—which they referred to as "coquik" service—the innovation was advertised by a coquí sitting astride a rocket that shot across the screen. Once again, the image represents the benefit being offered by coquí.net: not only can the coquí travel through an expanding domain, but new technological developments will allow this movement to be faster and more efficient.

More recently, the help page of the site has begun to incorporate similar imagery. Users who click on the help button connected to the coquí on the welcome page encounter a rather different representation of the creature:

as with the coquí leaping into cyberspace that no longer appears on the site, this coquí soars through the cosmos in the foreground of the image and moves away from the globe depicted in the background. It is being pursued by a spaceship, which apparently is firing lasers at it, and the phrase "HELP... HELP... HELP..." appears diagonally above its head. In this case, the representation speaks to the potential hazards of the coquí's expanding domain: as users move through cyberspace, they may encounter unexpected dangers. Because of its insertion at the top of the help page, however, this image does not imply that such threats should impede exploration. Instead, this section is designed to offer the necessary access to assistance that will allow users to overcome any difficulties that they may encounter. In this case, more importantly, the coquí is not characterized as the invading element whose survival depends on its ability to adapt to a new environment. In fact, the conventional paradigm of the deterritorialized immigrant is inverted: the coquí maintains its native status and the other creatures it encounters in its travels are portrayed as alien forces. The perils the coquí may encounter, therefore, are not attributed to its status as a foreigner but to the inhospitable aggression of the other inhabitants of its expanded domain. The coquí can move freely through the cosmos in its natural state without the need of a spaceship or any protective apparatus and can simultaneously protect itself from more denaturalized forces through its access to the coquí-net.

Of course, this use of iconography should be considered in the context of coquí.net's content, avowed function, and apparent usage. As I mentioned earlier, the site is a gateway that acts as the launch page for the company's Internet access and contains links to media and companies in Puerto Rico. Their site has featured language such as "Providing the Finest Internet Access to all of Puerto Rico" and "Providing Internet Access to Puerto Rico and the Caribbean." Hence, it is a tool that allows users to easily connect to Puerto Rican industry and infrastructure from anywhere in the world, whether they are located in Puerto Rico or in the diaspora. According to coquí.net, the site is utilized predominantly by individuals who were born or lived in Puerto Rico or who have close relatives on the island. More specifically, although the service does not require users to provide demographic information or personal histories, most of the patrons of the "micoquí.com" feature (through which users can personalize their access of the site) identify themselves as current or former residents of the island. In this sense, coqui.net provides its users with the ability represented symbolically through its iconography: they are able to both travel beyond the island and stay connected to it.

## Where No Coquí Has Gone Before: The Enduring Island and the Performance of Community

In the end, the representation of diasporic identities on the Internet both reaffirms and reconfigures existing paradigms of community self-definition. Although this assertion should seem relatively self-evident given the existing research on the topic, the specific use of Puerto Rican insularity in this process proves more significant. Despite the changes in demographics and in the mechanisms of self-representation, the island continues to function as a principal trope in Puerto Rican self-fashioning. On the one hand, this ongoing function of insularity can be viewed as a continuity within the cultural discourse. The global *island* of cyberspace carves out or demarcates a space on the Web that highlights and preserves a separate, distinctive puertorriqueñidad while at the same time facilitating and inherently insisting on connections with the world (real and virtual) beyond it. That is, these constructions draw on and contribute to the complex representations of the island that had already become a defining characteristic of Puerto Rican subjectivity. However, insularity also codifies the dynamics of the formation and maintenance of community in the diaspora. The reterritorialization of the island in cyberspace demarcates a delimited space that is both separate and connected to a wide array of locations. In this sense, via the Internet, insularity achieves the paradoxical otherness alluded to in the epigraph quoted from "La otra isla de Puerto Rico." Through the ambiguity of his title, Manuel Ramos Otero questions the idea of the homeland as the exclusive (or even primary) locus of enunciation of Puerto Rican discourse. In cyberspace, the ambiguity of the island's otherness does not destabilize the definition of the community but instead becomes part of the semantic code through which virtual spatiality is produced.

Through this combination of real and imagined spaces, the global and virtual island conforms to Foucault's definition of a heterotopia: "The heterotopia is capable of juxtaposing in a single real place several spaces, several sites that are in themselves incompatible. . . . Either their role is to create a space of illusion that exposes every real space . . . as still more illusory . . . or else . . . to create a space that is other, another real space, as perfect, as meticulous, as well arranged as ours is messy, ill constructed and jumbled. This latter type would be the heterotopia, not of illusion but of compensation, and I wonder if certain colonies have not functioned somewhat in this manner."[46] Based on this understanding of the construction of space, a new relationship emerges between insularity in cyberspace and its rhetorical predecessors. Not only do the virtual islands analyzed here enact the spatialized demarcation of communal relationships described by both Lefebvre and Foucault, but they also function as heterotopias in that they codify the very dynamics of spatiality through which the community defines itself. These virtual islands are spaces that simultaneously foster separation from and connection to alternative locations. Moreover, the very processes of globalizing identities are codified through these representations of insularity. In this sense, as with More's *Utopia*, the island acts as a heuristic device through which an idealized version of the community can be enacted. These virtual islands also closely parallel Pedreira's *Insularismo* in that the island constitutes a device through which Puerto Rican self-fashioning is achieved. Rather than being bound to a particular definition of geographic determinism, the reterritorialization of the island in cyberspace dialogues with the practices of globalization as it simultaneously carves out new real-and-imagined spaces of puertorriqueñidad. Hence, virtual insularity highlights the processes through which Puerto Rican spatiality is produced and reconfigured.

The prevalence of the cosmos as a recurring theme in the Web pages discussed above is also evidence of this function. Whether as background image or represented as the new domain of the coquí, the iconographic location of virtual islands in outer space underscores the desire to construct an alternative spatiality that transcends existing boundaries and thus cannot be contained by traditional geographical configurations of community. In this sense, the representation of Puerto Rican spatiality on coquí.net, while clearly playful and humorous, can also be seen as quite astute. The cosmocoquí soaring through extraterrestrial space dramatizes the reterritorialization of virtual islands. Not only does the coquí now have access to the world without having to abandon its native habitat, but its movement extends beyond the conventional parameters of human experience. The construction of Puerto Rican spatiality on the Internet offers the coquí's human counterparts the promise of a similar transglobal (or even extraglobal) mobility. The insularity of cyberspace maintains the specificity of the Puerto Rican cultural landscape while also facilitating unlimited connections to and movement through a more universalized space. In fact there is an inherent homology between the diaspora, the Internet, and the performance of community in a globalizing world. The construction of virtual islands in cyberspace occurs at the point of convergence between the dream of the diaspora and the utopia of the information age: they are a clearly demarcated nonspace that is located both nowhere and everywhere, and they allow for the simultaneous permanent connection to the homeland without compromising the unfettered movement toward and through other places.

The importance of the diaspora in discourses of self-definition is becoming increasingly undeniable. Not only is the population of Puerto Ricans living outside the island almost as large as that of those who reside permanently in Puerto Rico, but the increased mobility and developing technologies have also engendered the constant and virtually instantaneous exchange of information among communities in spite of the distances between them. In a sense, insularity is rendered insufficient and anachronistic. At the same time, nevertheless, the island as a national allegory has proven surprisingly malleable, and, once again, appears available to an innovative reinterpretation of its significance. Through the construction of virtual islands, the spatialized locality of Puerto Rican discourse is reterritorialized in a global context.

## Virtual Islands and Translocal Caribeñidad

In the face of growing emigration and globalization, a tension inevitably develops between conventional demarcations of identity and the contemporary conditions of Caribbean communities. As I have argued here, however, insularity and translocality are not necessarily incompatible. The iconography of Puerto Rican Web sites offers a particularly rich and salient example of how spatiality is reterritorialized in this new context. Nonetheless, contemporary Cuban, Dominican, and Puerto Rican literary and cultural texts increasingly engage the rhetoric of insularity in dynamic and innovative ways. They do not subscribe uncritically to the fetishistic attachment to geographic models. Instead, they underscore the very paradoxical status that islands acquire in a translocal context. In this way, insular tropes codify the experience of demographic and geopolitical shifts and their impact on Caribbean identities.

# Conclusion:
# Beyond the Island

As I have asserted throughout this study, islands are the most salient feature of the Antillean landscape. At the same time, their prominence is also equally apparent in discourses of national and regional self-definition. Just as insular geography delineates the social space of the Caribbean, the rhetoric of insularity demarcates Caribbean identity and authority. According to cultural discourse, what makes Antillean people who and what they are can be understood as a direct result of insular existence. In a similar fashion, in his exchange with Juan Ramón Jiménez cited earlier, José Lezama Lima insists that insularity defines Caribbean (self)expression. In this manner, beyond the specific traits associated with them, islands become the symbol of Antillean legitimacy and authority.

The collection of contemporary Cuban art of the Museo Nacional de Bellas Artes (National Museum of Fine Arts) in Havana includes a work by Antonio Eligio Fernández, commonly known as Tonel. The piece is a large installation that sits on a wall of the museum. From a distance, the image is readily recognizable as a map of the world (figure 4).

A close examination of the piece reveals that the map is comprised entirely of small, wooden carvings in the shape of the island of Cuba (figure 5). The installation also includes the title of the piece, *Mundo soñado* [Dream World], in large block letters beneath the map.[1] Through this image, Tonel symbolically depicts Cuba's ideal vision of globalization: the island of Cuba remains wholly unaltered and, in this state, it remaps the rest of the world.

Of course, Tonel's piece offers a playful—or perhaps melancholic—commentary on the discrepancy between the dominant rhetoric of Cuban nationalism and the emergent world order. Even as the internal reality of the island is significantly reshaped by post-Soviet restructuring, Cubans

Figure 4. Tonel, *Mundo soñado*. Installation, Contemporary Cuban Art Collection, Museo Nacional de Bellas Artes, Havana, 2003. Ink and wood, Dimensions variable.

continue to dream of a world in which their perfectly preserved autochthony serves as the principal model for global development. Rather than be subsumed by the capitalism and neoliberalism of external powers, Tonel's image depicts a hyperbolic inversion of the more common patterns of transnational interactions and their cultural impact.

At the same time, however, *Mundo soñado* also underscores another prevalent phenomenon in Caribbean cultural discourse: the representations of the island allows Cuban, Dominican, and Puerto Rican artists and writers to achieve something symbolically that is otherwise unattainable. They can envision an alternative relationship between territory and power and thereby carve out a legitimate (and legible) space for themselves. In the face of political factors that might call their self-determination into question, these groups can demarcate their cultural autonomy through the supposed relationship between insular terrain and identity. Consequently, insularity can be understood as a mode of post-colonial self-fashioning: it fosters and sustains the articulation of local subjectivity and nationalism in spite of the historical influence of external, imperial powers in the region.

Indeed, this function of insularity may explain its continued deployment under changing conditions that would presumably render it inappro-

Figure 5. Detail from Tonel's *Mundo soñado*, featuring the depiction of the island of Cuba and the reproduction of that depiction in order to comprise the surrounding continental land masses. (N.B. The other Antilles—perhaps because these smaller islands could not be as easily represented through multiple reproductions of the Cuban cartographic image—are distinctly absent.)

priate or anachronistic. The instances of spatial incongruity that I have addressed in this study inevitably raise the question of why insularity persists as a principal category of self-definition despite its extraordinary polyvalence, contradictory status and even geographic irrelevance. Queer authors challenge the hegemonic equation of insular space and normative sexuality, yet they construct their critique in terms of a rhetorically equivalent spatiality. The presence of an adversary within the borders of the island is refuted, not by means of an alternative configuration of national territoriality, but through the performative reassertion of insular sovereignty. The increasing translocality of Caribbean spaces does not immediately displace insularity as a central mode of self-representation; instead, insularity is reconfigured—either productively or problematically—in response to this shift. These cases therefore demonstrate that the importance of insularity transcends the particular circumstances of geography.

In fact, the extension beyond the conventional island-nation points to the ability of insular self-fashioning to stage the fundamental drama of Caribbean identity. Insularity continues to function as a principal mode of self-definition because of its compensatory potential: Hispanic Antillean authors and artists can lay claim to the overt demarcation of insular space in order to symbolically negate the islands' imperfect or incomplete historical status as independent nations. Recent political and demographic changes increasingly belie the underlying conceit that the nation and the island should be perfectly equivalent. In doing so, they both play into and work against the fetishistic attachment to insular identification that evolves in the absence or lack of overt national authority.

In this manner, moreover, Hispanic Caribbean self-fashioning offers a compelling case study of local specificity and national persistence in the face of increasing transnationalism, neoliberalism, and geopolitical restructuring. According to many scholars, the role of the nation has significantly diminished. Michael Hardt and Antonio Negri, for example, assert that the nation-state has become increasingly irrelevant in the current organization of capital and power. Nevertheless, the idea of the nation and its affective power still thrive in spite of the relative disappearance of traditional borders that has been engendered by increasingly transnational markets and by the concomitant flow of capital and movement of labor. Historically, subjectivity and identity have been constructed in terms closely linked to conventional definitions of nations and nationalism. Accordingly, however retrograde it may seem, the attachment to political borders persists. The nation therefore remains highly crucial as the primary space of subject formation even as its precise position is radically redefined in an increasingly globalized world.

To some extent, this phenomenon can be traced throughout the contemporary landscape.[2] The conflict between traditional and emergent paradigms, however, becomes even more acute in those contexts in which nationalism tends to be viewed as a failed, impossible, or troublesome project. In political terms, only a small portion of the contemporary globe can reasonably lay claim to a firmly established (and relatively stable) national history that can now alternately be embraced or discarded. Of course, the cases examined here do not fall into this category. I contend, however, that this quality makes them more relevant rather than less so: through their investment in a system that has often led to disenfranchisement and disadvantage, they highlight the essential potential and limits of that system. My analysis, moreover, specifically focuses on populations and instances in which the ideals articulated by the dominant nationalist agenda prove, at best, problematic. In the case of queer sexuality, contested spaces, and the diaspora, the proposed subject is one that could not realistically be inserted into the identity demarcated by conventional narratives of insularity. The desired subjectivity, therefore, is one that is at odds with the established vision of national spatiality. Given this vexed relationship, these cases call attention precisely to the limitations and contradictions that are fundamentally produced and reproduced by this vision.

The significance of these examples thus stems from an underlying condition—the perpetual reinscription of a rhetoric of identity that is ill-equipped to produce the desired subjectivity—along with a natural geography that heightens the visibility of processes of self-fashioning. Because of the clear demarcation of insular terrain and the role of insularity in Hispanic Caribbean cultural discourse, national configurations of self-definition prove especially persistent. The preservation of traditional spatiality (albeit delimited in terms of alternate spaces or places) constitutes a palimpsestic resurgence of the underlying nationalist paradigms that have neither been fully established nor completely eradicated; the unrealized project of the nation is thus reenacted through the (re)assertion of insular autonomy. Under these conditions, the rhetoric of insularity continually performs the national specificity and legitimacy that were never firmly founded and simultaneously negotiates emergent transnational and global paradigms of identity. In this fashion, contemporary reconfigurations of insularity dramatize the central conflict of postcolonial nationalisms in the Hispanic Caribbean.

Consequently, despite the diminishing centrality of insular geography as a universal characteristic of Caribbean experience, cultural discourse has not truly moved beyond the island. Even if the Antilles are not wholly identified with the fixed and bound terrain of insular geography, literary, and cultural production continues to engage insularity as a mode that must be suitably reproduced, modified, or supplanted. In a contemporary context, geographically determined models are often inherently inappropriate or counter-productive. Nevertheless, insular tropes and the notion of bound demarcation endure as principal methods of Hispanic Caribbean self-fashioning. Hence, cultural discourse beyond the island has not necessarily moved away from the concept of Antillean spatiality as a privileged site of community formation. In the end, islands act as a discourse machine that persistently produces authoritative identity in the Hispanic Caribbean.

# Notes

## Preface

1. I do not mean to suggest that they do not perform a similar function in other literary traditions. Nevertheless, my study will be limited to the manifestation and implications of this function in the writing of Europe and the Americas.

2. As has been widely documented, Defoe's account was probably inspired by the historical account of Alexander Selkirk. Selkirk, a Scottish sailor, was shipwrecked and stranded for several years on one of the Juan Fernández islands, off the coast of Chile. In fact, one of the islands in the group was subsequently renamed Alejandro Selkirk Island. Another, Isla Más de la Tierra, is also known as Robinson Crusoe Island—thus underscoring the supposed connection between the historical experiences and Defoe's fictional account.

3. It should be noted that remote oceanic islands and deserted islands are not perfectly equivalent. As Mary Louise Pratt has demonstrated, for example, imperial eyes often have the uncanny ability to see only the natural landscape, rendering its inhabitants invisible. In this manner, oceanic islands that are viewed as distant, isolated, and even "uninhabitable" paradoxically can contain substantial native populations. Although these islands presumably lie outside the everyday experience of the travelers that arrive from distant lands, the exact opposite is true for the residents of populated islands. Within the literary tradition of insular tales I am discussing here, however, the question of native inhabitants is either elided or is a source of tension in the narrative or drama depicted. Hence, the islands are portrayed as relatively uninhabited, even if that depiction would be refuted by extratextual demographic analysis.

4. Of course, Shakespeare's drama precedes Defoe's by about a century. Defoe's novel may have drawn on earlier literary precursors such as *The Tempest* that offer tales of shipwrecks and characters stranded on deserted islands. Nevertheless, as Deleuze's discussion of the trope affirms, *Robinson Crusoe* is frequently cited as the paradigmatic example of such tales. Hence, I cite Shakespeare's play—perhaps, anachronistically—as a text that parallels the subsequent novel.

5. Most notably, Ernest Renan and Aimé Césaire have both written alternative version of Shakespeare's play.

6. As Mary Pat Brady cogently argues in her work, space becomes an urgent issue in Chicano literature because of the repeated reterritorialization of the terrain historically

tied to the Mexican cultural homeland. In this context, the myth of Aztlán challenges the historical processes through which people of Mexican descent have been perpetually distanced (in both geographic and temporal terns) from their place(s) of origin.

## 1. Between Island and Nation

1. Flaherty, *Once On This Island*, 6.
2. The *Requerimiento* recited by the Spanish conquerors, for example, expressed their desired intention to civilize the peoples they encountered and incorporate them as subjects of the Spanish crown. Officially, the conquistadores were expected to read this proclamation to the inhabitants of the lands that they were claiming. In practice, however, the fulfillment of this requirement revealed a slightly different relationship with the native population than the one suggested by the language of the text. Not only would the document presumably be incomprehensible to its implied audience (since they were written in a language that they could not understand), but the conquistadores frequently performed the ritual well before approaching the inhabitants themselves. In this sense, the performance of the ritual inaugurates the imperial enterprise that follows: the project of colonization is expressed in terms of civilization, education, and indoctrination, which would require careful interaction and negotiation with the colonized subjects, but is more generally realized through the unequivocal imposition of Spanish imperial power that obviates or elides the authoritative exchanges implied by the stated objectives.
3. In the Spanish American context, the term *criollo* refers to an individual of European descent who is born in the Americas. According to the hierarchy of colonial society, these individuals were considered inherently inferior based on the circumstances of their birth. As products of American terrain, they belonged to a lower social class than their ethnically equivalent counterparts who had been born in Europe and migrated to the New World.
4. Of course, unlike most of Latin America, Cuba and Puerto Rico did not establish their independence from Spain at the beginning of the nineteenth century. Instead, they remained Spanish colonies until the conclusion of the Spanish-American War in 1898. Although this difference in political conditions radically alters the context in which identities are articulated, it does not impede the construction of homologous discursive practices in Cuba, Puerto Rico, and the incipient Latin American nations. Given both this understanding and the interpretation of "nationalism" advanced within postcolonial studies, the terms "nation" and "national identity" are used here anachronistically to refer to the practices that exist even in the absence of a formally established nation.
5. The principal issue debated is whether the Caribbean is restricted to the Antilles or if the continental nations with Caribbean coastlines also constitute part of the region. Nevertheless, the question of the inclusion of individual nations in the region is not based solely on their proximity to Caribbean waters. Some scholars have argued that areas beyond the Caribbean Sea should also be considered part of the region based on historical and cultural commonalities.

On the other hand, the location of an island within the West Indies does not necessarily guarantee its regional classification either. In the introduction to Juan Flores's *Divided Borders*, Jean Franco notes the curious exclusion of Puerto Rico from a map of Latin America that includes the other Hispanic Antilles: "As I walked alongside the map tracing the waterways, cities and mountains from Tierra del Fuego to Cuba I noticed something odd about the Caribbean—Puerto Rico was missing" (9).

6. Similar cases of the conflict between Balkanization and unification could be cited outside the Caribbean. I mention it here, however, since it constitutes the basis for the polemic within Caribbean definitions. Nevertheless, the specific situation of the Caribbean and its relationship to parallel dynamics in other geographic areas will be addressed in this chapter as well.

7. Benítez Rojo, *The Repeating Island*, 1.

8. Although the original conquest and colonization of the region occurs under Spanish rule, other European nations struggle for control throughout the sixteenth, seventeenth and eighteenth centuries. As a result, Spain retains control of three of the four major Antilles, and the remaining islands are divided among the French, the English, and the Dutch.

9. It should be noted that the relationship between canonicity and Caribbean literature is far from irrelevant in Torres Saillant's study. Nevertheless, he stresses that scholars should not depart from a comparison that seeks to equate Caribbean works with canonical ones, since this approach diminishes their capacity to truly evaluate these works. Furthermore, in his conclusions, he proposes that such an in-depth analysis of works in acanonical terms may reveal the underlying value system that causes certain literary traditions to be privileged while others are marginalized. That is, by developing a literary analysis that does not depend on canonical thinking, critics may foster an ability to deconstruct established Western canonicity.

10. Torres Saillant, *Caribbean Poetics*, 14.

11. Ibid., 17.

12. Ibid., 23.

13. Jiménez visited Cuba in 1937, and this visit prompted the publication of *Coloquio* first in 1937, in *Revista Cubana* in 1938 and then by Colección Valoración Literaria. Subsequently, the piece is also included in several anthologies of Lezamian prose.

14. Lezama, *Coloquio*, 3 (my translation).

15. Ibid., 6 (my translation).

16. Cruz-Malavé, *Primitivo implorante*, 34 (my translation).

17. Through a comparison with other categories established by Lezama, Cruz-Malavé offers a more sophisticated understanding of the rhetorical function of the *mito del insularismo*. He demonstrates that the elevation of Cuban ontology through insularity develops concurrently with the subordination of other ontological categories, such as *sensibilidad negra*. That is, although insularity is postulated in order to subvert hierarchies that marginalize Cuban poetic expression, it simultaneously creates alternative hierarchies that marginalize certain forms of this expression (39).

18. XX states that the siesta can be used to transform one's relationship with death and a suicidal impulse, through concentrating on the topic. Although it is unclear why the siesta constitutes the necessary moment for such reflection, XX's prescription definitively establishes it as a privileged—and, of course, specifically tropical—experience.

19. Lezama, *X y XX*, 136 (my translation).

20. Ibid., 141 (my translation).

21. Pedreira's essay actually predates Lezama's articulations on the subject: *Insularismo* is published in 1934 and *Coloquio* in 1937. Moreover, it is quite possible that Lezama's thinking on insularity was influenced in part by Pedreira's text.

## NOTES TO CHAPTER 1

22. Within *Insularismo*, there is some discrepancy as to the exact status of this essence. On the one hand, Pedreira insists on its existence and the need to rediscover and recuperate it. At certain moments in the essay, however, he suggests that Puerto Ricans must create such an essence. Nevertheless, despite these contradictions, Pedreira definitively postulates the emergence of a Puerto Rican essence as a key element in his prescription. Consequently, the reversal of historical processes constitutes a necessary prerequisite to (re)initiating its evolution—even if this reversal is ultimately designed to recover something that ostensibly never existed. In other words, the solution Pedreira proposes remains relevant to my analysis, even if his argument relies on mutually contradictory claims.

23. Unless otherwise indicated, all quotations of Pedreira's text in English are taken from Rivera Serrano's translation.

24. As Pedreira himself avows in other sections of the text, the exterior is not associated consistently with peril or threat within the Puerto Rican psyche. In fact, in the chapter entitled, "Nos coge el holandés" (The Dutchman Will Catch Us), he cites an example of the jubilation brought by arriving ships during a specific historical period: "En el aislamiento impenetrable en que vivía nuestra colonia, ponía una nota pintoresca la visita de cualquier barco anunciada clamorosamente a campana herida, mientras el pueblo aglomeraba en la bahía gritando entusiasmado: "¡Velas! ¡Velas!" (Pedreira, *Insularismo*, 111). [Such an occurrence, clamorously announced for all to hear as people gathered at the bay shouting enthusiastically, "Ships! Ships!" provided a lively interval during the impenetrable isolation in which the colony lived.] (Pedreira, *Insularismo: An Insight*, 94) Nevertheless, Pedreira argues that the fear of the exterior instilled in the Puerto Rican mentality by specific historical experience can be seen as a paradigmatic manifestation of a more general unwillingness—or, at the very least, lack of desire—to explore and connect with the world beyond the island's borders.

25. Pedreira, *Insularismo*, 115.

26. Pedreira, *Insularismo: An Insight*, trans. Aoife Rivera Serrano, 97.

27. The other principle metaphor in *Insularismo* is one of illness. Although a complete discussion of the implications of this metaphor are beyond the scope of this project, several significant scholarly works address such metaphors in other texts. See, for example: Elaine Scarry, *The Body in Pain*; Michael Solomon, *The Literature of Misogyn*; and Susan Sontag, *Illness as Metaphor*.

28. Pedreira, *Insularismo*, 14 (my translation).

29. Ibid., 145.

30. Pedreira, *Insularismo: An Insight*, 128.

31. Flores, *Divided Borders*, 18.

32. Benítez Rojo, *Isla que se repite*, xiv.

33. Benítez Rojo, *Repeating Island*, 11.

34. Ibid., 10.

35. Although both possibilities exist independently, the may also coexist. That is, a border may both reinforce and subvert existing definitions of national identity. Anzaldúa characterizes her own identity in terms of living on the border. She argues that this existence generates alternative subjectivities but also simultaneously precludes others. In his work, *An Other Tongue*, Alfred Arteaga argues that a single sign can have multiple referents and thus combine contradictory functions. Hence, through the concepts of nation, ethnicity, and alterity, the border is inscribed in terms that control access to subjectivity.

At the same time, however, the reterritorialization of these concepts can circumvent this control and cause the borders of subjectivity to become permeable.

36. Derrida, "Signature, Event, Context," 317.

37. It should be noted that the canonical status of Hostos's work is established in part by Pedreira. I would argue, of course, that Pedreira's identification of Hostos as a founding father of Puerto Rican literature is no mere coincidence but, instead, that Hostos's treatment of insularity as a defining rhetorical trope advances Pedreira's own project. That is, Hostos constitutes a literary "beginning"—in Edward Said's sense—for Pedreira since he originates a trajectory that would lead to *Insularismo*.

38. For a contemporary, critical edition of *Album* and *Aguinaldo puertorriqueño*, see: Emilio M. Colón. *Primicias de las letras puertorriqueñas*.

39. I will return to a more detailed discussion of this trajectory and its implications in *Enriquillo* in chapter 3.

40. At a conference on Caribbean literatures held at Emory University (April 1999), Rodríguez reflected on the prevalence of insular imagery in her writing and in the work of other Caribbean authors. She suggested that the centrality of the island has limited the ability of these writers to construct visions of the region.

## 2. OUT ELSEWHERE

1. Of course, scholars such as Samuel Delany, Judith Halberstam, Martin F. Manalansan, and José Esteban Muñoz have carefully explored the complex way in which gay culture is represented and reterritorialized in the mainstream media. That is, increasing visibility does not necessarily imply changing attitudes toward homosexuality.

2. As Halberstam cogently asserts in her work, *In a Queer Time and Place*, critical analyses of space often obscure or mask the underlying intersections with questions of queer temporality. That is, they focus on the cultural logic of spatio-temporal politics and poetics in a manner that effaces questions of identity or non-normative subjectivity. Halberstam points out that, although many theories of space are indebted to Foucault's essays and lectures on heterotopias, few scholars have rigorously examined the inexorable links between this work and Foucault's more widely read scholarship on sexuality and the formation of the state.

3. Most notably, homosexuals were persecuted, forced to wear the (now infamous) pink triangle and sent to concentration camps under the Nazi regime. I do not mean to suggest that the example of the treatment of gay men in Cuba is unique. Instead, I propose that the insular context heightens the visibility (and insistence on) the intersection of masculinity, normativity, and nationalism.

4. Lugo Ortiz, "Community," 129.

5. Although the drama premiered in 1958, the published version of the text did not appear until the following year.

6. Gelpí, *Literatura y paternalismo*, 123–24 (my translation).

7. Barradas, *Apalabramiento*, 27 (my translation).

8. The proposed role of the *nuevos narradores* is also enhanced by the constructions of a poetics of innovation in the collection itself. In *Apalabramiento*, Barradas not only presents an analysis of current narrative trends but charts the development of Puerto Rican literature. His depiction of a generation of narrators who rewrite the paradigms of

their predecessors is reinforced, moreover, by the anthology's overt insertion into national literary history. The work is juxtaposed with René Marqués's *Cuentos puertorriqueños de hoy*. The subtitle of *Apalabramiento*, "Diez cuentistas puertorriqueños de hoy," destabilizes this totalizing reification of the genre; Barradas reconfigures the title so that the collection offers a finite set of current examples of the Puerto Rican short story rather than purporting to offer a definitive compilation thereof.

9. Barradas, *Apalabramiento*, 27 (my translation).

10. Cabrera Infante, "The Death of Virgilio," 10. The "Death of Virgilio" is published as an introduction to the anthology *Cold Tales*, which is a translation of *Cuentos fríos* and other stories not included in the original Spanish edition.

11. Kanzepolsky, "Virgilio Piñera," 149 (my translation).

12. Cristófani Barreto, "Cuentos fríos," 33 (my translation).

13. Santí, "Carne y papel," 58 (my translation).

14. Ibid., 63.

15. Several critics—Latin Americanists as well as those working in other fields—have explored this relationship between biographical interpretation and queer analysis of the writing of a homosexual author (whether openly so or closeted). In her discussion of the work of Gabriela Mistral in *A Queer Mother for the Nation*, for example, Licia Fiol-Matta offers a rigorous and subtle analysis of this relationship. She presents a compelling reading of Mistral's poetics that dialogues with biographical information but that does not allow this information to become a reductive critical lens.

16. Quiroga, "Fleshing Out," 176.

17. Quiroga, *Tropics of Desire*, 121.

18. Moreiras, *Tercer espacio*, 311 (my translation).

19. Piñera, *Poesía*, 25.

20. Piñera, "La isla en peso and Other Poems," unpublished manuscript. (The English text for Piñera's poetry cited here has been provided by Mark Weiss. His translation of "La isla en peso" will be included in his anthology of contemporary Cuban poetry, "The Whole Island," which will be published by University of California Press in 2008.)

21. Piñera, *Poesía*, 32.

22. Piñera, "La isla," trans. Mark Weiss.

23. Piñera, *Poesía*, 38.

24. Piñera, "La isla," trans. Mark Weiss.

25. Piñera, *Poesía*, 29. It should be noted that this passage in "La isla" has been interpreted as a criticism of Lezama's Baroque style. Even if we accept this interpretation, nevertheless, Piñera's criticism of Lezama is based on an inappropriate incorporation of foreign elements.

26. Piñera, "La isla," trans. Mark Weiss.

27. Piñera, *Poesía*, 36.

28. Piñera, "La isla," trans. Mark Weiss.

29. Piñera, *Poesía*, 30.

30. Piñera, "La isla," trans. Mark Weiss.

31. Piñera, *Poesía*, 35.

32. Piñera, "La isla," trans. Mark Weiss.

33. Martin, "Sexualities," 115.

34. Piñera, *Cuentos fríos*, 93.

35. Piñera, *Cold Tales*, 126.

36. Piñera, *Cuentos*, 11.
37. Piñera, *Cold Tales*, 7.
38. Piñera, *Carne de René*, 15.
39. Piñera, *René's Flesh*, 5.
40. Piñera, *Carne de René*, 24.
41. Piñera, *René's Flesh*, 14.
42. Although the portrait is not identified as the work of a specific artist, it depicts—according to the description—the classic image of the martyr's body as punctured by multiple arrows.
43. Piñera, *Carne de René*, 98.
44. Piñera, *René's Flesh*, 104.
45. Piñera, *Carne de René*, 167.
46. Piñera, *René's Flesh*, 159–60.
47. Piñera, *Carne de René*, 161.
48. Piñera, *René's Flesh*, 152.
49. Piñera, *Carne de René*, 257.
50. Piñera, *René's Flesh*, 250.
51. Piñera, *Carne de René*, 76–77.
52. Piñera, *René's Flesh*, 66–67.
53. Piñera, *Carne de René*, 90–91.
54. Piñera, *René's Flesh*, 80.
55. Prieto, *Body of Writing*, 138.
56. The precise geopolitical location of the island is not specified, but several critics have noted a possible historical referent in Cuba. As in other places, individuals with socially stigmatized illnesses in Cuba were often placed in an isolated sanitarium. These locations, which were purportedly once used for patients suffering from leprosy, became clinics in which individuals who had tested positive for HIV were forcibly interned.
57. Several scholars have noted the symbolic significance of characters' names. The text often underscores the ironic use of names or nicknames that underscore precisely what the character lacks or fails to achieve. The character Caimán could therefore be understood as a reference that links the island and its habitants to Cuba since the name was sometimes linked to Cuba (along with the Cayman Islands) during the Colonial Period. The island is thus identified as the antithesis of its historical referent, as the incarnation of what Cuba lacks or has failed to become. And Guillermina de Ferrari has noted, more specifically, the references in the novel that evoke the mandatory *reclusorios* that were established in Cuba for AIDS patients during the 1990s .
58. Sarduy, *Pájaros*, 32.
59. Sarduy, *Beach Birds*, unpublished manuscript, 14. The translations of Sarduy's work (including the rendering of the title as "Beach Birds") have been provided by Suzanne J. Levine and Carol Maier. The passages cited here are from their translation of the novel, which will be published by Otis Books/Seismicity Editions in 2007. An excerpt also appeared in *Fiction Magazine* (vol 19, no. 2, 2005).
60. In his work on medieval literature, Michael Solomon juxtaposes the terms *illness* and *disease*. According to his definitions, disease expresses an otherness that is not present in illness. That is, in contrast with earlier ideas of infirmity—conventionally understood as the result of an internal imbalance—the concept of disease develops based on the notion of infection in which an external agent invades the body and contaminates it.

61. Sarduy, *Pájaros*, 46.
62. Sarduy, *Beach Birds*, trans. Levine and Maier, 20–21.
63. Psychoanalytic studies in particular have focused on the function of memory. Most scholars argue that memory constitutes a narration of past events that is circumscribed by the narrator's current psychological state as much as by historical occurrences. Based on her study of trauma, for example, Cathy Caruth asserts that the nature of memory defies historical accuracy: "the event is not assimilated or experienced fully at the time, but only belatedly, in its repeated possession of the one who experiences it" (Caruth, *Trauma*, 4). According to this evaluation, what is recorded is the experience of trauma rather than the historical events that produced this experience.
64. It should be noted that the inclusion of Bola de Nieve in this supposed youthful memory, the famous Cuban singer and piano played, is one of the cultural references that specifically associates the location of the narrative with Cuba.
65. Sarduy, *Pájaros*, 12.
66. Sarduy, *Beach Birds*, trans. Levine and Maier, 12.
67. Sarduy, *Pájaors*, 40.
68. Sarduy, *Beach Birds*, trans. Levine and Maier, 18.
69. Sarduy, *Pájaros*, 124–25.
70. Sarduy, *Beach Birds*, trans. Levine and Maier, 72.
71. Sarduy, *Pájaros*, 125.
72. Sarduy, *Beach Birds*, trans. Levine and Maier, 72.
73. The term "global divas" is a deliberate reference to Martin F. Manalansan IV's book of the same title. I invoke the title to suggest that the negotiation of queer sexuality and transcultural discourse that Manalansan analyzes in the case of gay Philippino men can elucidate a reading of the intersection of queer sexuality and space in *Sirena Selena*.
74. The title of the English translation is *Sirena Selena*, thus preserving the use of the protagonist's drag name and the initial rhyme of the original title in Spanish. It should also be noted that the term "Sirena" in Spanish refers to either a mythical Siren (as in the creatures that attempted to lure sailors—such as Ulysses—to their deaths) or to a mermaid.
75. Santos Febres, *Sirena Selena*, back cover.
76. Santos Febres, *Sirena Selena vestida de pena*, 20.
77. Santos Febres, *Sirena*, 12.
78. Santos Febres, *Sirena Selena vestida de pena*, 21–2.
79. Santos Febres, *Sirena*, 13.
80. I will return to this scene in my next chapter and discuss how it spatializes international relations. I introduce it here, nonetheless, as a salient and pithy example of the equation of heteronormativity and national development as well as the anxieties provoked by the potential permeability of the island-nation.
81. Luibhéid, *Entry Denied*, ix.

## 3. Dancing with the Enemy

1. Sublette, *Cuba Classics 2*, back cover. The packaging of the album highlights a temporal and spatial displacement. The front cover of the album features a blurred image of a couple dressed in cabaret style costumes. Rather than present the contemporary context in which this music would be performed or listened to, it evokes instead the circum-

stances of night clubs, such as the Tropicana, that are generally associated with tourists and a small, privileged class in a pre-Revolutionary Cuba. In this sense, the image underscores the fetishistic relationship with the island that, according to Silvia Spitta, is often found in the diaspora. Hence, the cover image alludes to the very temporal and spatial division between contemporary Cuban and U.S. cultures that the album is designed to overcome.

2. Of course, the transcultural (and extrapolitical) mobility of music has been analyzed much more rigorously by numerous scholars. Scholars such as Frances Aparicio, Rey Chow, Ruth Glasser, and Fernando Reyes Matta have astutely examined the complex ways in which music functions in particular transcultural and political contexts. I do not intend to offer a similar study of Cuban popular music in this case. Instead, I would simply like to underscore how Sublette uses both the supposed local specificity and potential universality of music to highlight a paradoxical spatial(ized) relationship between Cuba and the United States.

3. The term "pa'lante-pa'trás"—which literally translates to "forward-back"—refers to the basic step used in salsa dancing. As with similar dances, the dancing pair steps backwards and forward in unison, which requires that each movement be matched by an equal and opposing one: the partner must take an equivalent step backwards in order to complement and/or counter the forward step of the other, and then the two must repeat the combination in the opposite direction.

4. At times, the divisiveness within the newly formed Haitian republic only contributed to Dominican discomfort since both Henri Christophe and Alexandre Pétion sought to solidify and expand their respective domains.

5. Wucker, *Why the Cocks Fight*, 13.

6. Balaguer, *La isla al revés*, 83 (my translation).

7. Of course, Balaguer is not the only leader to express anxiety over the corrupting influence of Haitians. Moreover, whether or not the Haitians are specifically identified as the source of corruption, the anxieties surrounding racial, ethnic, and religious purity can be traced throughout Dominican history. In a bitterly ironic incident, for example, Trujillo offers over 100,000 visas to German-Jewish refugees following the Evian Conference in 1938. Not only did this policy help to improve the dictator's image but he presumably believed that the Jewish immigrants would advance his own ethnic cleansing project by "whitening" the Dominican population.

8. The most prominent members of colonial society were those individuals who had been born and educated in Spain. The criollos—who were also ostensibly of purely Spanish or European descent—were considered inferior on the basis of having been born in the New World. These individuals nonetheless enjoyed a higher social status than those of "mixed" or purely indigenous racial heritage.

9. Ramón Menéndez Pidal, for example, accuses Galván of lying based on his alteration of the events recorded in Las Casas's text.

10. Sommer, *Foundational Fictions*, 233.

11. Galván, *Enriquillo*, 63.

12. Galván, *Cross and the Sword*, 4.

13. Galván, *Enriquillo*, 282.

14. Galván, *Cross and the Sword*, 150.

15. Galván, *Enriquillo*, 309.

16. Galván, *Cross and the Sword*, 169.

17. Galván, *Enriquillo*, 225.
18. Galván, *Cross and the Sword*, 110.
19. Galván, *Enriquillo*, 241.
20. Galván, *Cross and the Sword*, 121–22.
21. Galván, *Enriquillo*, 265.
22. Galván, *Cross and the Sword*, 139.
23. Galván, *Enriquillo*, 322–3.
24. Galván, *Cross and the Sword*, 178.
25. Galván, *Enriquillo*, 330–1.
26. Galván, *Cross and the Sword*, 184–85.
27. Galván, *Enriquillo*, 376.
28. Galván, *Cross and the Sword*, 216.
29. Galván, *Enriquillo*, 535.
30. Galván, *Cross and the Sword*, 324.
31. Galván, *Enriquillo*, 540.
32. Galván, *Cross and the Sword*, 327.
33. Galván, *Enriquillo*, 539.
34. Galván, *Cross and the Sword*, 327.
35. Of course, this Europeanization has been effected already in Las Casas's account.
36. As Patricia Seed has cogently argued, the ideologies of the Conquest can be traced in both the arguments that aver the humanity of the Indians and those that negate it. Given that Spanish imperial practices were legitimated through evangelical claims, it became necessary for colonial authorities to imbue the conquered subjects with reason. That is, the defense of indigenous humanity did not constitute an act of charity but, instead, the expression of an ideological strategy. Hence, the arguments that establish indigenous humanity can be equated with those that insist on the inferior nature of Indians, since both reflect the underlying ideological interests of their respective advocates. In this way—as I have argued elsewhere—the representation of indigenous subjectivity in colonial discourse becomes a rhetorical strategy that reflects the ideological project of its author. (Goldman, "El otro," 163.)
37. As I assert in chapter 1, the work of canonical nineteenth century authors such as Salvador Brau, Gertrudis Gómez de Avellaneda, Eugenio María de Hostos, and Cirilio Villaverde addresses the foundational question of insular spatiality in a manner comparable to Galvan's.
38. The Cuban Constitution and Platt Amendment favored exchanges between the two countries, and the United States continued to enjoy a privileged relationship with Cuba until 1959.
39. The building officially houses the U.S. Special Interest Section of the Swiss Embassy. Nevertheless, it is often referred to as the U.S. embassy and is known as the place where Cubans who want to emigrate seek visas to enter the United States.
40. Elián González gained international notoriety in 1999 when he was rescued at sea after his mother died attempting to reach the United States. In the subsequent months, he became the object of an international custody battle. The issue was finally resolved when armed officers entered the family home in Miami, removed Elián, and returned him to the Cuban authorities.
41. According to section 7 of the Platt Amendment (1901), the U.S. government would have the right to purchase or rent Cuban territory in order to maintain indepen-

dence and protect the Cuban people. The agreements signed by President Theodore Roosevelt and the Cuban Senate in 1903 stipulated that the Cuban government would rent the land in Guantánamo "por el tiempo que las necesitare." [for as long as needed.] (Suárez, *A escasos metros*, 216). In 1934, many of the exclusive rights granted to the United States by these documents were abolished by President Franklin D. Roosevelt, but the provisions for the naval base remained unaltered.

42. The English translation was published in 2001; the original text was first published in 1998.

43. In fact, the book is primarily dedicated to the first two members of the Brigada de la Frontera [Border Brigade] who were killed by gunshots emanating from the base in the 1960s: "A Ramón y Luis, cuyas jóvenes vidas fueron vilmente cesadas desde ese pedazo de tierra nuestra usurpado por los yanquis." [To Ramon and Luis, whose young lives were vilely stopped from within this piece of our land that has been usurped by the Yankees] (Suárez, *A escasos metros*, front matter).

44. As I have discussed earlier, during the decades immediately following the revolution, homosexuality is equated with counterrevolutionary sedition—an equation that is exemplified through the incarceration of homosexuals along with other political dissidents in the UMAP military reeducation camps. Consequently, Diego's overtly homosexual behavior and discourse renders him suspect. Nevertheless, David's initial assessment is reinforced by Diego's access to illicit materials (i.e., books and other reading material not approved by the Communist Party, a bottle of whisky), his attitude and his admission that he has had problems with the system in the past. As the relationship evolves, however, David begins to value Diego's perspective. In the end, the film presents this new ideological position—one that reconciles both David's militant commitment to the Cuban Revolution and Diego's criticisms—as a corrective vision that will foster the continued development of the revolutionary project. In this way, *Fresa* presents a modified vision of Cuban communism that can overcome both the errors of the past and the difficulties of the Special Period.

45. Gutiérrez Alea, *Fresa y chocolate*.

46. Gutiérrez Alea, *Strawberry and Chocolate*. (I have elected to use my own translation rather than provide the corresponding dialogue from the captions included in the film. The film's translation of specific words and pharses from this scene—in particular, the rendition of the final line as "Cause it wasn't rammed up his ass!"—might prove misleading in the context of my argument. Admittedly, that translation captures the aggression of Miguel's exclamation, but it does not underscore the relationship between insular and corporeal penetration as clearly as the Spanish. Of course, as both translations of the phrase suggest, Miguel's condemnation of Diego points to a homophobic equation of sexuality, masculinity, and nationalism in which male penetration is seen as fundamentally incompatible with the project of the Cuban Revolution.)

47. As I have suggested in the preceding chapter, according to Miguel's assertion, homosexuality stands in opposition to the revolution as an outside influence that threatens its ideals. In *Tropics of Desire*, José Quiroga offers an insightful analysis of how the relationship between queer subjectivity and revolutionary ideals is constructed in the film. Although I will not closely examine this aspect of the film here, I would like to underscore how Miguel postulates the conflict in terms of a necessary division between the internal mission of communism and the external threat that must be prevented from invading the appropriate body politic.

48. Gutiérrez Alea died during the filming and the movie was completed by his collaborator, Juan Carlos Tabio.

49. Gutiérrez Alea, *Guantanamera*.

50. Ibid. (In this case, the translation is taken form the subtitles included in the international release of the film.)

51. Joseíto Fernandez's "Guajira guantanamera" draws upon traditional forms of folkloric Cuban music and presents a bucolic and idyllic vision of a young woman from the easternmost province of the island. At the same time, it is widely considered as a protest song (a status that tends to be partially attributed to Pete Seeger's rendition of it at a concert in Carnegie Hall in 1963) that ironically situates this folkloric vision of Cuba in the very place of U.S military occupation. (Sánchez Oliva and Moreaux Jardines).

52. "Gitmo" is a term used colloquially by military personnel to refer to the Naval Base. I use it here to distinguish the space and spatiality of the base from that of the province of Guantanamo.

53. Sorkin, *A Few Good Men*, 51. In the film, Jessep (played by Jack Nicholson) delivers an altered version of this line in which he claims to eat breakfast three hundred yards from four thousand Cubans.

54. I do not mean to suggest that these texts offer a more accurate picture of the area. In fact, one might argue that the dominant U.S. portrayal of Cuba favors the depiction of excessive proximity. Nonetheless, I cite these texts here because they present a vision that productively complicates and complements the one depicted in Cuban cultural discourse: that is, they emphasize the very conditions that their Cuban counterparts tend to obviate.

55. Arenas, *Antes que anochezca*, 190.

56. Arenas, *Before Night Falls*, 163–64.

57. Arenas, *Antes que anochezca*, 190–91.

58. Arenas, *Before Night Falls*, 164–65.

59. The U.S. Air National Guard Base Muñoz in San Juan, for example, was once occupied by proindependence activists.

60. When the United States first took control of the island, they established a military government under which the Puerto Rican people had no formal autonomy or representation. Between 1900 and 1952, the U.S. government passed several laws that addressed this situation. Most notably, perhaps, all Puerto Ricans were granted U.S. citizenship (with limited privileges as nonresidents) in 1917 and the island became a Commonwealth (Estado Libre Asociado) in 1952 following a popular plebiscite.

61. Maldonado Denis, *Puerto Rico*, 179–85.

62. "La isla nena" is an epithet often used to refer to Vieques. In addition to connoting affection, it characterizes the smaller island as a daughter of the larger principal island of Puerto Rico.

63. The volume includes essays such as "Historia de un pueblo-símbolo [History of a Town-Symbol]," "Vieques plantea el colonialismo [Vieques Raises the Issue of Colonialism]," and "Colonial Naval Desnuda [Naval Colony Exposed]."

64. González, "A Town of Tents," A1.

65. Hernández, "A Tiny Island," 8.

66. The resident commissioner is the appointed representative of the Puerto Rican government in the U.S. Congress. According to Public Law 600, this individual has the right to address Congress but cannot vote.

67. U.S. House of Representatives, "Readiness Implications," 77–78.

68. González, "A Town of Tents, 12.
69. González, "A Town of Tents," 12.
70. As I contend in chapter 1, Pedreira criticizes the unwillingness of Puerto Ricans to explore (literally and figuratively) beyond the boundaries of the island. He invokes the historical threat of pirates that awaited intrepid travelers off the coast as a symbol of the unhealthy relationship the residents have traditionally cultivated with their insular circumstances.
71. González, "A Town of Tents," 10.
72. As a version of the name that the Arawaks used before Columbus's arrival, Borinquen is generally considered to be a particularly heart-felt way of referring to Puerto Rico. Although it is often used with little or no strong political implications, the affective significance can imbue it with an anti-imperialist charge.
73. Soja, *Thirdspace*, 87.

## 4. OUT OF PLACE

1. According to the 2000 U.S. Census, the population of Puerto Rico was approximately 3.8 million (a slight decline) and the number of Puerto Ricans residing in the United States had reached 3.4 million. Based on the specific trends of birth rate and migration, moreover, several analysts have suggested that the population in the United States will exceed that of the island within fifty years. In the following chapter, I will return to this demographic shift and offer a more in-depth analysis of how the particular migratory patterns and growing diasporic community engender a discourse (and iconography) of translocal insularity. For the moment, I would like to cite this statistic as the most extreme and striking example of the decentering of the island as the principal location of Caribbean communities.
2. The use of the term Latino's Inc. is a deliberate reference to Arlene Dávila's book of that title and to her argument about the relationships among the representation of Latino culture, mass media and marketing.
3. Suro, *Strangers among Us*, 316.
4. Hijuelos, "North to Home," 15.
5. McWilliams, *North from Mexico*, 9.
6. Similar strategies can be found in the works such as *La guagua aérea* and *The Commuter Nation*. That is, these titles deploy a metaphor of movement rather than reference a fixed geographic location. I will return to this question of translocal paradigms of self-definition later in the chapter. For the moment, I would like to underscore the specific textual corpus (and genealogy) that is evoked by Hijuelos's title.
7. It should be noted that the strategy of reflecting on his own experience in a specific place is typical within Morris's writings. Several of his essays examine what particular spaces—such as Southern graveyards—signify for the author. Nevertheless, in *North toward Home*, Morris evokes both "familiar" and "foreign" settings in the construction of his own subjectivity. In this way, more importantly, the author's definition of "home" is advanced by his personal migration through these juxtaposed spaces.
8. Stapinski, "Generación Latino," 62.
9. Ibid., 64.
10. Ibid., 68.

11. Quite literally, he appeared in numerous magazine and newspaper articles that discussed the Latin music explosion. A particularly salient example of this paradigmatic status is his appearance on the cover of *Time*. The issue featured an article by Christopher Farley that focused on Martin as one of the most prominent examples of the purported Latin pop phenomenon.

12. The appearance at the Grammy Awards Ceremony is especially significant since it is frequently discussed as a turning point in Martin's cross-over success. At the same time, however, the particular metamorphosis I describe is also representative of a recurring trend in the signer's career.

13. Goodman, "La explosion," 22.

14. Stapinsky identifies Lou Bega's father as German and his mother as Sicilian. According to the biographical information included on the artist's Web site, however, his father was born in Uganda and moved to Germany later in life. The question of inclusion or exclusion of the African heritage in constructions of Bega's identity—and, of course, the consequent racialization of him—are worthy of further consideration. Nevertheless, my analysis here will be limited to the undisputed fact that he is not Latino.

15. Spahr, "Bega's Mambo," 50.

16. Ibid.

17. I am particularly grateful to my colleague, Robert Rushing, for pointing out the emblematic significance of this phrase.

18. Of course, the most extreme example of this phenomenon can be found in locations such as Las Vegas, where the majority of the architecture and urban landscape produces a hyperbolic exopolis. Mike Davis has cogently analyzed the human and environmental costs of Las Vegas and its ultimate inability to fully divorce itself from the natural order. What interests me about the built environment in this case, nonetheless, is the presumed link between the disruption of normal spatiotemporal structures and capitalist consumption.

19. Hennessy, *Profit and Pleasure*, 109–10.

20. Rivera, *Family Installments*, 299.

21. The implications of Puerto Rican and Dominican migratory patterns and their impact on recent cultural production will be addressed more thoroughly in the following chapter. I would, however, like to mention two highly relevant examples in which this relationship with insularity constitutes a principal theme or focus within the narrative itself: Luis Rafael Sánchez's "La guagua aérea" and Manuel Ramos Otero's "La otra isla de Puerto Rico." Both Sánchez and Ramos Otero construct a discourse of national identity based on movement through distinct insular topographies and, in doing so, fundamentally reterritorialize the rhetoric of insularity.

22. García, *Dreaming*, 5–6.

23. After the publication of her essay in the PMLA, Chow's emblematic analysis of the cover image on (certain editions of) *Of Grammatology* was challenged by other scholars. In her response, however, Chow defended her claims and insisted that the image was nonetheless representative of a larger trend in Derrida's argument.

24. García, *Dreaming*, 7.

25. Indeed, the use of letters as a literary device is often at odds with their supposed communicative function. In his analysis of the intersections between epistolary writing and sexuality, for example, Patrick P. Garlinger discusses the ironic ability of letters to underscore the very displacement that they are intended to diminish.

26. García, *Dreaming*, 7.
27. Ibid., 119.
28. Ibid., 195.
29. Obviously, one could interpret this problem in more psychoanalytic terms and argue that Lourdes is projecting her feelings onto her visions of her father. That is, the information that Jorge del Pino threatens to share with his daughter is, in fact, knowledge that Lourdes already possesses but cannot accept consciously. However, even if the connection is understood as one between Lourdes and her own subconscious, the danger still lies in its capacity to prove too successful.
30. The problem of bilingualism is a common theme in transcultural literature, and the treatment of the issue in *Dreaming* follows the established paradigm. As I will argue here, however, it becomes part of a larger expressive dilemma in García's novel.
31. García, *Dreaming*, 10.
32. Ibid., 81.
33. Ibid., 237.
34. Ibid., 235.
35. Ibid., 144.
36. Ibid., 139.
37. Ibid., 233.
38. Ibid., 76.
39. As Patricia Parker has argued in her work, *Literary Fat Ladies*, the expansion and restriction of feminine flesh is a prominent theme within Western literature. According to Parker, since women's bodies have been a traditional focus of normativity, cultural stability is achieved and maintained through the circumscription of them. Feminist scholarship in the emergent field of Fat Studies has further interrogated the social norms and expectations that have historically been attached to gendered body images in various cultures. A woman's body thus becomes a contested space, and the negotiation of her corporeal boundaries reflects a process through which normative subjectivity is contested, reaffirmed, and modified. Furthermore, the uncontrolled expansion of a female subject threatens the established order. Similarly, the historical connection between women and hysterical disorders has been discussed extensively by psychoanalytic and feminist critics.
40. García, *Dreaming*, 74.
41. The organization of the novel in terms of sections and the titles of the chapters can be apprehended in the table of contents. The division of chapters into subsections (and the individual titles assigned to certain subsections) is not indicated in the table of contents but is clearly marked in the body of the text.
42. According to the author, this structure evolved over the rewriting of the novel. Originally, she had only planned to include the text from a single letter, but she decided to develop the correspondence further and subsequently organized them as a framing device (López, "And There is Only My Imagination," 108).
43. The intervening three epistolary chapter, as they appear in the novel, are: "Celia's Letters: 1942–1949," "Celia's Letters: 1950–1955," and "Celia's Letters: 1956–1958."
44. García, *Dreaming*, 245.
45. Davis, "Back to the Future," 60.
46. Arango, "To Write in Cuba," 123.
47. According to Carl Jung, the process suggested by the title is wholly commensurate of the semantics of dreams: each individual generates a system of symbols that must

be deciphered in light of personal experiences. Hence, García's title would simply constitute a description of how the universal processes of encoding and decoding are being rendered in the novel.

48. López, "And There is Only My Imagination," 109.

49. Foucault, "Of Other Spaces," 24.

50. Not all caribeña narratives insist unequivocally on the island as the exclusive destination of a trajectory of self-definition or space of subject formation. In fact, many works by contemporary authors attempt to challenge the centrality of the island. In addition to examples cited earlier, alternative trajectories of self-definition and demarcations of space can be found in works such as Achy Obejas's *Memory Mambo*, Ana Lydia Vega's *Encancaranublado*, and Judith Ortiz Cofer's *An Island Like You*. These works fundamentally question the centrality of the traditional insular rhetoric, yet they continue to engage it in a manner that reinforces its significance. Even in their contestatory approach, therefore, these novels offer further evidence of the problematic persistence of insularity in U.S.-Caribbean writing.

## 5. Virtual Island

1. Fornet, "Bridging Enigmas," 3.

2. As I mentioned in chapter 3, the Special Period refers to the years following the dissolution of the Soviet Union, during which the Cuban government loosened restrictions on international funds, investment, and trade in order to compensate for the loss of Soviet support. The measures were initially presented as a temporary solution designed to meet the immediate financial exigencies of the country. By the beginning of the twenty-first century (when *Aunque estés lejos* was made), however, the more liberal commercial regulations had become commonplace, and the government had not presented an alternative economic model to supplant the increased role of international investment.

3. Although the *III* suffix would ordinarily suggest an intervening *Nueba Yol II*, no such film was ever produced. The 1998 film follows directly from the first, but the director elected to title it in this matter because of the negative connotations often associated with sequels.

4. As Frank Bonilla and Ricardo Campos have clearly demonstrated in their groundbreaking work on Puerto Rican migration, the relocation of large numbers of workers to the United States was systematically fostered during the 1930s and 1940s.

5. In fact, according to the 2000 U.S. Census, the number of Puerto Ricans residing in the United States now exceeds those residing in Puerto Rico.

6. Sánchez, *Guagua aérea*, 15.

7. Sánchez, "Airbus," 29.

8. Sánchez, *Guagua aérea*, 17.

9. Sánchez, "Airbus," 50.

10. Sánchez, *Guagua aérea*, 20.

11. Sánchez, "Airbus," 51.

12. Sánchez, *Guagua*, 21.

13. Sánchez, "Airbus," 51.

14. Sánchez, *Guagua aérea*, 23.

15. Sánchez, "Airbus," 51.
16. Ramos Otero, *Página*, 11. (my translation)
17. Ibid., 16.
18. Ibid., 19.
19. Ibid., 12.
20. Ibid., 15.
21. Ramos Otero, "Caribbean Dislocations," 112.
22. By referring to the figures as cartoon-like, I do not mean to suggest that they are parodied or ridiculed in this representation. I am referring here to the fact that these depictions resemble the anthropomorphic renditions of the coquí rather than the biological specimens found throughout the island.
23. Lury, "Object of travel," 95.
24. The plural in Spanish is "coquíes." Nevertheless, I will render the plural as coquís here to reflect the incorporation of the Spanish term into English discourse and grammar.
25. Of course, local folklore and symbolism are very often the sources of souvenir objects. The commodities produced by this tendency, however, are not always valued by local consumers. On the contrary, a stark contrast can frequently be traced between those cultural functions associated with these objects that are enacted by members of the community and the packaging of the same objects for foreign consumers. In fact, studies such as *Being Indian in Hueyapán* and the ethnographic film *Cannibal Tours* highlight the complex processes through which members of a community perform their cultural practices in order to meet the expectations of an external consumer but which are completely disconnected from quotidian existence. What is striking in this case, therefore, is the appeal of these objects to members of the local community as well as visitors and/or emigrants.
26. I would like to thank Arnaldo Cruz Malavé, who brought the proliferation of the coquí in Hawai'i to my attention.
27. Hawai'ian environmental organizations—as with many similar groups elsewhere—have aggressively asserted their concerns about the perils of globalization. Therefore, the campaign against the coquí must be understood in the larger context of the desire to preserve the existing ecological system. Consequently, the condemnation of all recently arriving species is based on the perception of them as a potential threat to that stability. Nevertheless, the prejudicial subtext that can be read in the attitude toward the coquí should not be ignored.
28. www.hear.org/frogs.
29. Most of the methods to eradicate the coquí's presence in Hawai'i have not proven successful. Recently, therefore, HEAR and other environmental organizations have begun to consider alternative strategies for coping with the unwelcome immigrant population.
30. www.hear.org. (emphasis in original)
31. Morales Carrión, *Puerto Rico*, 348.
32. I do not mean to suggest that Lefebvre makes this assertion about islands per se. Instead, as I will argue here, a careful analysis of insular space in terms of Lefebvre's theory of spatiality suggest that it functions in this manner.
33. It should be noted that this reaction to an idealized, allegorical space is not uncommon. In fact, the Garden of Eden may stand as a paradigmatic case of such a response in Judeo-Christian traditions. That is, many readers interpret the place described as a fictional heuristic device that comments on existence in the natural world by depict-

ing a place that only exists outside of it. Others, however, have insisted on the literal component of the allegory and have engendered extensive discussion as to the precise location where the garden may have once existed.

34. The word "pal" is a contraction of "para el" that connotes a sociolinguistic speech pattern or orality, and the term "boricua" is derived from the pre-Columbian name of the island, Boriquén, and is generally synonymous with Puerto Rican. Although it is certainly susceptible to patterns of linguistic change and shifting connotations, "boricua" is most commonly used as a particularly patriotic or passionate way of describing individuals and other objects.

35. In particular, the earliest versions of Internet communication were sponsored by the U.S. Department of Defense as part of a project designed to decentralize information. As the department became increasingly dependent on data storage and transferal, they became concerned that the highly localized gathering of information in a single system would make them vulnerable to a site-specific attack. Hence, they began to develop a network of connections and routers that allowed information to be stored in several remote servers that were readily accessible to computers in multiple locations.

36. Early versions of Internet services allowed one to access specific networks and pursue information by following text-based links. You could, for example, enter the Library of Congress database and scroll through the menus until you reached the desired line of information, and select the link that would then produce a new page of text. Internet service providers also offered chat functions, which approximated the more recent space of the cyber-chat room. Again, however, these functions incorporated text only. Hence, although one could communicate with other individuals over long distances in real time, this ability did not differ significantly from the capabilities of the telephone or teletype machines used by the hearing impaired.

37. In her chapter, "Welcome to the Global Stage," Juana María Rodríguez offers a thorough and lucid discussion of the complex ways in which traditional structures of identity are both reinforced and subverted by the technology and practices of the Internet.

38. When I was first researching this topic, I identified this particular site as one of the most relevant ones to my topic. More recently, however, I have not been able to access it.

39. The bohío refers to the traditional huts associated with the folkloric past of Puerto Rico. Although these structures are rarely found in contemporary society as residential dwellings, they often appear in more commercial contexts as a symbol of cultural heritage.

40. As Johannes Fabian has argued, anthropological discourse has traditionally constructed its object of study in terms of an anteriority. That is, although the anthropologist conducts fieldwork in real time and analyzes a culture that is contemporaneous with his/her own, the discourse and methodology of the discipline conventionally have characterized the observed culture as primitive and has evaluated it as a precursor rather than as a coeval alternative. Similarly, in this case, the two locations occupy the same space and time yet are represented in terms of a temporal trajectory that leads from Puerto Rico to New York.

41. The term "boricua" in Spanish can be either male or female but it also can act as either an adjective or a noun. In this case, therefore, it may be an adjective that modifies the noun New York. Conversely, New York may be behaving as an adjective that modifies the noun boricua (meaning a person of Puerto Rican descent).

42. A full analysis of the politics of the Internet is beyond the scope of this project. Nevertheless, the proliferation of pornography, Web-cams that broadcast over the Internet, and the extraordinary anxiety around anonymity and identity security all point to the tenuous spatiality of cyberspace. The value of cyberspace lies precisely in its ability to provide unfettered fluidity of movement without completely dislodging existing boundaries; but the precarious balance between the two must be vigilantly maintained.

43. http://www.boricuadesterrao.com/About_Us.html.

44. In fact, the company differentiates itself from providers of cultural artifacts that appeal to the exclusive prestige or cult value of more expensive items. Hence, the Internet is presented as the most appropriate forum for the exchange of commodities that the company offers.

45. The coqui.net data mentioned here was collected between March 2001 and February 2002. In addition to the instances mentioned, the statistics on usage and similar information may no longer be current.

46. Foucault, "Of Other Spaces," 25–27.

## Conclusion

1. The most logical (idiomatically correct) translation of the title, *Mundo soñado*, would probably be "Dream World," as indicated above. It should be noted, however, that the original Spanish uses the past participle, "dreamt," rather than a phrase such as "mundo de sueño." That is, the title in Spanish does not simply indicate that the image depicted is a dream world; instead, it specifically characterizes it as a world that someone (an unnamed, invisible subject) has dreamt.

2. Scholars such as Antoinette Burton, Anton Appadurai, and Etienne Balibar, for example, have elucidated the complex ways in which conventional nationalist ideas (and ideals) continue to wield affective power even as the political landscape is being reshaped by postnationalist and transnational paradigms.

# Bibliography

Almendros, Néstor, and Orlando Jiménez-Leal. *Mauvaise Conduite [Improper Conduct]*. New York, NY: Cinevista Video, 1984.

Alonso, Carlos J. *The Spanish American Regional Novel: Modernity and Autochthony*. Cambridge and New York: Cambridge University Press, 1990.

Alonso, Manuel A. *El Gíbaro: cuadro de costumbres de la isla de Puerto Rico*. San Juan: Instituto de Cultura Puertorriqueña, 1974.

Althusser, Louis. *Lenin and Philosophy, and Other Essays*. Translated by Ben Brewster. New York: Monthly Review Press, 1971.

Alvarez, Julia. *How the García Girls Lost Their Accents*. New York: Plume, 1992.

———. *Something to Declare*. Chapel Hill, NC: Algonquin Books of Chapel Hill, 1998.

Anderson, Benedict. *Imagined Communities: Reflections on the Origin and Spread of Nationalism*. Rev. ed. London and New York: Verso, 1991.

Anzaldúa, Gloria. *Borderlands/La Frontera: The New Mestiza*. San Francisco: Aunt Lute, 1987.

Aparicio, Frances R. *Listening to Salsa: Gender, Latin Popular Music, and Puerto Rican Cultures*, Hanover, NH: University Press of New England, 1998.

Appadurai, Arjun. *Modernity at Large: Cultural Dimensions of Globalization*. Minneapolis: University of Minnesota Press, 1996.

Arango, Arturo. "To Write in Cuba, Today." *SAQ* 96, no. 1 (1997): 117–28.

Arenas, Reinaldo. *Antes que anochezca: autobiografía*. Barcelona: Tusquets, 1992.

Arteaga, Alfred. *An Other Tongue: Nation and Ethnicity in the Linguistic Borderlands*. Durham: Duke University Press, 1994.

———. *Before Night Falls*. Translated by Dolores M. Koch. New York: Penguin Books, 1994.

Babín, María Teresa and Stan Steiner, eds. *Borinquen: An Anthology of Puerto Rican Literature*. New York: Vintage Books, 1974.

Balaguer, Joaquín. *La isla al revés: Haiti y el destino dominicano*. 10th ed. Santo Domingo: Libreria Dominicana, 1998.

Balibar, Etienne. *We, the People of Europe? Reflections on Transnational Citizenship*. Princeton: Princeton University Press, 2004.

Barceló de Barasorda, Angelina. Introduction. *Insularismo*. By Antonio S. Pedriera. Río Piedras: Editorial Edil, 1992.

Barradas, Efraín. *Apalabramiento: cuentos puertorriqueños de hoy*. Hanover, NH: Ediciones del Norte, 1983.

Bega, Lou. *A Little Bit of Mambo*. BMG Records, 1999.

Behar, Ruth. *Bridges to Cuba/Puentes a Cuba*. Ann Arbor, MI: University of Michigan Press, 1995.

Bejel, Emilio. *Gay Cuban Nation*. Chicago: University of Chicago Press, 2001.

Benítez Rojo, Antonio. *La isla que se repite: el Caribe y la perspectiva posmoderna*. Hanover, NH: Ediciones del Norte, 1989.

———. *The Repeating Island: The Caribbean and the Postmodern Perspective*. Translated by James E. Maraniss. Durham: Duke University Press, 1992.

Bermejo, Gonzalo. "Guantanamo: A Fence between Two Worlds." In *Reporting on Cuba*. Havana: Instituto del Libro, 1963.

Bhabha, Homi K. *Nation and Narration*. London and New York: Routledge, 1990.

Bonilla, Frank, and Ricardo Campos. *Industry & Idleness*. New York: Centro de Estudios Puertorriqueños, 1986.

Brady, Mary Pat. *Extinct Lands, Temporal Geographies: Chicana Literature and the Urgency of Space*. Durham: Duke University Press, 2002.

Brau, Salvador. *La vuelta al hogar y ¿Pecadora?*. Río Piedras: Editorial Edil, 1975.

Burnett, Mark. "Survivor (the Complete First Season)." In *Survivor*. U.S.: Paramount, 2004.

Burton, Antoinette M. *After the Imperial Turn: Thinking with and through the Nation*. Durham: Duke University Press, 2003.

Cabrera Infante, Guillermo. "The Death of Virgilio." In *Cold Tales*, 11–14. Hygiene, CO: Eridanos Press, 1988.

Carrero, Jaime. "Vieques Del Caribe." *Revista Chicano-Riqueña* 7, no. 3 (1979): 9–13.

Caruth, Cathy. *Trauma: Explorations in Memory*. Baltimore: Johns Hopkins University Press, 1995.

Césaire, Aimé. *Une Tempête: d'après "La Tempête" de Shakespeare: adaptation pour un théâtre nègre*. Paris: Éditions du Seuil, 1980.

Chatterjee, Partha. *The Nation and Its Fragments: Colonial and Postcolonial Histories*. Princeton: Princeton University Press, 1993.

Chekhov, Anton Pavlovich. *Three Sisters*. Translated by Stephen Mulrine. London: Nick Hern, 1994.

Chenevey McCoy, Mary Ellen. "Guantanamo Bay: The United States Naval Base and Its Relationship with Cuba." Diss, University of Akron, 1995.

Chow, Rey. "How (the) Inscrutable Chinese Led to Global Theory." *PMLA* 116, no. 1 (2001): 69–74.

———. "Silent Is the Ancient Plain: Music, Filmmaking, and the Conception of Reform in China's New Cinema." *Discourse: Journal for Theoretical Studies in Media and Culture* 12, no. 2 (1990): 82–109.

Clavigero, Francesco Saverio. *Historia antigua de México*. 8a ed. México: Porrua, 1987.

Clifford, James. *Routes: Travel and Translation in the Late Twentieth Century.* Cambridge: Harvard University Press, 1997.

Colón, Cristóbal. *Los cuarto viajes del Almirante y su testamento.* 10th ed. Madrid: Espasa Calpe, 1946.

Colón, Emilio M. *Primicias de las letras puertorriqueñas: Aguinaldo puertorriqueño (1843); Álbum puertorriqueño (1844); El cancionero de Borinquen (1846).* San Juan: Instituto de Cultura Puertorriquena, 1970.

*Coqui.net.* March 15, 2003, *http://www.coqui.net/.*

Cosgrove, Denis E. *Mappings.* London: Reaktion Books, 1999.

Crichton, Michael. *Jurassic Park.* New York: Knopf (Distributed by Random House), 1990.

Cristófani Barreto, Teresa. "Los cuentos fríos de Virgilio Piñera." *Hispamércia* 24, no. 71 (1995): 23–33.

Cruz-Malavé, Arnaldo. *El primitivo implorante: el "sistema poético del mundo" de José Lezama Lima.* Amsterdam: Rodopi, 1994.

D'Emilio, John. *The World Turned: Essays on Gay History, Politics, and Culture.* Durham, NC: Duke University Press, 2002.

Darwin, Charles. *On the Origin of Species.* New York: New York University Press, 1988.

Dávila, Arlene M. *Latinos, Inc.: The Marketing and Making of a People.* Berkeley: University of California Press, 2001.

Davis, Mike. *Dead Cities, and Other Tales.* New York: New Press (Distributed by W. W. Norton), 2002.

Davis, Rocío G. "Back to the Future: Mothers, Languages, and Homes in Cristina García's *Dreaming in Cuban.*" *World Literature Today* 74, no. 1 (2000): 60–68.

de Certeau, Michel. *Heterologies: Discourse on the Other.* Minneapolis: University of Minnesota Press, 1986.

de Ferrari, Guillermina. "Enfermedad, cuerpo y utopia en *Los pasos perdidos* de Alejo Carpentier y en *Pájaros de la playa* de Severo Sarduy." *Hispanic Review* 70, no. 2 (2002): 219–41.

Defoe, Daniel. *The Life and Strange Surprizing Adventures of Robinson Crusoe, of York, Mariner: Who Lived Eight and Twenty Years, All Aone in an Un-inhabited Island on the Coast of America, Near the Mouth of the Great River of Oroonoque, Having Been Cast on Shore by Shipwreck, Wherein all the Men Perished but Himself: With an Account How he Was at last as Strangely Deliver'd by Pyrates, Written by Himself.* Oxford: Oxford University Press, 1999.

Delany, Samuel R. *Times Square Red, Times Square Blue.* New York London: New York University Press, 1999.

Deleuze, Gilles. *Desert Islands and Other Texts, 1953–1974.* Cambridge, MA.: Semiotext(e), (Distributed by MIT Press), 2004.

Derrida, Jacques. *Margins of Philosophy.* Paper ed. Chicago: University of Chicago Press, 1986.

Diego, Eliseo, and Miguel Cossío Woodward. *Sobre literatura cubana: dos conferencias presentadas en el Instituto el 16 de octubre de 1980, Occasional Papers.* Stockholm: Institute of Latin American Studies, 1980.

James Dietz. *Economic History of Puerto Rico: Institutional Change and Capitalist Development*. Princeton: Princeton University Press, 1986.

———. "Puerto Rico's New History." *LARR* 19, no. 1 (1984): 210–22.

Eng, David L., and David Kazanjian. *Loss: The Politics of Mourning*. Berkeley: University of California Press, 2003.

Fabian, Johannes. *Time and the Other: How Anthropology Makes Its Object*. New York: Columbia University Press, 2002.

Farley, Christopher J. "Latin Music Pops." *Time* 1999, 74–9.

Ferré, Rosario. *Papeles de Pandora*. México: J. Mortiz, 1976.

Findlay, Eileen. *Imposing Decency: The Politics of Sexuality and Race in Puerto Rico, 1870–1920*. Durham: Duke University Press, 1999.

Fiol-Matta, Licia. *A Queer Mother for the Nation: The State and Gabriela Mistral*. Minneapolis: University of Minnesota Press, 2002.

Flaherty, Stephen, Lynn Ahrens, and Rosa Guy. *Once on This Island*. Secaucus, NJ (Warner Bros. Publications), 1990.

Flores, Juan. *Divided Borders: Essays on Puerto Rican Identity*. Houston: Arte Público Press, 1993.

Flores, Rosa. "Mi bohio nuyorquino." January 20, 2002 http://www.geocities.com/mibohio.

Fornet, Ambrosio. "Bridging Enigmas: Cubans on Cuba." *SAQ* 96, no. 1 (1997).

Foucault, Michel. *Madness and Civilization: A History of Insanity in the Age of Reason*. New York: Vintage Books, 1988.

———. "Of Other Spaces." *Diacritics* 16, no. 1 (1986): 22–27.

Franco, Jean. Introduction. *Divided Borders: Essays on Puerto Rican Identity*. By Juan Flores. Houston: Arte Público P, 1993.

Friedlander, Judith. *Being Indian in Hueyapan: A Study of Forced Identity in Contemporary Mexico*. New York: St. Martin's Press, 1975.

Galván, Manuel de Jesús. *The Cross and the Sword*. Translated by Robert Graves. Bloomington: Indiana University Press, 1954.

———. *Enriquillo: leyenda histórica dominicana (1503–1533)*. Madrid: Cultura Hispánica, 1996.

García Chichester, Ana. "Superando el caos: estado actual de la crítica sobre la narrativa de Virgilio Piñera." *Revista Interamericana de Bibliografía/Inter-American Review of Bibliography* 42, no. 1 (1992): 132–47.

García, Cristina. *Dreaming in Cuban*. New York: Ballantine Books, 1992.

García, Samuel. *Growing Up Nuyorican*. October 25, 2002, http://www.growingupnuyorican.com/.

Garlinger, Patrick Paul. *Confessions of the Letter Closet: Epistolary Fiction and Queer Desire in Modern Spain*. Minneapolis: University of Minnesota Press, 2005.

Gelpí, Juan. *Literatura y paternalismo en Puerto Rico*. San Juan: Editorial de la Universidad de Puerto Rico, 1993.

Ginzburg, Carlo. *No Island Is an Island: Four Glances at English Literature in a World Perspective*. New York: Columbia University Press, 2000.

Glasser, Ruth. *My Music Is My Flag: Puerto Rican Musicians and Their New York Communities, 1917–1940*. Berkeley: University of California Press, 1995.

Golding, William. *Lord of the Flies*. Harmondsworth: Penguin Books, 1960.

Goldman, Dara E. "El otro que no es uno: configuraciones retóricas en los estudios coloniales Recientes." *Cuadernos Americanos* 5, no. 71 (1998): 163–79.

———. " Los límites de la carne: los cuerpos asediados de Virgilio Piñera." *Revista Iberoamericana* 69, no. 205 (2003): 1001–15.

———. "Once on This Island: The Performance of Spatiality in Salvador Brau's *La Vuelta Al Hogar*." *Chasqui* 32, no. 1 (2003): 74–84.

———. "Out of Place: The Demarcation of Hispanic Caribbean Cultural Spaces in the Diaspora." *Latino Studies* 1, no. 3 (2003): 410–23.

———. "Virtual Islands: The Reterritorialization of Puerto Rican Spatiality in Cyberspace." *Hispanic Review* 72, no. 3 (2004): 375–400.

Gómez de Avellaneda y Arteaga, Gertrudis. *Sab*. Edited by José Servera. Madrid: Cátedra, 1997.

Gonzalez, David. "A Town of Tents and Civil Disobedience." *New York Times*, August 1, 2001.

González, José Luis. *El país de cuatro pisos y otros ensayos*. 7th ed. Río Piedras: Ediciones Huracán, 1987.

González Echevarría, Roberto. *La ruta de Severo Sarduy*. Hanover, NH: Ediciones del Norte, 1987.

———. *Myth and Archive*. New York and Cambridge: Cambridge University Press, 1990.

Goodman, Fred. "La Explosion Pop Latino." *Rolling Stone*, May 13, 1999, 21–22.

Gran Combo de Puerto Rico, El. *Nuestra Música*. Combo Records, 1998.

Gutierrez Alea, Tomás an Juan Carlos Tabío. *Guantanamera*. Havana: Vídeo ICAIC, 1995.

Gutiérrez Alea, Tomás, and Juan Carlos Tabío. *Fresa y chocolate [Strawberry & Chocolate]*. Distributed by Buena Vista Home Video: Miramax Home Entertainment, 1995. videorecording.

Guy, Rosa. *My Love, My Love, or, the Peasant Girl*. New York: Holt Rinehart and Winston, 1985.

Haines, Randa. "Dance with Me." Columbia/Tristar Home Video, 1998.

Halberstam, Judith. *In a Queer Time and Place: Transgender Bodies, Subcultural Lives*. New York: New York University Press, 2005.

Haraway, Donna J. *Modest_Witness@Second Milleniun.© Female Man_Meets_Oncomouse™ Feminism and Technoscience*. New York: Routledge, 1997.

Hardt, Michael, and Antonio Negri. *Empire*. Cambridge, MA: Harvard University Press, 2000.

Harvey, David. *Justice, Nature, and the Geography of Difference*. Cambridge: Blackwell Publishers, 1996.

Hawaiian Ecosystems at Risk. *Alien Caribbean Frogs in Hawaii*. May 13, 2003. http://www.hear.org/AlienSpeciesInHawaii/species/frogs/.

———. July 5, 2003. http://www.hear.org/frogs.

Hennessy, Rosemary. *Profit and Pleasure: Sexual Identities in Late Capitalism*. New York: Routledge, 2000.

Hernández, Raymond. "A Tiny Island, but a Cause So Celebre; from New York to Hollywood, Vieques Has Issues for Everyone." *New York Times*, July 15, 2001.

Hijuelos, Oscar. "North to Home." *George* 4, no. 7 (1999): 12–15.

Hostos, Eugenio María de. "Mi viaje al sur." In *Obras completas*. San Juan: Instituto de Cultura Puertorriqueña, 1969.

———. "La peregrinación de Bayoán." In *Obras completas, edición crítica*, 101–357. Río Riedras: Instituto de Cultura Puertorriqueña/Editorial de la Universidad de Puerto Rico, 1988.

———. "Diario (1866–1869)." In *Obras Completas (Edición Crítica)*. Río Piedras: Editorial del Instituto de Cultura Puertorriqueña/Editorial de la Universidad de Puerto Rico, 1990.

Hulme, Peter, and William H. Sherman. *The Tempest and Its Travels, Critical Views*. London: Reaktion, 2000.

Iglesias, Enrique. *Bailamos: Greatest Hits*: Fonovisa, 1999.

Isaacs, Jorge. *María*. Edited by Donald McGrady. Madrid: Cátedra, 1986.

Jameson, Fredric. *Postmodernism, or the Cultural Logic of Late Capitalism*. Durham, NC: Duke University Press, 1991.

Jung, Carl G. and Marie-Luise von Franz. *Man and His Symbols*. New York: Dell, 1975.

Kanzepolsky, Adriana. "Virgilio Piñera, la generosa provocación." *Hispamérica* 25, no. 75 (1996): 137–49.

Knapp, Jeffrey. *An Empire Nowhere: England, America, and Literature from Utopia to the Tempest*. Berkeley: University of California Press, 1992.

Knight, Franklin. *The Caribbean: Genesis of a Fragmented Nationalism*. New York: Oxford University Press, 1978.

Kolodny, Annette. *The Lay of the Land: Metaphor as Experience and History in American Life and Letters*. Chapel Hill, NC: University of North Carolina Press, 1975.

Kristeva, Julia. *Revolution in Poetic Language*. New York: Columbia University Press, 1984.

Kurlansky, Mark. *A Continent of Islands: Searching for the Caribbean Destiny*. Reading, MA.: Addison-Wesley Publishing Comany, 1992.

Lacan, Jacques. *Feminine Sexuality*. Translated by Jacqueline Rose. New York and London: W. W. Norton & Company and Pantheon Books, 1982.

Landow, George P. *Hypertext 2.0*. Rev., amplified ed. Baltimore: Johns Hopkins University Press, 1997.

Laó-Montes, Agustín, and Arlene M. Dávila. *Mambo Montage: The Latinization of New York*. New York: Columbia University Press, 2001.

Las Casas, Bartolomé de. *Historia de las Indias*. Caracas: Biblioteca Ayacucho, 1986.

Lefebvre, Henri. *Critique of Everyday Life*. London and New York: Verso, 1991.

———. *The Production of Space*. Oxford and Cambridge, MA: Blackwell, 1991.

Lenin, Vladimir I. *Collected Works*. London: Lawrence & Wishart, 1960.

Lezama Lima, José. *Coloquio con Juan Ramón Jiménez*. Havana: Publicaciones de la Secretaría de Educación, 1938.

———. *Analecta Del Reloj*. La Habana: Orígenes, 1953.

Little Louie and Marc Anthony. *When the Night Is Over*. WEA, Atlantic, 1991.

López, Iraida. "'. . . And There Is Only My Imagination Where Our History Should Be': An Interview with Cristina Garcia." In *Bridges to Cuba/Puentes a Cuba*, edited by Ruth Behar, 102–14. Ann Arbor: University of Michigan Press, 1995.

Lugo Ortiz, Agnes. "Nationalisms, Male Anxiety and the Lesbian Body in Puerto Rican Narrative." In *Hispanisms and Homosexualities*, edited by Sylvia Molloy and Robert Irwin, 76–99. Durham: Duke University Press, 1998.

Lugo-Ortiz, Agnes. "Community at Its Limits: Orality, Law, Silence and the Homosexual Body in Luis Rafael Sánchez's '¡Jum!'" In *¿Entiendes?: Queer Readings, Hispanic Writings*, edited by Emilie L. Bergmann and Paul Julian Smith, 115–36. Durham, NC: Duke University Press, 1995.

Luibhéid, Eithne. *Entry Denied: Controlling Sexuality at the Border*. Minneapolis: University of Minnesota Press, 2002.

Lury, Celia. "The Object of Travel." In *Touring Cultures*, edited by Chris Rojek and John Urry, 75–95. New York: Routledge, 1997.

Maldonado-Denis, Manuel. *Puerto Rico; una interpretación histórico-social*. Mexico D.F.: Siglo Veintiuno Editores, 1969.

Manalansan, Martin F. *Global Divas: Filipino Gay Men in the Diaspora*. Durham, NC: Duke University Press, 2003.

Marc Anthony. *Marc Anthony*. Sony Music, 1999.

Marqués, René. *Purificación en la calle del Cristo (cuento) y Los soles truncos (comedia dramática en dos actos)*. Río Piedras: Editorial Cultural, 1983.

Marshall, Paule. *Brown Girl, Brownstones*. New York: The Feminist Press at the City University of New York, 1981.

———. *Daughters*. New York: Plume, 1991.

Martin, Biddy. "Sexualities without Genders and Other Queer Utopias." *Diacritics* 24 (1994): 104–21.

Martin, Ricky. *Ricky Martin*. New York, NY: C2 Records/Columbia, 1999.

Martínez-San Miguel, Yolanda. *Caribe Two Ways: cultura de la migración en el Caribe insular hispánico*. San Juan: Ediciones Callejón, 2003.

Matos Rodríguez, Félix V. "New Currents in Puerto Rican History: Legacy, Continuity, and Challenges of the 'Nueva Historia'." *LARR* 32, no. 3 (1997): 193–208.

McWilliams, Carey and Matt S. Meier. *North from Mexico: The Spanish-Speaking People of the United States*. New, updated ed. New York: Greenwood Press, 1990.

Menéndez Pidal, Ramón. "Observaciones criticas sobre las biografias de Fray Bartolome de las Casas." In *Actas del Primer Congreso Internacional de Hispanistas*, edited by Frank Pierce and Cyril A. Jones. Oxford: Dolphin Book Co., 1964.

Miranda Bravo, Olga. *Undesirable Neighbors: The U.S. Naval Base at Guantánamo*. Havana: Editorial José Martí, 2001.

———. *Vecinos indeseables: la base yanqui en Guantánamo*. La Habana: Editorial de Ciencias Sociales, 1998.

Montrose, Louis. "The Work of Gender in the Discourse of Discovery." In *New World Encounters*, edited by Stephen Greenblatt, 177–217. Berkeley: University of California Press, 1993.

Morales Carrión, Arturo. *Puerto Rico, a Political and Cultural History*. New York: W. W. Norton, 1983.

More, Thomas. *Utopia*. Edited by Paul Turner. London: Penguin Books, 2003.

Moreiras, Alberto. *Tercer espacio: literatura y duelo en America Latina*. Santiago, Chile: ARCIS, 1999.

Morris, Willie. *North toward Home*. Boston: Houghton Mifflin, 1967.

Moschovitis, Christos, et. al. *History of the Internet: A Chronology, 1843 to the Present*. Santa Barbara: ABC-CLIO, 1999.

Muñiz, Ángel. "Nueba Yol." Ideal Enterprises, 1996.

———. "Nueba Yol III: Bajo La Nueva Ley." Ideal Enterprises, 1997.

Muñoz, José Esteban. *Disidentifications: Queers of Color and the Performance of Politics*. Minneapolis: University of Minnesota Press, 1999.

*Nyboricua*. Edited by Talí Lamourt. July 4, 2003, http://www.Nyboricua.com.

O'Rourke, Dennis. "Cannibal Tours." [Canberra] Santa Monica, CA: O'Rourke & Associates, Direct Cinema Ltd., 1987.

Obejas, Achy. *Memory Mambo*. Pittsburgh: Cleis Press, 1996.

Ortiz Cofer, Judith. *An Island Like You: Stories of the Barrio*. New York: Orchard Books, 1995.

Parker, Patricia A. *Literary Fat Ladies: Rhetoric, Gender, Property*. New York: Methuen, 1987.

Pedreira, Antonio S. *Insularismo*. Río Piedras: Editorial Edil, 1992.

———. *Insularismo: An Insight into the Puerto Rican Character*. Translated by Aoife Rivera Serrano. New York: Ausubo Press, 2005.

Pérez Firmat, Gustavo. *Life on the Hyphen: The Cuban-American Way*. Austin: University of Texas Press, 1994.

Pérez Prado, Dámaso. *Cuban Originals*: BMG Latin, 1999.

Pérez Viera, Edgardo. *Victoria de un pueblo: Crónica del Grito de Vieques*. San Juan: Editorial Cultural, 2002.

Piñera, Virgilio. "La isla en peso." In *Poesía y prosa*. La Habana: Ediciones R, 1944.

———. *Cuentos fríos*. Buenos Aires: Editorial Losada, 1956.

———. *Teatro completo*. Habana: Ediciones R, 1960.

———. *La carne de René*. Madrid: Ediciones Alfaguara, 1985.

———. *Cold Tales*. Translated by Mark Shafer. Hygiene, CO: Eridanos Press, 1988.

———. *René's Flesh*. Translated by Mark Shafer. Boston: Eridanos Press, 1989.

———. "La isla en peso." In "The Whole Island: Cuban Poetry Since 1944." Translated by Mark Weiss. Berkeley: University of California Press, [forthcoming].

Plato. *The Dialogues of Plato*. Translated by Benjamin Jowett. 4th ed. London: Sphere, 1970.

———. *The Republic*. Trans. Richard W. Sterling and William C. Scott. New York: Norton, 1985.

Pratt, Mary Louise. *Imperial Eyes: Travel Writing and Transculturation*. London and New York: Routledge, 1992.

Prieto, René. *Body of Writing: Figuring Desire in Spanish American Literature.* Durham, NC: Duke University Press, 2000.

Quammen, David. *The Song of the Dodo: Island Biogeography in an Age of Extinctions.* New York: Scribner, 1996.

Quiroga, José. "Fleshing out Virgilio Piñera from the Cuban Closet." In *¿Entiendes?: Queer Readings, Hispanic Writings*, edited by Emilie L. Bergmann and Paul Julian Smith, 168–80. Durham: Duke University Press, 1995.

———. "On the Weight of Insular Flesh." In *Hispanisms and Homosexualities*, edited by Sylvia Molloy and Robert Irwin. Durham, NC: Duke University Press, 1998.

———. *Tropics of Desire: Interventions from Queer Latino America.* New York: New York University Press, 2000.

Ramírez Berg, Charles. "Stereotyping in Films in General and of the Hispanic in Particular." In *Latin Looks: Images of Latinas and Latinos in the U.S.*, edited by Clara E. Rodríguez, 104–20. Boulder: Westview Press, 1997.

Ramos Otero, Manuel. *Página en blanco y staccato.* Santurce: Editorial Playor, 1987.

Renan, Ernest. *Caliban: A Philosophical Drama Continuing "the Tempest" of William Shakespeare, Publications, No. 9a.* New York: AMS Press, 1971.

Reyes Matta, Fernando. "The 'New Song' and Its Confrontation in Latin America." In *Marxism and the Interpretation of Culture*, edited by Cary Nelson and Lawrence Grossberg, 447–60. Urbana and Chicago: University of Illinois Press, 1988.

Ríos Ávila, Rubén. "The Origin and the Island: Lezama and Mallarmé." *Latin American Literary Review* 8, no. 16 (1980): 242–55.

———. "Caribbean Dislocations: Arenas and Ramos Otero in New York." In *Hispanisms and Homosexualities*, edited by Sylvia Molloy and Robert Irwin, 101–19. Durham, NC: Duke University Press, 1998.

Rivera, Edward. *Family Installments: Memories of Growing up Hispanic.* Hammondsworth, Middlesex and New York: Penguin Books, 1983.

Rivera, Juan Manuel. "*La pergrinación de Bayoán*: fragmentos de una lectura disidente." *Revista de crítica literaria latinoamericana* 15, no. 30 (1989): 39–55.

Rivera-Batiz, Francisco L. and Carlos Enrique Santiago. *Island Paradox: Puerto Rico in the 1990s.* New York: Russell Sage Foundation, 1996.

Rodó, José Enrique. *Ariel: Motivos de Proteo.* Edited by Ángel Rama. Caracas: Biblioteca Ayacucho, 1976.

Rodriguez, Juana Maria. *Queer Latinidad: Identity Practices, Discursive Spaces, Sexual Cultures.* New York: New York University Press, 2003.

Rodríguez, Reina María. *Ellas escriben cartas de amor.* La Habana: La Azotea, 1998.

———. "La poesía cubana hoy." Escribir otras islas: El Caribe hispánico hoy. Emory University, Atlanta. April 8, 1999.

———. *Violent Island and Other Poems.* Translated by Nancy Gates Madsen. Los Angeles: Green Integer, 2004.

Rodríguez Castro, María Elena. "Las casas del porvenir: nación y narración en el ensayo puertorriqueño." *Revista Iberoamericana* 59 no. 162 (1993): 33–54.

Rodríguez Vecchini, Hugo. "Back and Forward." In *The Commuter Nation: Perspectives on Puerto Rican Migration*, edited by Hugo Rodríguez Vecchini and William Burgos

Carlos Antonio Torre, 1–81. Río Piedras: Editorial de la Universidad de Puerto Rico, 1994.

Rosa, Richard. *Los fantasmas de la razón: una lectura material de Hostos*. San Juan, Puerto Rico: Isla Negra, 2003.

Saavedra, María Cristina. "The Impossible Island: The Intellectual and the Search for [the] Cuban Nation (Martí, José)." Diss, New York University, 1997.

Said, Edward W. *Beginnings: Intention and Method*. New York: Columbia University Press, 1985.

Sánchez, Luis Rafael. *En cuerpo de camisa*. 4th ed. Río Piedras: Editorial Cultural, 1984.

———. *La guagua aérea*. San Juan: Editorial Cultural, 1994.

———. "La Guagua Aérea/ The Airbus." Translated by Diana L. Vélez. *Caribbean Review*. 13, no. 3 (1984): 26–29, 50–51.

Sánchez Oliva, Iraida and Santiago Moreaux Jardines. *La Guantanamera*. La Habana, 1999.

Sandoval-Sánchez, Alberto. *José, Can You See? Latinos On and Off Broadway*. Madison: The University of Wisconsin Press, 1999.

———. "¡Mira, que vienen los nuyoricans!: el temor de la otredad en la literatura nacionalista puertorriqueña." *Revista de Crítica Literaria Latinoamericana* 23, no. 45 (1997): 307–25.

Sandoval-Sánchez, Alberto and Nancy Saporta Sternbach. *Stages of Life: Transcultural Performance and Identity in U.S. Latina Theater*. Tucson: University of Arizona Press, 2001.

Santí, Enrico Mario. "Carne y papel: el fantasma de Virgilio." *Vuelta* 18, no. 208 (1994): 58–63.

Santiago, Esmeralda. *America's Dream*. New York: Harper Collins, 1996.

———. *América's Dream*. 1st ed. New York: HarperCollins Publishers, 1996.

Santos-Febres, Mayra. *Sirena Selena*. Translated by Stephen A. Lytle. 1st ed. New York: Picador USA, 2000.

———. *Sirena Selena vestida de pena*. Literatura Mondadori. Barcelona: Mondadori, 2000.

Sarduy, Severo. "Beach Birds." Translated by Suzanne J. Levine and Carol Maier. Los Angeles: Otis Books/Seismicity Editions, [forthcoming].

———. *Escrito sobre un cuerpo: ensayos de crítica*. Buenos Aires: Editorial Sudamericana, 1969.

———. *De donde son los cantantes*. Serie del volador. 3. ed. México, D.F.: J. Mortiz, 1978.

———. *Colibrí*. Bibliotheca del fénice ; 21. 1a ed. Barcelona: Argos Vergara, 1984.

———. *Ensayos generales sobre el Barroco*. México: Fondo de Cultura Económica, 1987.

———. *Pájaros de la playa*. Barcelona: Tusquets Editores, 1993.

Scarry, Elaine. *The Body in Pain: The Making and Unmaking of the World*. New York and Oxford: Oxford University Press, 1987.

Seed, Patricia. "'Are These Not Also Men?': The Indians' Humanity and Capacity for Spanish Civilization." *JLAS* 25 (1993): 629–52.

———. *Ceremonies of Possession in Europe's Conquest of the New World, 1492–1640*. New York: Cambridge University Press, 1995.

Shakespeare, William. *The Tempest*, Roma Gill ed. Oxford: Oxford University Press, 1998.

Skinner, Lee. "Pandora's Log: Charting the Evolving Literary Project of Rosario Ferré." *Revista de Estudios Hispánicos* 29, no. 3 (1995): 461–76.

Soja, Edward W. *Postmodern Geographies: The Reassertion of Space in Critical Social Theory*. London and New York: Verso, 1989.

———. *Thirdspace: Journeys to Los Angeles and Other Real-and-Imagined Places*. Cambridge, MA: Blackwell, 1996.

Solomon, Michael. *The Literature of Misogyny in Medieval Spain: The "Arcipreste De Talavera" and the "Spill."* New York: Cambridge University Press, 1997.

Sommer, Doris. *Foundational Fictions: The National Romances of Latin America*. Berkeley: University of California Press, 1991.

Sonnenfeld, Barry. "Wild, Wild West." USA: Warner Bros., 1999.

Sontag, Susan. *Illness as Metaphor; and, Aids and Its Metaphors*. New York: Doubleday, 1990.

Sophocles. *The Theban Plays*. Translated by E. F. Watling. Harmondsworth: Penguin, 1986.

Sorkin, Aaron. *A Few Good Men*. Garden City, NY: Fireside Theatre, 1990.

Soto, Pedro Juan. *Usmaíl*. 4th ed. Rio Piedras: Editorial Cultural, 1974.

Spahr, Wolgang. "Bega's 'Mambo' Hit Crosses Boundaries." *Billboard*, August 7, 1999.

Spitta, Silvia. "Transculturation, the Caribbean and the Cuban-American Imaginary." In *Tropicalizations: Transcultural Representations of Latinidad*, edited by Frances Aparicio and Suzanne Chávez Silverman, 160–80. Hanover and London: University Press of New England, 1997.

Stapinski, Helene. "Generacion Latino." *American Demographics* 21, no. 7 (1999): 62–68.

Suárez Ramos, Felipa and Pilar Quesada. *A escasos metros del enemigo: historia de la Brigada de la Frontera*. La Habana: Verde Olivo, 1996.

Sublette, Ned. *Cuba Classics 2: Dancing with the Enemy*: EMI/Luaka Bop, 1991.

Suro, Roberto. *Strangers among Us: How Latino Immigration Is Transforming America*. New York: Alfred A. Knopf, 1998.

Tabio, Juan Carlos. "Aunque Estés Lejos." Alta/Tornasol Films, 2003.

Todorov, Tzvetan. *The Conquest of America: The Question of the Other*. Translated by Richard Howard. New York: HarperPerennial, 1992.

Torre, Carlos Antonio, Hugo Rodríguez Vecchini, and William Burgos, eds. *The Commuter Nation: Perspectives on Puerto Rican Migration*. Río Piedras, PR: Editorial de la Universidad de Puerto Rico, 1994.

Torres Saillant, Silvio. *Caribbean Poetics: Toward an Aesthetic of West Indian Literature*. New York and London: Cambridge University Press, 1997.

Tugwell, Rexford G. *The Stricken Land, the Story of Puerto Rico*. Garden City, New York: Doubleday & Company, Inc., 1947.

U.S. Bureau of the Census. *Census of Population and Housing, 1990 (U.S.): Subject Summary Tape File (SSTF) 14—Occupation and Industry*. Issued March 1995 ed. Washington, DC: U.S. Dept. of Commerce Bureau of the Census Data User Services Division (distributor), 1998.

United States House of Representatives. Committee on Armed Services. Subcommittee on Military Readiness. *Readiness Implications Concerning the Atlantic Fleet Training Center, Vieques, Puerto Rico: Hearing before the Military Readiness Subcommittee of the Committee on Armed Services, House of Representatives, One Hundred Sixth Congress, First Session, Hearing Held September 22, 1999.* Washington: U.S. G.P.O. : For sale by the U.S. G.P.O. Supt. of Docs. Congressional Sales Office, 2000.

Vega, Ana Lydia. *Encaranublado y otros cuentos de naufragio.* 4th ed. San Juan: Editorial Antillana, 1990.

Viera, Joseph M. "Matriarchy and Mayhem: Awakenings in Cristina García's *Dreaming in Cuban.*" *The Americas Review* 24, (1996): 231–42.

Viera, Joseph Martin. "Navigating the Straits of Florida: Gender, Politics and Culture in Cristina Garcia's 'Dreaming in Cuban'." Diss, Florida State University, 1996.

Villa, Raúl. *Barrio-Logos: Space and Place in Urban Chicano Literature and Culture, History, Culture, and Society Series.* Austin: University of Texas Press, 2000.

Villaverde, Cirilo. *Cecilia Valdés, o, La Loma Del Ángel.* Madrid: Cátedra, 1992.

Vitier, Cintio. *Lo cubano en la poesía.* La Habana: Instituto del Libro, 1970.

Walcott, Derek. *The Antilles: Fragments of Epic Memory (the Nobel Lecture).* New York: Farrar, Strauss, and Giroux, 1992.

West, Alan. *Tropics of History: Cuba Imagined.* Westport, CT: Bergin & Garvey, 1997.

White, Hayden V. *Tropics of Discourse: Essays in Cultural Criticism.* Baltimore: Johns Hopkins University Press, 1978.

Wucker, Michele. *Why the Cocks Fight: Dominicans, Haitians, and the Struggle for Hispaniola.* New York: Hill and Wang, 1999.

Yáñez, Mirta. "El indígena en la narrativa romántica latinoamericana: *Enriquillo* y *Cumandá.*" In *La narrativa del Romanticismo en Latinoamérica.* 147–54. La Habana: Letras Cubanas, 1989.

Zamora, Margarita. *Reading Columbus.* Berkeley: University of California Press, 1993.

# Index

Abu Ghraib, 130
*Advocate*, 62
AIDS, 88, 122, 217n. 57
Almendros, Néstor, 71
Alonso, Carlos J., 35
Alonso, Manuel, 51
Althusser, Louis, 128
Álvarez, Julia, 99, 160, 174–75
Anderson, Benedict, 38
Anzaldúa, Gloria, 49, 214n. 35
Aparicio, Frances, 219n. 2
Appadurai, Anton, 229n. 2
Arango, Arturo, 172
Arenas, Reinaldo, 135–36
Aristotels: units of time and space, 170
Arteaga, Alfred, 214n. 35
Atlantis, 11
Aztlán, 13, 212n. 6; and indigenous people, 13; indigenous characters, 116–17, 123

Balaguer, Joaquín, 112–13
Balibar, Etienne, 229n. 2
*Balseros*, 107
Barceló de Barasorda, Angélica, 45
Barcelona, 31, 33
Barradas, Efraín, 67, 215n. 8
Bega, Lou, 155–56, 224n. 14
Behar, Ruth, 162
*Being Indian in Hueyapán*, 227n. 25
Benítez Rojo, Antonio, 37, 46–48
Bejel, Emilio, 69
Bermejo, Gonzalo, 129
Bhabha, Homi 49, 104

Bildungsroman, 160
Biesenkamp, Goar, 156
Body, 77–78, 80–81, 83–84, 87, 91, 94, 99, 102–3, 168, 201, 217n. 42, 225n. 39, degraded, 89; and corporeal realization of desire, 79; and corporeal limitations, 80
Bonilla, Frank, 226n. 4
Border, 15–16, 28, 34, 48, 52, 57, 59, 69, 77, 98–100, 102, 108, 110–11, 116, 162, 179; contestation of, 48; political borders, 77, 108, 127, 145, 149, 190, 209; control of national borders, 98, 172; of the U.S., 127; (post)national borders, 106; control of political borders, 77, 99, 106–9, 190; officials, 99; border patrol, 100, 102; as contested space, 100; as a site of incarnation and implementation, 102; U.S. government within the national borders of Cuba, 126; and subdivision of Hispaniola, 109, 112; disputed borders, 116. *See also*, Guantánamo
Boricuadesterrao, 199, 200
Boundaries, 9–10, 15, 34, 48–50, 56, 59, 68, 77, 83, 92, 94, 101, 104, 109, 122, 146, 163, 170; 15, 34, 184; land-sea, 9–10, 48; corporeal, 82; political, 15, 106, 190; social, 97, 121; normative, 99; permeability of demarcated boundaries, 108; destabilization of insular, 169; of national discourse, 172
Boyer, Jean Pierre, 111
Brady, Mary Pat, 211n. 6

## 244 INDEX

Brau, Salvador, 50, 52–54, 220n37
Brigada de la Frontera, 221 n. 43
Burnett, Mark, 103
Burton, Antoinette, 229 n. 2

Cabrera Infante, Guillermo, 71
Campos, Ricardo, 226 n. 4
*Cannibal Tours*, 227 n. 25
*Caribeña*: popular culture, 59; fictions, 162, 173; cultures, spatiality, communities, 176, 177
*Caribeñidad*, 16, 30, 60, 65, 150, 159, 176; translocal, 180
Carnegie Hall, 222 n. 51
Carrero, Jaime, 139
Caruth, Cathy, 218 n. 63
Casas, Bartolomé de las, 113, 115, 117, 121, 219 n. 9, 220n35
Castro, Fidel, 63, 128, 129, 186
Césaire, Aimé, 211 n. 5
Chatterjee, Partha, 39
Chayanne, 148
"Che" Geuvara. *See* Guevara, Ernesto "Che"
Checkov, Anton Pavlovich, 66
Chenevey McCoy, Mary Ellen, 134
Chicano movement, 13
Christianity, 112–13
Christophe, Henri, 219 n. 4
Chow, Rey, 164, 219 n. 4, 224 n. 23
Citizenship, 58, 64, 95; global, 130; normative and appropriate citizens, 133, 134; U.S. citizenship in 1917 in Puerto Rico, 138
Clavigero, Francisco Javier, 124
Cold War, 108
Colonialism, 11–13, 34–35, 39, 52, 136, 141; colonial project 11, 35; colonial society, 53, 55, 113, 115, 123; ideological project, 35; colonial social order, 54; colonial Caribbean societies, 55; legacy of colonialism, 111–24; colonial subject, 113; colonial period, 113, 121; military colonization, 126; and civilization, 8–9, 11–12, 16; and narratives of modernity, 88
Colón, Emilio, 215 n. 38
Columbus, Christopher, 13, 34, 51, 52, 223 n. 72; *Diario*, 13

Commodification, 65, 149; commodities, 79, 139, 154; and marketing of Latino cultural production, 149–50; commercial marketing, 152, 156; cultural, 157; of Caribbean cultural production, 158; profit, 158, 229, 293; of Latino cultures in the U.S market, 159; of *latinidad*,159; and marketing of *latinidad*, 176, 223; cultural commodity, 157
Commuter Nation, The, 223 n. 6
Coquí, 189–193, 201–4, 227, 229
Corazón-throb, 157, 174
Cosgrove, Denis, 33
*Cosmopolitan*, 62
Crichton, Michael, 8
*Criollo*, 35, 204, 212 n. 3, 219 n. 8; *criollo* writers, 35
Cristófani Barreto, Teresa, 72,103
Cruz-Malavé, Arnaldo, 42, 53, 213 n. 17, 227 n. 26
Cruz Viera, Nazario, 143
Cuban Constitution, 220n38
Cuban Embassy (Algiers), 71
Cuban Missile Crisis, 107
Cuban music, 145, 209
Cuban Revolution, 63, 102, 107, 125, 173, 187, 221 n. 44; and Communism, 145; pre-Revolutionary Cuba, 219 n. 1; post-Revolutionary Cuba, 173; Special Period, 182, 226 n. 2; Communist Party in Cuba, 136, 221 n. 44
Culebra, 138–39, 143

Darwin, Charles, 8
Dávila, Arlene, 159, 178, 223 n. 2
Davis, Mike, 224 n. 18
Davis, Rocío G., 171
D'Emilio, John, 103
Defoe, Daniel: *Robinson Crusoe*, 11, 12, 211 nn. 2, 3, and 4
Delany, Samuel, 138, 215
Deleuze, Gilles: *Desert Islands*, 9–10, 11, 16, 211 n. 4
Derrida, Jacques, 49, 164, 224 n. 23
*Destierro*, 13
Diaspora, 16, 59–60, 103, 148–49, 161, 174–77, 179, 180, 182–84, 188, 195, 197–98, 202,–3, 205, 210, 219 n. 1; dias-

poric subjectivity, 60; challenges to insular self-fashioning, 180; space of homosexual self-fashinoning, 103; as a place of cultural production, 149; diasporic (self)expression, 173; postrevolutionary, 173; diasporic subject, 183

Displacement, 53–55, 74, 87, 91, 101, 103, 113–14 116, 122, 124, 144–45, 147, 151–52, 163–64, 171, 177, 185, 187, 191, 194–95, 200, 203, 231; of non-normative sexuality, 87, 111; and alienation, 112; non-normative, 87; temporal, 91, 114, 164; physical displacement and reterritorialization, 103; of the enemy, 147, 202; and strategies of repression, 113; temporal displacement of the narrative, 114; and themes of confinement, 159; domestic, 122

Dietz, James L., 138, 192

"El Escriba." 88. *See* Piñera, Virgilio
El Gran Combo, 65
Eligio Fernández, Antonio, 206
Elsewhereness, 58, 101, 105
Embargo, U.S. against Cuba, 136
Eng, David, 87, 103; mourning and loss, 87
Estado Libre Asociado, 222 n. 60. *See also* Free Associated State
Evian Conference (1938), 219 n. 7

Fabian, Johannes, 228 n. 40
Family establishment, 62, 65; nuclear family, 62; family and genealogy, 65; family ties, 111; Christian institution of the family, 112; central structure of production and reproduction, 62, immigrant families, 161
Farley, Christopher, 224 n. 11
Fernández, Joseíto, 222 n. 51
Fernández Retamar, Roberto, 12; *Caliban*, 13
Ferrari, Guillermina de, 217 n. 57
Ferré, Rosario, 64, 67
Figueroa, Angelo, 153, 154
Findlay, Eileen, 65
Fiol-Matta, Licia, 216 n. 15
Flaherty, Stephen, 212. See also *Once On This Island*

Flores, Juan, 212 n. 5
Fornet, Ambrosio, 180, 182
Foucault, Michel, 33, 49, 55, 62, 90, 115, 138, 203–04, 215 n. 2; on heterotopias of crisis and of divergence, 175
Foundation, 30, 44, 49, 51–52, 67, 74, 117, 152, 162; rhetoric of insularity as foundation for national discourses in the region, 30, 49; failed foundational drama, 54; foundational component, 93; foundational myth of Hispanic Antillean subjectivity, 104. *See also* Doris Sommer and foundational fictions, 49, 55, 124
Franco, Jean, 212 n. 5
Free Associated State, 137–39, 145, 199

Galván, Manuel de Jesús, 54–55, 113–25; and Amerindian legacy, 123; indigenous characters, 116–17, 123; indigenous subjects, Aztec legend, 124, 212 n. 6
García, Cristina, 59, 163–76
García, Samuel, 199
García Chichester, Ana, 70, 71
García Lorca, Federico, 71
García Passalacqua, Juan, 141
García Ramis, Magali, 67
Garlinger, Patrick P., 224 n. 25; and epistolary genre, 163–66, 170–73
Gaudí, Antonio, 31
Gelpí, Juan, 53, 66–67, 82–84
German Jewish refugees, 204
Ginzburg, Carlo, 194
Gitmo, 133–34, 222. *See also* Guantánamo
Glasser, Ruth, 219 n. 2
Golding, William, 11
Gómez de Avellaneda, Gertrudis, 54–55, 220n37
González, David, 143
González, Elián, 127, 220n40
González, José Luis, 64
González Echevarría, Roberto, 9, 88, 113
Goodman, Fred, 155
Grammy Awards Ceremony, 154, 224 n. 12
*Granma*, 130
*Granma Digital-Español*, 131
Growing Up Nuyorican, 199–200
Guantanamera, 182

246  INDEX

Guantánamo, 125–37, 146; Guantanamo Bay, 58, 128–31, 133, 136; Guantanamo Border, 129, 135
Guevara, Ernesto "Che," 63, 71
Gutiérrez Alea, Tomás, 102, 131–33, 222 n. 48
Guy, Rosa: *My Love, My Love*, 28; *Once on This Island*, 28–29, 53
Guy Tugwell, Rexford, 138

Haines, Randa, 148
Haiti, 151–71
Halberstam, Judith, 138, 215 n. 2
Hanks, Tom: *Cast Away*, 8
Haraway, Donna, 196
Hardt, Michael, 209
Harvey, David, 33
HEAR (Hawaiian Ecosystems at Risk), 190, 227 n. 29
Hennessy, Rosemary, 158
Hernández, Raymond, 142, 210
Heteronormativity, 62, 87, 218 n. 80; domesticity, 62; anti-gay policies, 63; displacement of non-normative sexualities, 63; national territory and normative subjectivity, 63; demarcation of national space, 68; demarcation of gender, 97
Hijuelos, Oscar, 151, 152
HIV, 217 n. 56
Homeland, 50, 168, 175, 199; sacred, 13, lost, 34, 194; as modern nations, 34; ancestral, 166; allegorical spatiality productively reterritorialized, 61; inaccessible, 162; desired connection to, 163; attachment to island, 173; to the legacy of insularity, 173
Homer, 186
Hostos, Eugenio María de, 50–54, 64, 206, 215 n. 37, 220n37
Hulme, Peter, 12

Iglesias, Enrique, 154–55, 158; and *Wild, Wild, West*, 154
Immigration and Naturalization Service (INS), 103; and U.S. immigration policies, 133, 134
Imperialism, 10, 11, 35, 39, 129, 137, 141, 176, 178, 193

Internet, 192–96, 199, 201, 204, 220n36; cyber-chat room, 228 n. 36; *The History of the Internet*, 195
Isaacs, Jorge, 53
Isla españada, la, 151
Islands: deserted, 8–11, 199, 211; inhabited, 9; as space and isolation, 8; as miniworld, 9; as sites of exile or banishment, 9, as island-prisons, 9, 168; continental and oceanic, 10; 211 n. 3; as mythical topos of individual and collective foundation, 11; intracontinental, 13; space of social formation, 57; and challenge to island-nation, 110–47, 179, 187, 204; and insufficiency of space, 10, 110; as sacred space of crisis, 175, global island of cyberspace, 203

Jackson, Michael, 154
Jameson, Frederic, 157
Jiménez, Juan Ramón, 41–43, 206, 213 n. 13
Jiménez Leal, Orlando, 71
Judeo-Christian traditions, 227 n. 33
Jung, Carl, 225 n. 47
*Jurassic Park*, 8

Kanzepolsky, Adriana, 71
Kazanjian, David, 87
Knight, Frank W., 38
Kolodny, Annette, 35
Kristeva, Julia, 166; on *jouissance*, 100
Künstlerroman, 160, 161
Kurlansky, Mark, 38

Lacan, Jacques, 54
Landow, George, 198
Laó-Montes, Agustín, 178
Latin American Studies Association, (LASA), 178–79
*Latinidad*, 148–50, 155
Latino culture, 149–62
Leal, Orlando, 71
Lefebvre, Henri, 30, 33, 193, 204, 227 n. 32
Lenin, Vladimir I., 128
Levine, Suzanne J., 89, 91, 93, 217 n. 59, 218 nn. 66–72

# INDEX

Lezama Lima, José, 41–44, 47, 70, 72, 206, 213 n. 17, 216 n. 25
Library of Congress, 228 n. 36
López, Iraida, 225 n. 42
*Lord of the Flies. See* Golding, William,
Lugo Ortiz, Agnes, 66, 68, 103
Luibhéid, Eithne, 77, 99, 102–3, 134
Lury, Celia, 227

Maier, Carol, 89, 91, 93, 217 n. 59, 218 nn. 66, 68, 70, and 72
Maldonado Denis, Manuel, 138
Malecón, 125
Manalansan, Martin, 103, 138, 144, 215 n. 1, 218 n. 73; on gay Philippino immigrants, 103; queer transnational sexuality and modernity, 103; queers of color, 103 Global Divas, 103, 144
Marc Anthony, 59, 154–55, 158
Mariel boatlift, 186
Marqués, René, 64, 66–68, 216 n. 8
Martí, José, 127
Martin, Biddy, 79, 140
Martin, Ricky, 59, 153–55, 158, 224 n. 12
Martínez San-Miguel, Yolanda, 186
McCreary Amendment, 102
McWilliams, Carey, 151–52
Menéndez Pidal, Ramón, 219 n. 9
Mi bohio neuyorkino, 196–98
Micoquí.com, 202
Military Readiness Subcommittee, 142
Miranda Bravo, Olga, 129, 130
Miró, William, 143
Mistral, Gabriela, 216 n. 15
Mito del insularismo, 213 n. 17; and Cruz-Malavé, Arnaldo, 213 n. 17
Montrose, Louis, 30
Morales Carrión, Arturo, 192
More, Thomas: *Utopia*, 12, 193–94, 204
Moreaux Jardines, Santiago, 222 n. 51
Moreiras, Alberto, 74
Morris, Willie, 152, 223 n. 7
Muñiz, Angel, 182, 183; *Nueba Yol, Nueba Yol III*, 226 n. 3 (chap 5)
Muñoz, José Esteban, 138; on disidentification, 79
Muñoz Marín, Luís, 138

Museo Nacional de Bellas Artes, 206; *Mundo soñado*, 206, 207, 229 n. 1
Mythology, 29; myth of Caribbean identity, 28; of insularism, 42; mito del insularismo;
mythical genesis of Puerto Rico, 139; mythical island, 173; demystification of migratory success, 182; mythological autochthony, 190, mythology of the coquí, 191

Nazi regime, 215
Negri, Antonio, 209
Neoliberalism, 158, 207, 209
New Man, 63
New World, 13, 34–35, 68, 219 n. 8
New York Boricua, 196, 198
*New York Times*, 142
Nicholson, Jack, 222 n. 53
*Nuevos narradores*, 67, 139, 215 n. 8

Obejas, Achy, 226 n. 50
Oedipus Rex, 101
*Orígenes*, 70
Ortiz Cofer, Judith, 226 n. 50
Orwell, George, 128

Page Law, 102
Pan-Caribbean identity, 37, 39; approach, 37; paradigm, 39; anticolonial nationalism, 39; identity as anti-imperial strategy, 39
Panama Canal, 138
Paris, 113
Parker, Patricia, 225 n. 39
Pedreira, Antonio Salvador, 44–46, 64, 143, 194, 213 n. 21, 214 n. n22–26, 215 n. 37, 223
*People en Español*, 153
Pérez Firmat, Gustavo, 162
Pérez Prado, Dámaso, 155, 156
Pétion, Alexandre, 219 n. 4
Piñera, Virgilio, 58, 64, 69, 70–88, 104, 140, 216 n. 25; and "El Escriba," 70
Plato: *Dialogues*, 11; *The Republic*; 11, 193
Poststructuralism, 88
Pratt, Mary Louise, 35, 211 n. 3

Presley, Elvis, 154
Prieto, René, 88
*Puertorriqueñidad*, 184, 191, 193, 203; iconography of, 191; cyber-construction of, 193; traditional locations of, 196

Quammen, David: *The Song of the Dodo*, 8–9
Queer subjectivity, 16; as a challenge to the equation island-nation, 16; aberrant others beyond insular borders, 87; non-normative sexualities, 62, 66, 87, 92, 101; removed from the dominant social space of the nation, 63; non-normative desires, 69; alternative subjectivity, 74; non-normative displacements, 82; queer fiction, 96; perpetual elsewhereness, 101; non-normative aberrant subjects, 102; queer sexuality as exile, loss, mourning, 87, 95; non-normative subjectivity, 215 n. 2
Quesada, Pilern, 130
Quiroga, José, 72–74, 154, 221 n. 47

Ramírez Berg, Charles, 150
Ramos Otero, Manuel, 67, 178, 186–88, 195, 203, 224 n. 21
Renan, Ernest, 211 n. 5
*Requerimiento*, 212 n. 2
*Revista Cubana*, 213 n. 13
Reyes Matta, Fernando, 219 n. 2
Ríos Ávila, Rubén, 43, 187
Rivera, Edward, 160, 174, 175
Rivera, John, 153
Rivera-Batiz, Francisco L., 183
Rivera Serrano, Aoife, 45, 214 n. 26
Rodó, José Enrique: *Ariel*, 12
Rodríguez, Juana María, 195, 228 n. 37
Rodríguez, Reina María, 27, 55, 215 n. 40; *Las islas*, 30
Rodríguez Juliá, Edgardo, 67
Romero Barceló, Carlos, 142, 144
Roosevelt, Franklin D., 138, 221 n. 41
Rushing, Robert, 224 n. 17

Saavedra, Maria Cristina, 173
Sagrada Familia, 31–33
Said, Edward, 171, 215 n. 37

Sánchez, Luis Rafael, 66–68, 104, 184–86, 224 n. 21
Sánchez Oliva, Manuel, 222 n. 51
Sandoval Sánchez, Alberto, 103
Sanes Rodríguez, David, 140–41
Santí, Enrico Mario, 72
Santiago, Esmeralda, 140
Santos Febres, Mayra, 58, 64, 69, 87, 95–102, 104
Sarduy, Severo, 58, 64, 69, 87–95, 104
Scarry, Elaine, 214 n. 27
Seed, Patricia, 34, 220n36
Seeger, Pete, 222 n. 51
Self-fashioning: Hispanic Caribbean, 27–28, 149, 179, 188, 209–10; insularity as central mode of self-definition, 15, 37, 48, 56–57, 59, 159, 162, 175–76, 179, 205–6; insularity as insufficient and limited;, 64–65, 69, 165–66; insular, 69, 109, 146; limits of normative self-fashioning, 63; translocal, 189; postcolonial, 17, 207
Selkirk, Alexander, 211
*Sensibilidad negra*. *See* Cruz-Malavé, Arnaldo, 213 n. 17
Shakespeare, William: *The Tempest*, 12–13, 29, 53, 89, 211; Ariel, 12, Caliban, 12; Duke of Milan,12; King Alonso, 12–13; Miranda, Prospero, 12
Sherman, William H., 12
Soja, Edward, 33, 146
Solomon, Michael, 214 n. 27; and illness and disease, 217 n. 60
Sommer, Doris, 53, 55, 157–58; and romance, 53, 55; family romance, 53; impossible romance, 53, national romance, 55; Latin American national romance, 114, 124
Sonnenfeld, Barry, 154
Sontag, Susan, 214 n. 27
Sophocles, 80. *See also* Oedipus
Sorkin, Aaron, 134, 222 n. 53
Soto, Pedro Juan, 139
Spahr, Wolfgang, 156
Spanish-American War, 68, 138, 197, 212 n. 4
Spitta, Silvia, 162
Stapinski, Helene, 152–53, 155

Structuralism, 88
Suárez Ramos, Felipa, 130, 221 n. 43
Sublette, Ned, 106, 218 n. 1
Suro, Roberto, 151–52
*Survivor*, 7, 103
Swiss Family Robinson, 8

Tabio, Juan Carlos, 181, 222 n. 48
Tel Quel group, 88
*Time*, 224 n. 11
Todorov, Tzvetan, 34
Tonel. *See* Eligio Fernández, Antonio, 206
Torres Saillant, Silvio, 39–41, 46–47
Trading With the Enemy Act, 146
Trasnationalism: transnational migration, 112; and "borderless" context, 100; capital, 100; mobility, 101, 174; context, 101; market, 209; and global paradigms of identity, 210
Trujillo, Rafael, 111, 219 n. 7

UMAP, 63, 94, 221 n. 44
U.S. Air National Guard Base Muñoz, 222 n. 59
U.S.-Cuba relations, 108, 130, 133; and the Platt Amendment, 220n38
U.S. Census, 223 n. 1, 226 n. 5

U.S. Department of Defense, 228 n. 35
U.S. House of Representatives, 210, 222 n. 67; and the Resident Commissioner of Puerto Rico, 210
U.S. invasion, 128
U.S. military, 109, 128–29, 131, 133–34, 138, 194; U.S. Naval Bases, 128, 133–34, 137–39; WWII War, 138; Korea War, 138; Vietnam War, 138
U.S. Special Interest Section, 126, 127, 220n39 (chap. 39)

Vega, Ana Lydia, 67, 226 n. 50
Vieques, 58, 137–46, 187
Viera, Joseph Martin, 172
Villa, Raúl, 178
Villaverde, Cirilio, 220n37

Weiss, Mark, 140, 216 nn. 22–32
West, Alan, 73
Wilde, Oscar, 71
Williams, Vanessa L., 148
Wucker, Michele, 112

Yáñez, Mirta, 123

Zamora, Margarita, 35